The
Girl on the
Magazine
Cover

CAROLYN KITCH

The

THE ORIGINS OF

Girl on the

VISUAL STEREOTYPES IN

Magazine

AMERICAN MASS MEDIA

Cover

The University of North Carolina Press Chapel Hill & London

© 2001
The University of North Carolina Press
All rights reserved
Designed by Richard Hendel
Set in Monotype Scotch and Kunstler types
by Tseng Information Systems, Inc.
Manufactured in the United States of America
The paper in this book meets the guidelines for permanence
and durability of the Committee on Production Guidelines for
Book Longevity of the Council on Library Resources.

Library of Congress Cataloging-in-Publication Data
Kitch, Carolyn L.
The girl on the magazine cover : the origins of visual stereotypes in
American mass media / Carolyn Kitch.
p. cm.
Includes bibliographical references and index.
ISBN 0-8078-2653-7 (cloth : alk. paper) — ISBN 0-8078-4978-2 (pbk. : alk. paper)
1. Women in mass media—History.   2. Mass media—United States—History.
3. Visual communication—United States—History.   4. Advertising—United States—
History.   5. Mass media and culture—United States—History.   6. Stereotype
(Psychology)—United States—History.   I. Title.
P94.5.W652 U655   2001
302.23′082′0973—dc21   2001027415

Portions of this manuscript have appeared previously
in somewhat different form:
Chapter 1 appeared as "The American Woman Series: Gender and Class in
The Ladies' Home Journal, 1897," Journalism & Mass Communication Quarterly 75,
no. 2 (Summer 1998): 243–62; most of Chapter 3 appeared as
"Destructive Women and Little Men: Masculinity, the New Woman,
and Power in 1910s Popular Media," Journal of Magazine and
New Media Research 1, no. 1 (Spring 1999), online at
<http//:nmc.loyola.edu/newmediajournal>;
and most of Chapter 7 appeared as "Family Pictures: Constructing
the 'Typical' American in 1920s Magazines," American Journalism 16, no. 4
(Fall 1999): 57–75. They are reprinted here with permission of the journals.

05   04   03   02   5   4   3   2

This book is dedicated to my parents,

the late Albert Kitch, who supported my hopes unconditionally,

and my mother, Aimee Lou Kitch, whose love of learning has been a

model for me and whose encouragement and presence in my life have

made everything possible. In so many ways, this is her work.

Contents

Acknowledgments, ix

Introduction, 1

Chapter 1. From True Woman to New Woman, 17

Chapter 2. The American Girl, 37

Chapter 3. Dangerous Women and the Crisis of Masculinity, 56

Chapter 4. Alternative Visions, 75

Chapter 5. Patriotic Images, 101

Chapter 6. The Flapper, 121

Chapter 7. The Modern American Family, 136

Chapter 8. The Advertising Connection, 160

Epilogue and Discussion, 182

Notes, 193

Bibliography, 221

Index, 239

Acknowledgments

This project began as my dissertation, and I am grateful to faculty at Temple University who played key roles in shaping the initial concept and offering suggestions for its future. Chief among them was my doctoral committee chair, Patricia Bradley, of the Department of Journalism, Public Relations and Advertising, who gave me the freedom to explore interdisciplinary studies while holding me to the highest standards of historical research and writing. I benefited from the diverse perspectives of other members of my committee, Paul Swann of the Department of Film and Media Arts, and Margaret Marsh and Allen Davis of the History Department. As a doctoral student at Temple, I was very fortunate to have funding from a Russell Conwell Fellowship that allowed me to devote my time to research. I also had valuable input from professors and peers in Temple's Women's Studies Graduate Certificate program, including Laura Levitt, Rebecca Alpert, and Elizabeth Abele. Although they were not involved in this particular work, other mentors shaped the scholar I became—including, at Temple, Barbie Zelizer and Benjamin Compaine, and, in the American Studies program at the Pennsylvania State University at Harrisburg, John Patterson and Theodora Rapp Graham.

During the years I spent revising the manuscript, I taught in journalism programs in which I had supportive colleagues. One of those programs was Northwestern University's Medill School of Journalism, whose magazine-department chair, Abe Peck, arranged for teaching-release time to help me complete an earlier stage of this project. I am grateful to him for his mentoring and continuing friendship, as I am for the collegiality of Bob McClory, Dick Schwarzlose, and Mary Ann Weston. I was fortunate to finish this book, as a member of the faculty, once again at Temple University's School of Communications and Theater. I appreciate the support I have received there from Deans Bob Greenberg and Concetta Stewart and department chairs Tom Eveslage and Karen Turner. I am particularly grateful for the encouragement I have received at Temple from Pat Bradley and Ed Trayes, two mentors and colleagues whose appreciation of the past has provided a model for my scholarship and teaching. My views have broadened through my involvement in Temple's American Studies program under Regina Bannan and Miles Orvell. I also have learned a great deal from students in my classes at Northwestern and Temple. Graduate students Alison Rice, Marie Suszynski, and Banu Akdenizli provided valuable assistance with research and manuscript preparation.

The following pages contain many images from very old media, and finding them—really *seeing* them in their original form (in an age of microfilm and digital imaging)—has been quite a journey in itself. Luckily I had the help of archivists, librarians, and corporate professionals who were generous with their time and advice. Cheryl Leibold of the Pennsylvania Academy of Fine Arts in Philadelphia and Ruth Bassett and Gail Stanislow of the Brandywine River Museum in Chadds Ford, Pennsylvania, allowed me to explore their institutions' archival holdings of work by a number of turn-of-the-century illustrators. I am especially grateful to those people who helped me to secure permissions to reproduce images and then to commission photographs of the images, including Bonnie B. Coles, senior research examiner in the Photoduplication Service of the Library of Congress, without whom I could not have published this book; Martha Sachs, curator of the Alice Marshall Women's History Collection at the Pennsylvania State University at Harrisburg, who has been involved with this project from its beginning; Tom Rockwell of the Norman Rockwell Family Trust; Suzanne Huntzinger of the Curtis Publishing Company; Elizabeth Aldred of the Norman Rockwell Museum at Stockbridge, Massachusetts; Neville Thompson and Gary Kulik of the Winterthur Museum, Garden and Library in Winterthur, Delaware; Paula DeStefano of the Delaware Art Museum; Lisa Romero of the D'Arcy Collection of the Communications Library of the University of Illinois at Urbana-Champaign; Bob Jackson of Time-Life Syndication; Scott Coleman and Elina Smith of Cluett, Peabody (The Arrow Company); Leslie Smith of *McCall's;* Yvette Miller of Gruner+Jahr; Sarah Scrymser of *Good Housekeeping;* Michele Gendron of the Free Library of Philadelphia; and Penelope Myers and David Dillard of Temple University's Paley Library. I also benefited from the resources in the Blitman Library of Temple's School of Communications and Theater and the guidance of librarian Lisa Panzer. I received helpful advice on how to proceed with the logistical aspects of my project from illustration historian Walt Reed, director of Illustration House in New York City; Terry Brown, director of the Society of Illustrators; and copyright attorney and illustrator Daniel

Abraham. I am particularly indebted to Georganne Hughes of Metro-photo in Hershey, Pennsylvania, who photographed many of the illustrations in this book, including the one that appears as the cover image.

Some parts of this manuscript have appeared previously as articles in scholarly journals. I am grateful to the editors, editorial boards, and reviewers of these publications for their constructive comments on earlier versions of this research, and I appreciate receiving the editors' permissions to allow this work to reappear in this book. For their guidance and permission I especially thank Jean Folkerts, editor, *Journalism & Mass Communication Quarterly;* Jennifer McGill, executive director of the Association for Education in Journalism and Mass Communication; Shirley Biagi, editor, *American Journalism;* and Kathleen Endres and Leara Rhodes, editors, *Journal of Magazine and New Media Research.*

I was very fortunate to find a university press that not only was willing to consider the sort of interdisciplinary communications history/American culture/gender studies work that this book is but also has been enthusiastic and supportive of it. For this I am grateful to editors Sian Hunter, Ron Maner, and Paul Betz and to the reviewers and editorial board of the University of North Carolina Press.

The late journalism historian Catherine Covert provided the theoretical perspective that underpins this book. Although I never knew her, I am indebted to her and thankful for the pioneering work she did. Over the past five years, I have presented my research in bits and pieces at academic conferences and have received much helpful feedback from scholarly colleagues nationwide, including Maurine Beasley, David Mindich, Carol Holstead, Patricia McNeely, Kathleen Endres, Therese Lueck, Sammye Johnson, Patricia Prijatel, David Sumner, David Spencer, Linda Steiner, Wallace Eberhard, David Sloan, Barbara Straus Reed, Leara Rhodes, Elizabeth Burt, Ann Colbert, Paulette Kilmer, and Tracy Gottlieb. I also am grateful to Tracy for first hiring me as an adjunct journalism professor at Seton Hall University more than a decade ago, when I was working as a magazine editor.

I have deep appreciation for the experience and insight I gained in that business. From 1983 to 1994, when I was on staff at *McCall's* and *Good Housekeeping* in New York, I had the privilege of learning from some of the industry's most distinguished and dedicated pros, including John Mack Carter, Barbara Blakemore, Mina Mulvey, Don McKinney, Lisel Eisenheimer, and the late Helen DelMonte. I mention these people in particular because they valued (and communicated to me) the lessons of the rich past of these magazines. Only when I left the business to go back to graduate school did I realize that I had been studying magazine history all along.

Finally, I am indebted to two people I "met" while I was a magazine editor even though they had died many decades earlier. One of them is Neysa McMein, who drew all of the covers for *McCall's* from 1923 to 1937, and the other is Jessie Willcox Smith, who drew all of *Good House-keeping*'s covers from 1918 to 1933. For eleven years, I walked around every day in hallways decorated with their artwork. Little did I know that they were leading me to this project, but they were. And so I thank them most of all.

The Girl on the Magazine Cover

Introduction

In the summer of 1998, *Time* magazine asked on its cover, "Is Feminism Dead?" The question stood out against a black background under the disembodied heads of Susan B. Anthony, Betty Friedan, Gloria Steinem, and . . . the television sitcom character Ally McBeal. The cover story nostalgically remembered the 1970s as an era when "feminists made big, unambiguous demands of the world. They sought absolute equal rights and opportunities for women, a constitutional amendment to make it so, a chance to be compensated equally and to share the task of raising a family. But if feminism of the 60s and 70s was steeped in research and obsessed with social change, feminism today is wed to the culture of celebrity and self-obsession." The article proclaimed that "[t]oday's feminists want to talk sex, not cents" and concluded that "much of feminism has devolved into the silly . . . a popular culture insistent on offering images of grown single women as frazzled, self-absorbed girls." [1]

In the "unambiguous" decade it recalled, *Time* itself had published a 1972 special issue that introduced "The New Woman" and devoted more than 100 pages to the movement, covering the day-to-day realities of ordinary women's lives as well as women's entry into the professions. It named women's rights activists its "Women of the Year" for 1975, spotlighting working women.[2] Just seven years later, however, a cover story announced "The New Baby Bloom," a trend in which "Career women are opting for pregnancy." As proof of this trend, its cover showed a beamingly pregnant actress Jaclyn Smith, whom the magazine called "Charlie's Angel turned Madonna."[3]

By the late 1980s, the magazine reported that "some look back wistfully at the simpler times before women's liberation" and proclaimed, "[f]eminine clothing is back; breasts are back; motherhood is in again."[4] In 1990, it published a special issue about young women who hoped "to achieve their goals without sacrificing their natures." This message was reinforced by ads from the issue's single sponsor, Sears. Displaying her bracelets, one young ad model said, "Sparkle comes from within. But a little outside help couldn't hurt." Another, cuddling her toddler at home, bragged, "I'm a senior partner in a very successful enterprise. My family."[5]

This seemingly drastic shift in media portrayals of women's lives was one theme in Susan Faludi's 1991 book *Backlash,* in which she analyzed cultural reactions to the gains of the women's movement.[6] She noted that mass media outlets such as *Time* contributed to as much as reported on the "backlash" against feminism. Ironically, the book's success drew as much attention to the "failure" of feminism as it did to the role of mass media in helping that process along, and in 1992 the magazine had Faludi on its cover, with an article that explained "why many women turned against feminism in the 1980s." The article took little note of real women, focusing instead on the popular culture imagery discussed in one part of Faludi's book and presenting it as evidence of cultural change itself. This sleight-of-hand occurred even in the "good news" sidebar collage of "Feminist Images"—a group of "successful independent women who found new answers and a vital balance"—which included television and movie characters (including Murphy Brown, Roseanne, and Thelma and Louise).[7]

The same conflation of popular culture imagery and women's realities characterized the 1998 issue that pronounced feminism "dead" and feminists consumed by silly self-absorption. Gone were the ordinary women worried about work and childcare; instead, the article's opening anecdotes featured rock singer Courtney Love and a host of actresses caught up in "[f]ashion spectacle, paparazzi-jammed galas, and mindless sex talk," with television character Ally McBeal as the Newest New Woman. A companion piece focused on today's teenagers, asking "What do the girls really want?" (a play on Spice Girls lyrics) but then analyzed young female *characters* on television, in the movies, and in song lyrics, interviewing only three actual girls (two of them about what they thought of television characters). "In an age in which image is often mistaken for both message and directive," the writer mused, "can girls truly tell if they're making up their own minds, even as they sing about telling people what they want?" The cover story concluded: "What a comedown for the movement."[8]

How did this happen—in the media and presumably in American society? Why were women themselves to blame? Why did the "death" of feminism make the cover of a national magazine? And why did its cover feature a succession of "types" and generations of women, represented by just their heads?

These questions are at the heart of this book, which examines what we think of as a modern-day issue by searching for its historical roots. It attempts to shed light on how women's visual and verbal media imagery evolved through the second wave of the American women's rights movement (and how and why that movement supposedly died) by revealing a very similar media story about women during the first wave. It argues that media stereotypes of women first emerged not in mass media from the 1970s to the 1990s but in mass media of the first three decades of the century. The women's heads that floated ominously on *Time*'s 1998 cover were types arranged in a pattern, from older, matronly activists to the dangerous but beautiful radical to the cute, skinny, sexually free girl. The same types appeared in the same order on magazine covers of the early twentieth century, during the peak and the aftermath of the suffrage movement.

Most scholars today are wary of what sociologist Gaye Tuchman called in 1978 "the reflection hypothesis" in which "the mass media reflect dominant societal values."[9] They caution that media imagery—including *Time*'s "news" reporting—is prescriptive rather than descriptive and that much is left out of the picture of American life they paint. In one of the first scholarly historical works on stereotypes of ideal womanhood, Mary P. Ryan warned that such images "must not be confused . . . with the actual life experience of women."[10]

As cultural theorists note, however, the media create as much as reflect reality, and their process of "selection and interpretation" is historically significant. "In a society as a whole, and in all its particular activities," wrote Raymond Williams in 1961, "the cultural tradition can be seen as a continual selection and re-selection of ancestors."[11] Indeed, what is so striking about *Time*'s treatment of feminism over the past three decades is that *Time* itself has so often covered the subject in terms of other popular culture imagery and that it pronounced feminism dead based on a shift in imagery, a new "popular culture insistent on offering images" that seem silly. In this evolving story, media imagery is not a "reflection" of the news; it *is* the news.

How mass media have pictured American women throughout the twentieth century—setting into place a visual vocabulary of womanhood that now seems natural—is the subject of this book, which seeks to understand how media imagery works to create, transform, and perpetuate certain cultural ideals rather than others. While the central question of this study is why, and how, feminism is recurrently pronounced alive and dead in mass media, this book is not only about women's imagery. It is also about men's imagery and about how gender tensions are resolved in media through an ideal of middle-class family life that seems (to us now) to be "typically" American. It argues that current media definitions of, and debates about, femininity, masculinity, class status, and Americanness have their origins in media of a century ago.

Though this study considers other forms of public communication, its focus is the American magazine. Magazines were the first truly mass medium in the United States, though they did not become large-scale operations until the 1890s, a century and a half into their existence. Like other industries, the magazine business grew rapidly between the close of the Civil War and the Progressive Era. In 1865, there were nearly 700 titles with a total circulation of about four million; forty years later, in 1905, there were some 6,000 magazines with a total audience of sixty-four million, averaging four magazines per household. By the same year, ten American magazines had readerships in excess of half a million, and the *Ladies' Home Journal* and the *Saturday Evening Post* each had passed the million mark.[12] It was also during this period that technological advances in engraving and printing enabled the high-quality mass-reproduction of artwork on magazine covers, first in two colors and then in four.[13]

The *Journal,* the *Post,* and other new titles such as *Munsey's, McClure's,* and *Cosmopolitan* existed in a symbiotic relationship with other aspects of mass culture.[14] When increasingly conglomerate corporations needed to launch major advertising campaigns in order to create demand for mass-produced goods, they found that magazines were the best way to reach a wide audience.[15] In turn, it was the financial base of national advertising that enabled magazine publishers to lower cover prices to ten and fifteen cents, pulling in huge numbers of readers from the swelling U.S. population and thus creating the broad consumer base corporate interests needed.[16] In its new alliance with American manufacturers, magazine publishing became, in fact, two businesses: that of selling magazines to readers and that of selling readers to advertisers.

Before either transaction could be made, magazines had to get readers' attention. Key to that accomplishment was the cover, which declared the magazine's personality and promise. It also made a statement about the intended reader. Most magazines did not vary their cover designs until the 1890s, when the cover became a selling tool.

Though photography was beginning to appear regularly in turn-of-the-century newspapers, the majority of magazines continued to use illustration on their covers because they were dealing in ideals rather than reality. The face of a woman could represent both a specific type of female beauty and a "style" that conveyed model attributes—youth, innocence, sophistication, modernity, upward mobility. (Chapter 3 explores how images of women were also used to convey the opposite, or loss, of these values.)

The illustrators who created the earliest such cover ideals developed distinctive styles that helped form individual magazines' editorial identities. Editors sought illustrators who had what *Ladies' Home Journal* artist Alice Barber Stephens called "a strong personality." [17] Most often that personality emerged through a "signature" type of woman's face, often identified by the artist's name. "The 'ideal American women' of [James Montgomery] Flagg and Charles Dana Gibson," note magazine historians John Tebbel and Mary Ellen Zuckerman, "became not only their trademarks but national institutions." [18] In 1915, when Irving Berlin wrote a song about a young man pining away for the ideal "girl," his title located her where most Americans would expect to find her—on the magazine cover.

Her various permutations were the first mass media stereotypes. "The strength of a stereotype," explains Teresa Perkins, "results from a combination of three factors: its 'simplicity'; its immediate recognisability [*sic*] (which makes its communicative role very important), and its implicit reference to an assumed consensus about some attribute or complex social relationships. Stereotypes are in this respect prototypes of 'shared cultural meanings.' " [19] Norman Rockwell gave the same explanation, recalling the lesson he learned when he began his career in the second decade of the century: "The cover must please a vast number of people (no matter how: by amusing, edifying, praising; but it *must* please) . . . it must have an instantaneous impact (people won't bother to puzzle out a cover's meaning)." [20]

Magazines paid well for artists who could make such an impact. In 1903, *Collier's* offered Charles Dana Gibson $1,000 apiece for 100 drawings, and other artists soon earned similar rates.[21] They earned even more, and gained additional fame, when the publishing companies reprinted their artwork and sold it to readers by mail order, as the old *Life* [22] did for Gibson and *Good Housekeeping* did for Jessie Willcox Smith. Top illustrators were "[b]illed as heroes" by their magazines, in which they were interviewed and where they received fan mail;[23] in the era that is now considered "the golden age of illustration," they had the status that would later be accorded to movie stars and athletes.

Advertisers of the day capitalized on this fame by hiring the same illustrators "to add luster to their product[s]."[24] During World War I, so did the U.S. government, for which illustrators lent their "signature" images to recruitment and fundraising posters. The sophisticated couples drawn by J. C. Leyendecker for the covers of the *Saturday Evening Post* also peopled his ads for Arrow Collar shirts. Smith's devoted mothers and adorable children, who appeared on every *Good Housekeeping* cover for sixteen years, also could be seen in her work for Ivory Soap. Coles Phillips's "Fadeaway Girls" blended into hosiery ads as well as the covers of *Life*. Howard Chandler Christy's "Christy Girl," who debuted in *Scribner's*, appeared on war posters to urge young men to enlist. The "Gibson Girl," who graced the pages of *Life* and *Collier's*, resurfaced on items from scarves to wallpaper and became the subject of plays and songs.

Particularly in the work of Norman Rockwell and J. C. Leyendecker, magazines offered visions of manhood as well as womanhood, and these ideals are discussed in the following chapters. Yet they emerged in ways that confirm historian Michael Kimmel's belief that—even while "[m]asculinity and femininity are relational constructs [and] the definition of either depends on the definition of the other"—cultural "definitions of masculinity are historically *reactive* to changing definitions of femininity."[25] When male figures appeared on covers, it was in response to ideas first inscribed in female figures.

Indeed, as the above examples suggest, feminine images dominated popular artwork of this era. These pictures conveyed ideas about women's natures and roles, but they also stood for societal values. The faces and figures of women had served this purpose in American culture long before the arrival of mass media. In early public art such as statues, flags, and coins, "the female body recurs more frequently than any other: men often appear as themselves, as individuals, but women attest to the identity and value of someone or something else," writes Marina Warner.[26] America itself has traditionally been depicted as a woman, in forms from Indian princess to Greek goddess.[27] So too has American progress. Since the seventeenth century, writes Mary P. Ryan, "different ideal types of femininity have marked America's growth from peasant to 'post-industrial' society."[28]

In her study of American imagery from 1876 to 1919, Martha Banta contends that, during this period of great societal change, *"the woman as image* [emphasis hers] was one of the era's dominant cultural tics. . . . However masculine the political and commercial activities that controlled 'the main world,' the images dominating the turn-of-the-century imagination were variations on the figure of the young American woman and permutations of the type of the American Girl." These symbols, Banta contends, embodied concerns about race, sexuality, consumption, and patriotism.[29]

Banta's point was illustrated—literally—on the covers of the era's popular magazines, where an idealized woman was used to signify broader concepts that spoke to an emerging American identity. That identity was both inclusive and exclusive, collective and "typical"; it was defined in terms of the shifting center of the country's demography. Illustration historian Susan Meyer notes that magazine cover art "provided the public with its first image of American ideals. . . . [T]he thousands of immigrants pouring into the country each day would find . . . prototypes after which they could pattern themselves."[30]

America's population growth, much of it from the massive waves of immigration in the years just around the turn of the century, was transforming the nature and needs of media audiences. In their quest to deliver vast audiences to their advertisers, the new magazines departed from the editorial format of the nineteenth century's most influential publications (such as *Scribner's* and *Harper's*), which published literary material for small but elite readerships who were urban, well educated, and affluent. Mass circulation magazines, by definition, served a more geographically and economically diverse readership, including new arrivals to the country and rural Americans who aspired to urbanity.[31] Their editorial content included practical advice (on housekeeping, fashion, health, and other matters), news of the world, and human interest features. The magazines also published fiction by respected authors and reproductions of fine artwork as part of their expressed mission to elevate the public.

This content combination was an early example of the ways in which twentieth-century mass culture would systematically blur the boundaries between "high" and "low" culture. It further instructed readers in upward mobility, showing them the lifestyles of the rich and fueling what Miles Orvell calls an "aesthetic of imitation" that "became the foundation of middle-class culture."[32] Magazines themselves were symbols of this process. In the middle-class home, "[t]he display of maga-zines signaled the couple's attainment and aspirations," notes Richard Ohmann; at the same time, "[t]he visual presentation of the magazine announced its own status as an elegantly made commodity that would grace a modern parlor."[33]

In the decades around the turn of the century, the two chief com-ponents of the upwardly mobile "aesthetic of imitation"—culture and consumption—were the province of women, who were homemakers, magazine readers, and shoppers. And both concepts were inscribed in the figures of women in popular culture imagery. More specifically, they were discussed through the idea of a "New Woman" who stood for change in women's lives and change in America.

While she represented societal change, the image of the New Woman varied significantly from the 1890s to the 1920s, expressed through a series of "types." Because these images appeared at particular times and in a particular order, they functioned not just as individual icons but rather as a symbolic system that visual theorists call "iconology." In this view, wrote Ernst Gombrich, an image "cannot be divorced from its purpose and requirements of the society in which the given visual lan-guage gains currency"—in other words, from its social, economic, and historical context—nor can its meaning be divorced from other images in the surrounding culture.[34]

Viewed over time, the New Woman offers a study in iconology. As a cultural construct, she conveyed opportunities for upward social and economic mobility while she also embodied fears about *downward* mo-bility, immigration, and the urbanization and corporatization of the lives of white American men. And she conveyed new social, political, and economic possibilities for womanhood. At many historical mo-ments, she seemed merely to "mirror" what was happening in society. Yet she (and the visions of masculinity that accompanied her) also served as a model for that society and as a cultural commentator through whom certain ideals came to seem "natural" in real life.

Between 1895 and 1930, the roles and status of American women underwent widespread discussion and some profound transformations. It was during these years that the Progressive reform and women's club movements enabled middle-class women to enter the political arena; that women made the final push for, and achieved, suffrage; that women entered college and the workforce, including new professions, in signifi-cant numbers;[35] that the American popularity of the works of Freud prompted an acknowledgment of women's sexuality; and that a new birth control movement enabled some women to express that sexuality more freely and safely.

It was also during this era when the term "feminist" first came into use. Women who described themselves with this word agitated for reforms broader than suffrage. Some of these activists were urban radicals and socialists, but feminism had a broader base as well. The reply to the title question "What Is Feminism?" in a 1914 *Good Housekeeping* article presumed readers' familiarity with the subject. The female writer's answer was similar to (and perhaps more generous than) replies to that question in mainstream media today:

> It's the woman's movement—It's the furthering of the interests of women—It's the revolt of the women—It's the assertion of woman's right to individual development—It's the doctrine of freedom for women—It's woman's struggle for the liberation of her personality— . . . there are as many definitions of feminism as there are feminists. Yet what distinguishes the contribution of the times on the subject is the really synthetic effort back of all the definitions, the effort to get "the woman question" assembled on a broader base than any from which it has as yet been projected. Higher education for women, economic opportunity for women, rights of person and property for women, political enfranchisement for women—all begin to be placed as parts of something greater, vaster. And for this something we seek the larger term.[36]

There was even broader support for the drive for women's suffrage, organized through the National American Woman Suffrage Association and other groups, which was at its peak and was widely discussed in the press. Though it still met with resistance from some women as well as men, the campaign that had begun with a handful of radicals at Seneca Falls in 1848 had gained momentum and nationwide support by the 1910s. Suffrage united women in an effort that, at least temporarily, transcended geography, race, and class: though they tended to organize separately from white middle-class women, African American women and working-class women were active participants in this cause.

At the same time, Progressive Era reform work literally moved women into the public sphere and brought women of different social and economic classes together. Kathryn Kish Sklar maintains that between 1890 and 1920 "[t]he crucial significance of women within

American grass-roots democracy was never better demonstrated."[37] Through settlement-house work and other social welfare work, some college-educated women created new professions based in reform.[38] But most female reformers were clubwomen, members of groups such as the Woman's Christian Temperance Union, the National Consumer's League, the Children's Aid Society, the National Congress of Mothers (later the PTA), and the Pure Food Association. By 1910, the General Federation of Women's Clubs had nearly a million members.[39]

These activists "defended the new ways in an old language,"[40] justifying their commitment to public work in maternal rhetoric that had reverberations throughout the twentieth century. Often this rhetoric appeared in popular women's magazines, and it tied "modern" women to the Victorian era's "cult of true womanhood" defined by "four cardinal virtues—piety, purity, submissiveness, and domesticity."[41] Nancy Cott explains that "[m]any women involved in club or reform activities were the first to say that their 'outside' interests were really undertaken in the service of the home, though on a larger scale."[42]

Such a strategy could be put to radical uses, as with upper- and middle-class women who claimed to be "protecting" their "weaker" working-class sisters by joining them in the labor agitation of the Women's Trade Union League. Yet other maternalist reform was reactionary, undertaken in the era when President Theodore Roosevelt (himself a Progressive reformer) publicly expressed concern over the decline in fertility rates among native-born white women in the face of increasing immigration.[43] Reformers urged middle-class women to make childbearing a priority while also making the goal of "assimilating immigrants into 'American' culture a vital part of their child welfare work."[44] These objectives were realized in settlements and in Mothers' Clubs at the same time they filled the pages of magazines.

Their nativism dovetailed with popular culture warnings about the virility of white manhood. Historians including Joe Dubbert and Peter Filene see this phenomenon of the century's first two decades as a "crisis of masculinity."[45] According to this theory, white men not only were threatened by the aggressiveness of the New Woman, who was invading their territory in education and business; they also had lost their sense of mastery in a changing workplace that was increasingly bureaucratic and in cities that were increasingly crowded and nonwhite.

"Experts" in the new field of psychology, who authored magazine articles and popular books, believed that the crisis of masculinity could be resolved through a "rugged" physical life and the acquisition of money and consumer goods, a combination of strength and status. Organizations such as the Boy Scouts and rough sports such as football became popular ways of socializing boys and young men into the rugged ideal and of removing them from the "feminizing" influence of mothers and female schoolteachers.[46] The call for a more hardy American masculinity reached a fever pitch in the years immediately preceding World War I. The ideal was cast in terms of the outdoorsman and the businessman—with both notions embodied in the figure of the suburban father.

By the 1920s, changing ideas about both femininity and masculinity had culminated in a revised and highly commercialized prototypical American family ideal. The urbanization and corporatization of America spawned exclusively white suburbs, a retreat from the city that brought about a "reprivatization of women's lives," writes Margaret Marsh.[47] At the same time, the popularization of Freudian psychology and the availability of birth control had led to increasingly "great expectations" of marriage, notes Elaine May, including sexual fulfillment and a "companionate" relationship between spouses.[48]

Women's duties within the home were changing as well. Popular magazines, borrowing from Progressive Era rhetoric, described housework as "domestic science" and homemakers as "domestic engineers." Despite the arrival of electricity in most American homes by the mid-1920s, homemakers spent fifty-three hours per week doing housework.[49] Motherhood became a similarly professional and full-time endeavor guided by the advice of psychiatrists and pediatricians. Those trends (reinforced in magazines) support the argument of Ruth Schwartz Cowan, who dates the "feminine mystique" to this era: "Whatever it was that trapped educated American women in their kitchens, babbling at babies and worrying about color combinations for the bathroom, the trap was laid during the roaring 20s, not the quiet 50s."[50]

How did this particular evolution of women's roles and women's lives occur? What happened to the New Woman? Why did the achievement of suffrage and the new movement called feminism "fail" in producing lasting change? These are among the central questions of American women's history. They are also the same questions that *Time* magazine asked about feminism when it pronounced its death in 1998.

Many women today believe that feminism is in fact still alive, no matter what *Time* says. Similarly, a number of historians contend that neither the suffrage movement nor the first wave of feminism failed, arguing that their gains continued to benefit and influence women in the middle decades of the century.[51] Yet neither wave of the movement truly transformed women's social and economic status, particularly in terms of family life. In both eras, the political promise of a New Woman dissipated while the concept remained evident in popular culture.

Imagery in 1920s mass media, which included movies as well as magazines, suggested that the New Woman had undergone a remarkable evolution—from a serious-minded college (or working) woman to a carefree, scantily clad "flapper" who existed to wear modern clothes, have fun, and, ultimately, catch a man who would support her. "The flapper symbolized a solipsistic, hedonistic, and privatized femininity, a gay abandonment of social housekeeping, women's organizations, and dogged professionalism," writes Mary P. Ryan.[52]

The transformation of first-wave American feminism from a collective movement to a matter of personal style involved a thorough redefinition of early feminist goals: a redirection of women's societal participation from voting to spending, a recasting of sexuality as silly sexiness, an educational shift away from reform and toward consumerism. The close parallels between media imagery and the actual behavior of Americans enabled media of the era to "report" these changes as reality. But these redefinitions were, to a great extent, constructed and articulated in mass media themselves.

This is precisely the case Susan Faludi has made about the role of mass media in the "backlash" against the second wave of the American women's movement. Indeed, the very same media redefinitions of the meaning of the New Woman in media of the first three decades of the century can be seen in *Time*'s treatment of feminism during the last three decades.

Tracing the visual representation of this transformation is the goal of this book. Its subject is a broad period of history and a vast body of media, and the visual and verbal texts discussed here are clearly selective, not exhaustive. Yet all of the images were chosen through extensive research into their biographical, institutional, and historical contexts—that is, the artists, the magazines, and the culture and politics of the era. A range of primary sources from the artists' own era as well as secondary sources (the work of other historians) were used to "read" the imagery with regard to those contexts.

Studying mass media requires "a kind of intellectual bricolage" (to borrow T. J. Jackson Lears's description of his own history of advertising).[53] That is true of this work, which draws on scholarship in the fields of history, literature, and sociology as well as communication; it is theoretically grounded in visual and rhetorical theory as well as cultural studies.[54] Methodologically, it is less a "content analysis" (in which certain specific elements are quantified within a given text) than what journalism historian Marion Marzolf called "content assessment"—a process of "reading, sifting, weighing, comparing and analyzing the evidence in order to tell the story."[55]

The following chapters survey the emerging "types" of womanhood and manhood in the new century, visions that appeared on magazine covers between 1895 and 1930. Each image or set of images is discussed in terms of its institutional setting (the magazine's editorial and advertising pages as well as its audience) and its historical moment. Two of the chapters, 5 and 8, explain how these stereotypical ideals that emerged in magazines moved easily into and among other aspects of American popular culture.

Chapter 1, "From True Woman to New Woman," deals with middle- and working-class aspirations during the earliest period of New Womanhood, the 1890s. It takes a very specific focus, a yearlong series titled "The American Woman," drawn for the *Ladies' Home Journal* by Alice Barber Stephens throughout 1897. These were Victorian images, showing women in corseted, neck-to-floor dresses, with serious expressions on their faces. Yet they were symbolically transitional for three reasons: they depicted women both inside and outside the home; they suggested the close relationships between and among women that characterized nineteenth-century society but were to a great extent lost in the modern era; and they included representations of upper-, middle-, and working-class women, conveying a fluid and inclusive notion of class. These illustrations—and their editorial and advertising context in the *Journal*—defined the first-generation New Woman as both a proper homemaker and a modern shopper.

Chapter 2, "The American Girl," examines the eponymous creation of Charles Dana Gibson, one of the best-known images of American womanhood ever drawn, and her successors in cover art. The Gibson Girl rose to national fame in the pages of *Life* and *Collier's* during the opening years of the twentieth century. This tall woman with an aristocratic bearing and an upswept hairdo was upscale and aloof, representing the lifestyle to which the "rising" classes might aspire. The Gibson

Girl spawned imitations that also came to be known by the names of their creators: the Fisher Girl, drawn by Harrison Fisher for the *Saturday Evening Post*, the *Ladies' Home Journal*, and *Cosmopolitan;* and the Christy Girl, drawn by Howard Chandler Christy for *Scribner's* and other titles during the 1900s and 1910s. Fisher's "girl" was less haughty and more blushingly pretty than Gibson's, somehow demure and sensual at the same time. The Christy Girl seemed friendly, perky, and approachable. Both of them played sports and went to college during an era journalist Dorothy Dix called "the Day of the Girl." [56]

Their evil opposites are discussed in Chapter 3, "Dangerous Women and the Crisis of Masculinity," which surveys images of modern women as beautiful but dangerous creatures who overpowered and used men. In various forms of popular culture of the 1910s, including Broadway revues, sheet music, and film, the New Woman was shown as a temptress and a golddigger. The same theme surfaced in magazine illustration. James Montgomery Flagg drew "vamps" — young women with saucy expressions, bare shoulders and legs, and provocative poses — for the covers of *Judge* and *Life*. The latter magazine also featured the work of Coles Phillips, known for his "Fadeaway Girls," slim young women whose dress patterns merged with their backgrounds. Though they were beautiful, they were often cruel: one of Phillips's recurring motifs was that of a vain young woman surrounded by tiny men, depicted as bugs caught in her web, as small suitors bearing gifts, as little faces she crossed off on a calendar.

Imagery depicting such sex-role reversal was linked partly to the theories of Sigmund Freud, newly popular in America, and to debates about the "feminization" of American culture as women seemed to become more socially and politically powerful. But the image of the dominating woman had to do with more than gender tensions; she symbolized white manhood endangered, the possibility of "race suicide" in an era of immigration. To counter this dominating woman, a parallel set of images of manhood emerged in popular culture of the era, and they were articulated by J. C. Leyendecker for the covers of the *Saturday Evening Post:* the businessman, who exhibited a fashionable, moneyed sense of style, and the athlete, who embodied muscular ruggedness.

The political forces that supposedly threatened white manhood during the second decade of the century are explored in Chapter 4, "Alternative Visions," which considers types of womanhood that were represented in the population and yet were not regularly represented in mass-circulation magazines. This chapter examines the depiction of suffragists, immigrants, prostitutes, and African American women on the covers of three smaller-circulation magazines, the *Woman Citizen*, the *Masses*, and the *Crisis*—imagery that both challenged and reinforced the stereotypes in mainstream media.

This alternative imagery, along with the "crisis of masculinity," largely disappeared from American popular culture during World War I. Instead, men were strong and women were angelic on the war posters drawn by almost all of the era's top illustrators. This work is surveyed in Chapter 5, "Patriotic Images." Organized by Charles Dana Gibson, who served as director of the government-appointed, wartime Division of Pictorial Publicity, the illustrators created recruitment and relief appeals that were displayed in towns and cities throughout the country. This chapter explores the thematic similarities between the artists' editorial work and war work, as well as some telling contradictions.

Magazine imagery after the war depicted two primary versions of womanhood, seemingly opposite images that were in fact complementary. One was the "Flapper," the subject of Chapter 6, which focuses on the work of a single illustrator, John Held Jr. (though it also discusses the portrayal of flappers in movies). Held's cartoon characters, which appeared mainly on the cover of *Life*, inhabited a now-familiar picture of the "Roaring Twenties," when carefree women had nothing better to do than drink gin, neck in the backseats of cars, and dance all night. Paradoxically, this sexually free woman was almost asexual-looking in Held's drawings: she was flat-chested, skinny, and hipless, with awkwardly long legs and arms.

At the very same time, other media imagery suggested a return to motherhood and family happiness. The construct of a "new family" involved ideas about not just womanhood, but also manhood and childhood. Chapter 7, "The Modern American Family," examines the cover imagery and editorial context of three magazines whose circulations soared during the 1920s.

In the work of Neysa McMein, the exclusive cover artist for *McCall's* from 1923 to 1937, the woman of the 1920s was a self-possessed, mature New Woman, depicted as an individual in a modern world. Jessie Willcox Smith, *Good Housekeeping*'s exclusive cover artist from 1918 to 1933, also drew female figures but featured mainly children, adorable cherubs who could have been any reader's child; in her illustrations, children came to stand for womanhood. And on the covers of the *Saturday Evening Post*, boyhood came to stand for manhood. Continuing the masculine gender–construction work begun in the *Post* by Leyendecker, Norman Rockwell envisioned masculinity in the modern era. His subjects were emblematic of a new middle-class suburban lifestyle, based on an idealized version of the small town.

Chapter 8, "The Advertising Connection," documents this aspect of the careers of five of the cover artists, J. C. Leyendecker, Coles Phillips, Jessie Willcox Smith, Norman Rockwell, and Neysa McMein. This section reveals the extent to which "signature" magazine cover imagery traveled quickly into the broader commercial culture. It notes the thematic connections between each artist's editorial and advertising imagery, assessing the possible consequences of such message-blurring.

The concluding chapter provides a brief survey of media imagery of the rest of the century, drawing on the work of other scholars who have studied television portrayals of women. It notes the staying power of certain gender notions and the striking representational parallels of both "waves" of feminism—confirming journalism historian Catherine Covert's point that, when viewed through the lens of women's experience, the past is "marked by repeated episodes and recurring motifs."[57]

Raymond Williams argued that "it is with the discovery of patterns of a characteristic kind that any useful cultural analysis begins."[58] The significance of the artwork discussed in the following chapters has less to do with imagery than with iconology, with how mass media make meaning in patterns that develop in response to particular cultural tensions but have the potential to recur as those tensions resurface over time. The larger picture of the girl on the magazine cover helps us understand her daughters and granddaughters in mass media—and their continuing symbolic uses in American culture.

From
True Woman to
New Woman

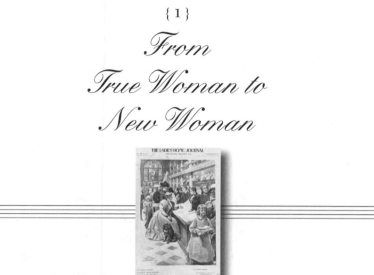

Throughout 1897, the *Ladies' Home Journal* ran a series of six full-page illustrations collectively titled "The American Woman." Drawn by Alice Barber Stephens, an artist with a national following (one journalist of the day called her "the dean" of female illustrators),[1] the images were promoted by the *Journal* as "something never hitherto successfully accomplished. . . . Mrs. Stephens portrays six types of American Woman as she is."[2] Four ran as the frontispiece, a "second cover" that bore the magazine's logo and date and that readers were encouraged to cut out and hang in their homes as art.

These works were seen by an audience that was, by nineteenth-century media standards, huge: the *Journal* reached some 850,000 readers and would be the first magazine to reach the million circulation mark just six years later.[3] Given that advances in printing technology had only recently made the mass reproduction of high-quality artwork possible in magazines, the series was among the first visual commentaries on gender—on what an "American Woman" looked like—in a truly national mass medium.

The six settings of the series mapped out the figurative and literal territory open to the proper young woman at the close of the nineteenth century. Its themes placed her both inside and outside the home in familial, social, and commercial surroundings while depicting her role and activity in each of those settings. Collectively the six pictures portrayed a woman whose "place" in American life was changing, though through a gradual rather than radical transformation, an integration of old and new images and roles. This transition had to do not only with gender roles but also with the social and economic aspirations of a growing American middle class.

As the Victorian era gave way to modernity, the *Ladies' Home Journal* was itself a blend of the old and the new. Like other early mass-circulation magazines, it was priced cheaply, selling at ten cents an issue or a dollar for a year's subscription—one-third the price of the more elite (and soon-to-expire) *Godey's Lady's Book*.[4] Its inside pages featured the latest in dresses, hairstyles, decorating, and, most of all, modern consumer products. Yet the *Journal*'s editorial voice was conservative. Despite his insistence that he was a new type of editor—"not an oracle removed from the people, but a real human being"—editor Edward Bok addressed his readers in the tone of a minister or schoolteacher, holding forth on morality and manners.[5] Some of the regular features were more empathetic, especially those written by Isabel Mallon, who dispensed advice under both her own name and the byline Ruth Ashmore.[6]

As the *Journal*'s circulation grew, its audience necessarily became more demographically diverse, including readers with a range of incomes, lifestyles, and political inclinations. The target audience suggested by the magazine's editorial and advertising content was somewhere in the center of that range: in her study of the magazine, Jennifer Scanlon describes its readership in this era as "white, native-born, middle-class women, who lived with the uncertain legacies of the nineteenth-century women's rights movement and who tried to find a comfortable role in the rapidly changing world of the expanding middle class."[7]

Alice Barber Stephens was herself part of the "rising classes" (she was born before the Civil War in a farm family of nine children) whose sensibilities were nevertheless shaped by the Victorian era and the conservative Philadelphia society to which she had risen.[8] She was a member of the first class of women admitted to the prestigious Pennsylvania Academy of the Fine Arts, where she trained under the painter Thomas Eakins, and by 1897 she was an instructor at the School of Design for Women and a leader in the Philadelphia art community. Her work, done in what one art historian calls a style of "sincerity and good taste,"[9] appeared not just in the *Journal* but also in *Scribner's, Cosmopolitan, Life, Century, Leslie's Weekly,* and the various *Harper's* magazines.[10]

By the time her series appeared in the *Journal*, Stephens was married and the mother of a four-year-old son, a living example of the New Woman who combined family and career. Her private life was publicized as evidence of her worthiness as an artist. The *Philadelphia Press Fiction Magazine* declared: "In Alice Barber Stephens there is a confluence of two of the most noble strains in humanity—the mother and the artist. Both qualities are creative.... Together they have given her love, happiness, work that is a joy and compensation for leisure and ease and a full, well rounded life." [11] In terms of both her professional reputation and her personal background, Stephens was an ideal choice for the task at hand: to create a series of pictures of the New Woman who held on to old values as she entered the new century. Her own combination of a career (albeit a cultured one) and family life made her a transitional role model; her rise from humble and rural origins to artistic acclaim and financial success surely prepared her to understand readers' desires for upward mobility as Americans became increasingly urban and acquisitive.[12]

Stephens's illustrations were different than those of any other artist discussed in this book. Some of her successors in cover art (especially Norman Rockwell) created "narrative" scenes featuring more than one person, yet they suggested spontaneous interaction, slices of everyday life caught happening. Stephens's illustrations were also slices of life, but their presentation was much more formal. They were tableaux, framed, populated, and staged so as to create a "scene" in the theatrical sense. By using this Victorian pictorial convention, Stephens placed her work in the professional realm of fine art and anchored it, stylistically and culturally, in the late nineteenth century.

In the artist's tableaux, ideological messages emerged less from the figures of individual women than from the entire setting. The meaning of "the American woman" had to do not so much with her looks, but rather with her location and context; it was defined by where and in whose company she appeared, and by what she did there. Three of Stephens's scenes showed women literally inside the home, and the other three showed them outside it. Several of the images commented not only on their subjects' physical and societal "place" as women but also on their economic status, containing clues that suggested the possibility of financial improvement. Though the settings varied, they were all noticeably feminine spaces, filled with women's faces—scenes in which men, if present at all, were secondary characters. They were spaces in which the reader could comfortably imagine herself.

The American Woman series appeared in the *Journal* every other month in 1897, beginning with the January issue and ending in November, portraying women in society, in religion, in the home, in summer, in business, and in motherhood. These various aspects of readers' lives were also addressed in articles and advertisements inside the magazine.

Although the magazine acknowledged the phenomenon of a New Woman and her involvement in public life, its editorials routinely promoted the Cult of True Womanhood. In addition to the characteristics with which historian Barbara Welter has defined this nineteenth-century ideal—piety, purity, submissiveness, and domesticity—Karen Blair adds "society"s emphasis on training young ladies in the arts, especially vocal and instrumental music, literary study, drawing, painting, and dance." [13] Such qualities made women the ruling moral force of the home, a private sphere separate from the male world of commerce. *Journal* editor Edward Bok, writing in the September 1897 issue, described the "true" American woman as "the home-loving woman, the woman fond of her children, and with a belief in God." [14] These qualities were represented in half of Alice Barber Stephens's American Woman series.

To the late-twentieth-century viewer, Stephens's illustration called "The Woman in Religion" (Figure 1.1) seems as if it must have been mistitled. Yet it would have made sense to readers of the *Journal* in 1897. It showed a small room in a home and four generations of females: a woman sewing, an older woman reading aloud, an elderly woman lying in bed, and a little girl crouched on the floor. "Religion" as it was represented in this picture was the province of women and something that naturally took place at home. The title suggested that what one woman was reading aloud was the Bible, and what the viewer was seeing were daily devotions, taking place in the course of family caregiving and homemaking.

The seated woman also could have been reading the *Journal* aloud, since the magazine regularly ran "Bible lessons" by the revivalist preacher Dwight Moody. The scene perfectly illustrated his viewpoints. In the September 1897 issue, Rev. Moody explained that the real test of readers' faith lay in the feeling they brought to their daily activities: "[H]ow sorely we need the keeping power of a holy presence in our lives

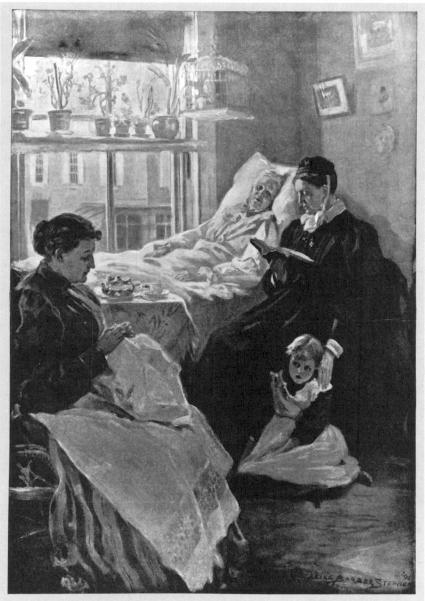

THE AMERICAN WOMAN
A SERIES OF TYPICAL SKETCHES
BY ALICE BARBER STEPHENS

II—THE WOMAN IN RELIGION

Figure 1.1. Alice Barber Stephens, "The Woman in Religion,"
The Ladies' Home Journal *(Mar. 1897). Courtesy, The Winterthur Library:*
Printed Book and Periodical Collection.

to make them lights in the world about us . . . it is the privilege of us all to live useful lives . . . and to be a blessing in our homes." [15]

The magazine celebrated everyday spirituality in its articles. An 1897 Easter feature about a Moravian community in Pennsylvania— with drawings by Alice Barber Stephens—offered "a graphic picture of the religious customs of these devout people." The February issue contained a hymn (for readers to sing at home) written "especially for the *Journal* . . . to supplement Mr. Moody's Bible Class." In the December issue, a New York City rabbi described the ideal Jewish woman in a way that echoed the magazine's philosophy: "The sphere of the Jewess is her home," he wrote. "The home is the Jewish woman's church." [16]

The inclusion of Judaism as part of the *Journal*'s discussion of religion is interesting in light of the fact that the majority of Jewish women in New York City (or Philadelphia) in 1897 were working-class or "rising" middle-class. Stephens's visual representation of feminine faith was notable for the plain dress of the women and the drab room in which they sat; this was not an upper-class home. In contrast to the main theme of the *Journal*'s editorial and advertising pages—that readers should aspire to a "better" life defined by material goods—the magazine's treatment of religious faith provided validation for at least one noncommercial aspect of the lives of the less well-to-do.

Home again was painted as a feminine world in Stephens's "The Beauty of Motherhood" (Figure 1.2), showing a young mother seated in front of a piano. The ball on the floor marked the parlor as the baby's territory as well as the woman's. But the father was nowhere to be seen, just as parenting advice in articles referred to female parents only. A "Suggestions for Mothers" column answered questions on topics from first aid to education to candy consumption. Ads addressed readers as mothers of children who needed breakfast cereals, special soaps, rockers, play clothes, even carpeting so they could crawl on the floor. The magazine further "look[ed] after the interests of the children" by publishing fairy tales for their mothers to read to them.[17]

The piano in this picture functioned as more than a backdrop. It indicated that this baby was born to a mother with the taste to value and the money to afford culture and that they lived in a proper home. Pianos were part of the material culture that signified that women, and the household as a whole, had attained middle-class manners. And women's association with the musical arts was so much a part of femininity that throughout popular culture of the late nineteenth century,

THE LADIES' HOME JOURNAL

Vol. XIV, No. 12   PHILADELPHIA, NOVEMBER, 1897   YEARLY SUBSCRIPTIONS, ONE DOLLAR
                                                            SINGLE COPIES, TEN CENTS

COPYRIGHT, 1897, BY THE CURTIS PUBLISHING COMPANY   ENTERED AT THE PHILADELPHIA POST-OFFICE AS SECOND-CLASS MATTER

THE AMERICAN WOMAN

A SERIES OF TYPICAL SKETCHES

BY ALICE BARBER STEPHENS

VI—THE BEAUTY OF MOTHERHOOD

The earlier illustrations in this series were:

I—THE WOMAN IN SOCIETY   -   -   JANUARY
II—THE WOMAN IN RELIGION   -   -   MARCH
III—THE WOMAN IN THE HOME   -   -   MAY
IV—THE AMERICAN GIRL IN SUMMER   -   JULY
V—THE WOMAN IN BUSINESS   -   -   SEPTEMBER

Figure 1.2. Alice Barber Stephens, "The Beauty of Motherhood,"
The Ladies' Home Journal *(Nov. 1897). Courtesy, The Winterthur Library:*
Printed Book and Periodical Collection.

the piano (in both visual and verbal imagery) came to stand for True Womanhood itself. Women learned how to play the instrument so that they could perform "parlor music"—a reference to the room where the family gathered, sometimes with visitors, and were musically entertained by the mistress(es) of the home.[18]

Such entertainment was the theme of Stephens's third domestic illustration, "The Woman in the Home" (Figure 1.3), which celebrated not just music, but other aspects of culture, as a natural part of home life: while the daughters played and sang, the mother did needlework; the father and son read; and the paintings on the walls suggested art appreciation in this household. Still, the nature of this tableau—the central position of the young women at the piano and the more passive and quiet activities of the other family members—echoed Ruth Ashmore's assertion in the June 1897 issue that in the American home, "the sister rules," at least socially.[19]

As suggested by the lamplight and shadows, this drawing could have illustrated an article in the January 1897 issue of the *Journal* titled "These Long Evenings in the Home," which urged readers to develop a "plan of literary and musical evenings at home" that would involve the entire family. The author, a "Prof. A. S. Isaacs," noted that these activities need not be limited to people who were well off or already well educated: "the great mass of the people . . . have warm longings for culture," he wrote. A regular editorial feature of "Literary Talks" gave advice on fiction; the magazine also had a "Literary Bureau" that advised readers on which books to buy—and then sold them to them by mail order.[20] Edward Bok believed that fine art and music could improve the home life and lift the spirits and minds of the "rising" classes, as they had in his own life as an upwardly mobile Dutch immigrant. The *Journal* sold prints of art masterpieces by mail order, and its Educational Bureau provided free musical training (with a home-study option) to young women, who qualified by selling subscriptions.[21] Bok regularly printed sheet music inside the magazine, and advertisers promoted music-training courses and pianos.

The fact that young women were shown at the center of this upward mobility contained a subtle challenge to the Cult of True Womanhood. The singing girls in Stephens's drawing were not helpmeets, background figures like the mother; instead, they were the primary characters in her rendition of refinement and self-improvement. They were girls who might do enough reading at home to want to go to college, pictured in

THE AMERICAN WOMAN
A SERIES OF TYPICAL SKETCHES
BY ALICE BARBER STEPHENS

5   III—THE WOMAN IN THE HOME

Figure 1.3. Alice Barber Stephens, "The Woman in the Home,"
The Ladies' Home Journal *(May 1897). Courtesy, The Winterthur Library:*
Printed Book and Periodical Collection.

an era when young women began entering universities in record numbers and when magazine articles and artwork began to regularly refer to "the college girl." While these young women were, like the figures in the other two domestic scenes, shown as True Women, they could become New Women if they left home.

The woman depicted in the outside world in "The Woman in Society" (Figure 1.4) was there for a conventionally feminine purpose, socializing. Yet this cover showed at least one woman, perhaps a maid, present *in* society and not *of* society. Her attention was focused on a female figure with an enormous coat, a woman shown, significantly, *arriving* in society, about to ascend stairs . . . but not before glancing backward, directly at the reader.

This triple act of looking—the reader's view of an image in which the servant admired the society woman, and the society woman looked out at the reader—created a class continuum full of possibilities. It also was an extremely early example of evidence supporting the theoretical notion that there is a "female gaze" that can transform the meaning of a seemingly traditional image. In her now-classic 1975 essay, film scholar Laura Mulvey contended that the camera (due to the male perspective of filmmakers and the assumption of a male audience) has a "male gaze," a phenomenon in which viewers see female characters through the eyes of the male characters and their male creators. John Berger similarly has argued that female viewers take a man's point of view, seeing images of other women as the same figure they know themselves to be, "the surveyed female." [22] Yet here was a tableau of women (men were literally in the margins) created by a female artist for a female audience, and—like "The Woman in Religion"—it had a specifically feminine meaning. Stephens was echoing a point Ruth Ashmore made in her column: "The power of men, socially, is limited; it is womankind who rules in society, and who decides whether or not such or such a girl shall be admitted." [23]

The issue of admission to "society," the chance for upward mobility, was indeed the subtext of the picture, as it would be in magazine cover imagery by other early-twentieth-century artists who conveyed economic aspirations through women's faces and figures. The difference between Stephens's articulation of this goal and those of the artists discussed in the next chapter was that, here, it was a conversation (within the image and within the magazine) entirely among women, and it was a scenario in which women were the ones rising, the actors rather than the

THE LADIES' HOME JOURNAL

Vol. XIV, No. 2   PHILADELPHIA, JANUARY, 1897   YEARLY SUBSCRIPTIONS, ONE DOLLAR
SINGLE COPIES, TEN CENTS

COPYRIGHT, 1897, BY THE CURTIS PUBLISHING COMPANY   ENTERED AT THE PHILADELPHIA POST OFFICE AS SECOND-CLASS MATTER

THE AMERICAN WOMAN
A SERIES OF TYPICAL SKETCHES
BY ALICE BARBER STEPHENS

1—THE WOMAN IN SOCIETY

Figure 1.4. Alice Barber Stephens, "The Woman in Society,"
The Ladies' Home Journal *(Jan. 1897). Courtesy, The Winterthur Library:*
Printed Book and Periodical Collection.

acted-upon. This difference would be seen in the work of other female illustrators drawing for women's magazines, whose work is discussed later in this book.

The class continuum represented in this image was suggested else-where in the magazine as well. Advertisements targeted both afflu-ent readers and those just making ends meet: products ranged from fine stationery and ladies' tailoring to absorbent socks and "A Good Cheap Desk." Similarly mixed messages appeared in editorial matter. A fashion feature pictured "the latest Paris designs" as a glimpse of exclusivity, yet offered patterns for twenty-five cents by mail order.[24] Household-hints columns cast advice in terms of how the reader's *ser-vants* should perform their duties, though instructions were presented in a direct, how-to manner.[25] A series written by an architect described houses that could be built for as little as $1,000 (a third of the average cost of a Philadelphia home and lot).[26] Etiquette columns told readers how to address their maids and what to wear on an ocean voyage, yet they also explained what "RSVP" meant and how a woman should be-have when encountering her employer in public.[27]

Such contradictions were smoothed over by the magazine's promo-tion of, to again use Miles Orvell's term, an "aesthetic of imitation," its repeated message that readers could rise socially or create the illusion of rising economically, through emulation.[28] One feature showed readers the "Inside of a Hundred Homes," explaining: "These pictures give a woman an opportunity to look into one hundred of the most tastefully furnished and decorated homes of America. . . . [Y]ou will be surprised at the new ideas they will give you."[29] Ads offered imitations of material culture of the wealthy at affordable prices. One sold "fine china [and] rich cut glass" at "prices 25 per cent lower than elsewhere"; another offered silk gloves for twenty-five to fifty cents; a third featured "New York Fashions Within the Reach of All." Even a lawn seed ad promised "A Beautiful Lawn in whose rich green velvety depths The Lawns of Old England have thus far found their only rival."[30]

The lawn seed ad is a humorous example of the Anglophilia that still characterized the culture of imitation in the pages of the *Journal* even as the Victorian era drew to close. The magazine's literary col-umnist touted British novelists, while society writers offered "personal glimpses" into the lives of royalty. One feature promised to "take its readers on the English throne with Her Majesty, and let them see what Victoria has seen since she became Queen." Readers who wishfully put themselves in the place of the ballgoer in "The Woman in Society" might also have imagined themselves a part of the ballroom scenes depicted in an article in the same issue (written "by an eyewitness") reporting on the Prince of Wales's visit to America.[31]

The *Journal* was not short on American patriotism, however, as evidenced by the July issue. Inside the magazine was a statistical piece explaining why the United States was "The Greatest Nation on Earth" and an article describing "The Women's Patriotic Societies" of America."[32] And on the frontispiece was Stephens's "The American Girl in Summer" (Figure 1.5). Throughout popular culture, the New Woman was characterized as uniquely American. She was a symbol of freedom—not only of women from old-fashioned gender roles, but also of the modern American twentieth century from the Victorian nineteenth century. Yet because she challenged propriety, she was a symbol that the conservative *Journal* used uneasily.

A century later, Stephens's rendering of "The American Girl in Summer" hardly seems to contain improper or challenging ideas. The picture showed three seemingly affluent and decorous young women happily chatting outdoors. The ocean could be seen behind them, and a puddle of water and wet umbrella lay in front of them. Although the friends were sheltered in the image, they had been out walking before they were caught in the rain.

What was "new" about this image in 1897? The title contained a clue. Aside from "The Beauty of Motherhood," in which the subject, by virtue of her maternal status, was clearly a woman, this was the only one of Stephens's illustrations without "woman" in its title. This difference is rhetorically significant in linking the picture's subjects to the newly popular "girls" of Charles Dana Gibson in *Life,* the beginning of a visual type that would soon also be taken up by magazine illustrators Harrison Fisher and Howard Chandler Christy. Their eponymous Girls were not actually girls but rather young women between adolescence and marriage. Some of them were shown in college settings with other girls, in the company of friends but not parents; most were shown in the outdoors, a setting characterized by nature rather than domesticity.

The notion of the American Woman as an outdoor girl was further suggested by some of the *Journal*'s contents. A feature in the May issue on camping outdoors assumed the magazine's typical service format: how to dress, what sorts of sanitary problems might arise, what food to take, how to pitch the tent. An outdoorswoman was the target of

THE LADIES' HOME JOURNAL

Vol. XIV, No. 8   PHILADELPHIA, JULY, 1897

YEARLY SUBSCRIPTIONS, ONE DOLLAR
SINGLE COPIES, TEN CENTS

COPYRIGHT, 1897, BY THE CURTIS PUBLISHING COMPANY

ENTERED AT THE PHILADELPHIA POST OFFICE AS SECOND-CLASS MATTER

THE AMERICAN WOMAN

A SERIES OF TYPICAL SKETCHES

BY ALICE BARBER STEPHENS

IV—THE AMERICAN GIRL IN SUMMER

The earlier illustrations in this series were:
I—THE WOMAN IN SOCIETY - JANUARY
II—THE WOMAN IN RELIGION - MARCH
III—THE WOMAN IN THE HOME - MAY

Figure 1.5. Alice Barber Stephens, "The American Girl in Summer,"
The Ladies' Home Journal (July 1897). Courtesy, The Winterthur Library:
Printed Book and Periodical Collection.

ads in other issues for ice skates, boots and skirts for walking, dress shields that guarded against "excessive perspiration," and bicycles. Every issue the magazine published in 1897 contained ads for bicycles and all sorts of related products, including corsets that produced a "bicycle waist" as "graceful as the New Woman." [33]

Marketers cast these activities not as a new form of freedom for women but as the epitome of femininity and good taste. They also presented outdoor life—true leisure in an industrial era—as proof of social status. One ad proclaimed, "The Stearns Bicycle captures a woman's heart. There's such a light, graceful, chic appearance in its make-up that the least susceptible maid or matron falls in love at first sight." Another ad for a "silk walking skirt" promised that the $5 item "will be worn this season by every lady who pays any claim to style." [34]

No matter how stylish her motives, however, the woman to whom these ads appealed had a life physically freer than her mother's had been. That freedom (indeed, nature itself) was upsetting to Edward Bok. One of his most strongly worded editorials was on the very subject that had inspired Stephens's July 1897 illustration. The following month, Bok suggested that "the American girl in summer" was not a carefree creature but an accident waiting to happen. He argued that the open air tempted young women to abandon propriety for more primitive pleasures. He advised mothers to erect "social fences" around their teenaged daughters. And at the end of the long piece, Bok turned his advice directly to the American Girl herself, whom he nearly threatened:

> Little licenses seem so much more natural in summer when we live an outdoor life. We feel that we can be more unconventional. We can be, but it is just when we are most unconventional that we are in greatest danger of going just a little beyond the point where we know and feel we ought to stop. It is a magnificent tribute to a girl's character when she can be unconventional and yet preserve in every sense the dignity of girlhood. That is what commands the highest respect for a girl. It is a very fine line which divides unconventionality in a girl's deportment from a certain license and freedom of action, which is so fraught with danger—a very, very fine line. And yet on one side of that line lies a girl's highest possession: her self-respect, and on the other side her loss of it. That line is the fence, and a girl cannot be too careful about removing one stone from it. . . . No greater satisfaction than this can come to a woman: the consciousness that she

preserved, at all times in her girlhood, the precious possession of her future womanhood. And one little slip can dim that satisfaction.[35]

This sermon suggested the extent to which the cultural construct of the New Woman lived uncomfortably in the pages of the *Ladies' Home Journal*. Linked to American "freedom," she was a useful symbol in a magazine with a growing circulation of upwardly mobile readers, many of them immigrants or children of immigrants. Yet her very freedom threatened the definitions of domesticity and respectability that were the core of the *Journal*'s editorial content, not to mention its editor's own philosophies about womanhood.

If the outdoor girl troubled Edward Bok, he was even less fond of the working woman. For years he maintained the stance he had taken in an 1893 editorial that "[t]he poorest, hardest-working woman in her home is a queen of independence compared to the woman in business."[36] That phrase was the title of the sixth image in Stephens's series.

The setting for "The Woman in Business" (Figure 1.6)—which showed an upper-middle- or middle-class woman being served by working women in a department store—was the great Wanamaker's Store in Philadelphia. This was perhaps the most fitting symbolic image for the cover of a mass circulation magazine at the turn of the twentieth century, given the structural, cultural, and commercial similarities between magazines and such retail spaces. The word "magazine" itself comes from the French word (*magasin*) for storehouse, and both the great stores and the new mass periodicals displayed an abundance of goods divided into "departments."[37] Like the tableau of a Wanamaker's window in Philadelphia (or R. H. Macy's in New York, Jordan Marsh in Boston, or Marshall Field in Chicago), Stephens's detailed scene of the store's main floor was a snapshot of well-ordered plenitude.[38]

And, as in her "Woman in Society" cover, the image is full of female faces, confirming that both the department store and the *Journal* catered to women. Early department stores provided a wide range of feminine amenities, such as ladies' lunchrooms, nurseries, concerts, art exhibitions, and libraries.[39] Film theorist Anne Friedberg argues that at the turn of the century, this new kind of public space for women allowed them to experience the "mobile gaze" that men, free to explore public areas, had always had.[40] Through Stephens's picture, the female readers of the *Journal* gained that mobile gaze, the shopper's survey of a place created specifically for women. This image, though, offered more than

THE LADIES' HOME JOURNAL

Vol. XIV, No. 10   PHILADELPHIA, SEPTEMBER, 1897   YEARLY SUBSCRIPTIONS, ONE DOLLAR SINGLE COPIES, TEN CENTS

Copyright 1897, by The Curtis Publishing Company   Entered at the Philadelphia Post-Office as Second-Class Matter

THE AMERICAN WOMAN

A SERIES OF TYPICAL SKETCHES

BY ALICE BARBER STEPHENS

V—THE WOMAN IN BUSINESS

The earlier illustrations in this series were:

I—THE WOMAN IN SOCIETY   JANUARY
II—THE WOMAN IN RELIGION   MARCH
III—THE WOMAN IN THE HOME   MAY
IV—THE AMERICAN GIRL IN SUMMER -   JULY

Figure 1.6. Alice Barber Stephens, "The Woman in Business,"
The Ladies' Home Journal *(Sept. 1897)*. *Courtesy, The Winterthur Library:*
Printed Book and Periodical Collection.

the shopper's perspective on such a place; it showed not one but two ways for a turn-of-the-century woman to enter the public sphere.

The customer, seated at the center, did represent one of these ways, which was consumption. The female shopper created yet another philosophical problem for Bok, given his insistence that women belonged at home. Richard Ohmann notes that for the editor "[t]o stand by the genteel ideology would have been to disavow the one essential—if unstated—premise of the [mass circulation] magazines' economic practice: that their readers and especially their women readers were eager and adventurous consumers. As consumers they had to go out into the world." [41] In "The Woman in Business," the shopper was shown making this necessary journey in a reassuring way. Propriety was encoded in the seated woman's dress, in the fact that she had been allowed to bring her little dog inside, in the churchlike stained-glass window, in the deference of the salesclerks, and in the background sea of female faces.

But the well-dressed, comfortably seated customer was not the subject of Stephens's illustration. The title—"The Woman in Business"— guided the reader's eye to the other type of American Woman of 1897 shown in this image, the expressionless, plainly attired clerks standing along its edge. At first glance, their appearance, as plain as the woman in the margin of "The Woman in Society," seems as if it would have assuaged Bok's concern "that the image of the working woman had begun to entice those who did not have to work." [42] Even so, their mere presence in the picture was evidence that women were entering the public sphere not only through the indulgence of buying mass-produced goods but also through the work of selling them. And that second role suggested a new opportunity for some of the *Journal*'s readers.

In her history of urban working-class women, Kathy Peiss notes that by the turn of the century, "the saleslady had become a fixture of the retail emporium, a much coveted position for young working women." [43] Wanamaker's provided its female employees with a dormitory, a medical clinic, a pension plan, athletic facilities, a savings bank, even debates on women's suffrage. [44] Department stores hired mainly native-born Americans and English-speaking immigrants likely to "rise." [45] The women in Stephens's image were such candidates, looking as "American" (i.e., white and European), if not as well dressed, as their customers. Thus the tired little working girl in front could be seen as the future: in a generation, *she* could be on the other side of the counter.

What is more, the comingling of women of different income statuses depicted in this illustration was actually happening to an increasing extent in American cities. Such meetings occurred when women who had to go out in public crossed paths with women who chose to go out in public. In the coming decade, the Progressive reform and women's club movements would intentionally bring these two groups together, as upper-middle- and middle-class homemakers engaged in efforts to improve the lives and opportunities of working women, especially immigrants. Their effort would, if only temporarily, redefine class as a continuum, rather than a set of discrete categories. Stephens advanced this idea by showing "The American Woman" on both sides of the department-store counter, in roles (not opposite, but related) that increased the chances that anyone in the *Journal*'s rapidly broadening readership would be able to imagine herself in the picture.

Both the department store and the mass circulation magazine were sites of identity formation for Americans of various classes. For this reason, "the woman in business" was symbolically important. She was the embodiment of the mixed messages contained inside the *Journal* about the roles and class of its readers.

For instance, at the same time the magazine disparaged working women, it offered them service editorial and steady encouragement. One striking example of this contradiction appeared on each issue's editor's page, a solicitation presented as a series of success stories. One revealed that "A young girl of eighteen earned forty dollars one week in July doing some simple work for the JOURNAL.... There are hundreds of dollars waiting to be earned by girls and women. And the JOURNAL's Circulation Bureau will tell them how." Another entry told of a young woman who was able to buy special Christmas gifts for her family because of the extra money she made selling subscriptions.[46] By working as a seller, in other words, a woman could become a shopper who owned things, a transaction that could make the notion of class quite fluid.

The implication of these notices, and of other features, of course, was that women's earnings were pin money. Yet by 1897, despite Bok's continuing praise for women who devoted themselves solely to home and family, the *Journal* had conceded that even respectable women worked. A feature in the April issue suggested what sorts of lunches women could pack to take to work with them. In a December article, Ruth Ashmore proclaimed that a woman "need no longer shrink, hesitate, stammer and blush when some one discovers that she earns her own living. The world has grown older, and the civilization of to-day recognizes and respects the working girl." [47]

As the nineteenth century came to a close, the *Journal* acknowledged that women's place in American society was broadening, and Stephens's drawings effectively delivered that news. While several of them portrayed ideal womanhood in terms of class status defined by possessions—a message that would become even clearer in future visual types of the American woman—these works showed the True Woman giving way to a New Woman. The illustrations' younger female characters in particular appeared in transitional settings that prepared them to leave the home and go out into the world. The American Woman series froze late-nineteenth-century women's lives in tableaux that, when viewed as a series, suggested that American womanhood was not at all static.

It was strangely prophetic, however, that when Ruth Ashmore finally contradicted her boss by approving of "the woman in business," she called her the working *girl*. Indeed, as the American Woman's sphere widened and her opportunities grew in real life, she was increasingly portrayed in popular culture as a girl. In the new century, a group of male illustrators would rise to fame and fortune by showing the public what that new American Girl looked like.

The American Girl

While it showcased the American Woman of Alice Barber Stephens during the late 1890s, the *Ladies' Home Journal* also was publishing the
work of an artist whose fame would eclipse hers in the opening years
of the new century. In February 1903, when the *Journal* became the
first magazine to reach a circulation of one million, it was "Mr. Gibson's
American Girl" who was on its cover (Figure 2.1). The two artists' work
differed not just in content, but also in style and effect: while Stephens's
oil paintings placed realistic-looking women in tableaux, Gibson's pen-
and-ink cartoons represented a *type,* a single repeatable idea that was
inextricably linked with his own name.

The Gibson Girl—sometimes an entire person and sometimes just a
head, as on the February 1903 *Journal* cover—looked quite similar from
one drawing to the next, and this consistency made her the first visual
stereotype of women in American mass media. Her rapid rise to fame
created a blueprint for the commercial uses of such a stereotype. "Before Gibson synthesized his ideal woman," wrote a newspaper reporter
looking back from the vantage point of the 1920s, "the American girl
was vague, nondescript, inchoate; there was no type of her to which one
could point and say, 'That is the typical American girl.'" [1]

The artist's biographer, Fairfax Downey, described the Gibson Girl
image that appeared, for the first time, in an 1890 issue of *Life:* "a tall,
radiant being, her gaze clear, fearless and direct, her nose slightly and
piquantly uptilted. Her lips fine-modelled and alluring. Her soft hair
crowning a serene brow and caught up into a dainty *chignon.* The grace-

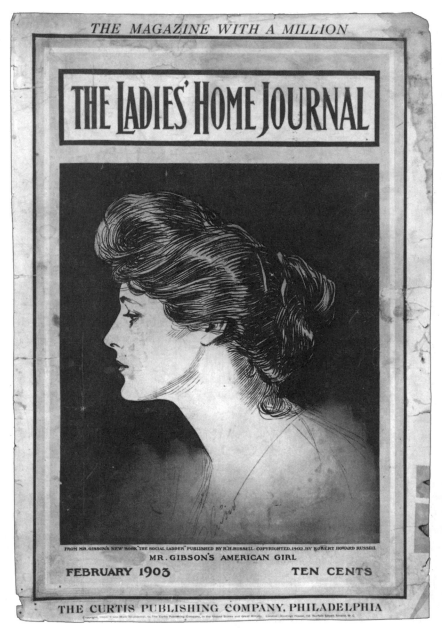

Figure 2.1. Charles Dana Gibson, "Mr. Gibson's American Girl,"
The Ladies' Home Journal (Feb. 1903). Courtesy of the Alice Marshall
Women's History Collection, Penn State Harrisburg;
photo by Georganne H. Hughes, Metrophoto.

ful column of her neck rising from the décolletage that barely concealed her delicately-rounded bosom. Her slim waist emphasized by the bodice cut of her gowns, gowns still with the vestige of a bustle and with full, smoothly-fluent skirts."[2] Gibson would make minor alterations over the next two decades—she would dress in more comfortable clothes, and her hairdo would become less towering and more functional, especially when she took up bicycling, golf, tennis, and swimming. Yet she was always well dressed and self-possessed. And, though in her "fearlessness" she rarely smiled, she was unfailingly beautiful.[3]

Gibson's vision of her appeared in many popular periodicals, including *Century, Scribner's,* the several *Harper's* magazines, *Cosmopolitan,* the *Ladies' Home Journal, Good Housekeeping, McCall's, Leslie's Weekly,* and *McClure's.*[4] She was most closely associated, however, with *Life* in the 1890s and *Collier's,* which in 1903 contracted with Gibson for 100 illustrations at $1,000 apiece.[5] *Life* was then a humor magazine that occasionally included serious political and social commentary; *Collier's,* though it later would engage in muckraking, was primarily a general interest title that published quality fiction.[6]

Some commentators have credited Gibson with visually defining not only the ideal American woman, but an entire era, with "intuitively absorbing the yearnings of his time and crystallizing them into captivating pictorial images."[7] The Gibson Girl and her world did represent a coveted social status, to which the artist himself had risen. Gibson was born in 1867 into a family that had been in Boston since 1634 but nevertheless was "of very modest means"; his father, a Civil War veteran, was a salesman. The son was talented and ambitious. During the years he studied in New York, Paris, and London, he gained entry to the highest artistic circles, earning the advice and friendship of impressionist William Merritt Chase, portraitist John Singer Sargeant, sculptor Augustus Saint-Gaudens, and painter Edwin Austin Abbey. Gibson's 1895 wedding further enhanced his social reputation: his bride was Irene Langhorne, a nationally famous beauty who, two years earlier, had led the Grand March with social arbiter Ward McAllister at New York's Patriarch's Ball. This was the society Gibson recreated in the pages of popular magazines. Literary scholar Ernest Earnest described Gibson's pictorial landscape as "the world pictured by Edith Wharton in *The House of Mirth* (1905) and *The Reef* (1912) and in her autobiography, [*A Backward Glance*]."[8]

In the early years of the twentieth century, the New York social elite were celebrities, writes historian Lois Banner. "On Sundays and holidays, upper Fifth Avenue, where the palaces of the wealthy were located, was thronged with crowds trying to catch a glimpse of the American aristocracy. When a major society wedding took place, the police had to be called to keep order among the curious outside the church." Women occupied a key place in this world, and beauty was their greatest asset: "[I]n the pages of the popular press it was the wives—and especially the daughters—of the wealthy who were featured . . . coverage accorded the reigning New York beauty approached that given to public figures in politics or the arts." [9]

By searching for beauty standards specifically in the small world of the native-born, white upper class, the press created a selective view that paralleled President Theodore Roosevelt's public worry about "race suicide." His concern—that whites were having fewer children while millions of eastern European immigrants arrived in the United States each year and bore large families—was echoed by the "scientific" arguments of eugenicists in newspapers and magazines and was justified in terms of the strength of country as a whole. [10] Physical beauty was a measure of fitness, character, and Americanness.

This standard applied to men as well as women. In announcing its acquisition of Gibson as a regular contributor, the editors of *Collier's Weekly* told the story of his rise to fame and fortune and reassured its readers, "His family is of good American stock, the male members having generally combined physical strength with marked intellectual traits. Gibson himself, standing over six feet and of powerful frame, is a typical specimen of his race. 'I often feel,' he said with a smile, 'that it is absurd for a big fellow like me to play at work with a little pencil.'" [11]

As if to justify this unmasculine work, he created for his Girl a tall, broad-shouldered, good-looking beau who came to be known as the "Gibson Man." Modeled on the artist himself and his best friend, writer Richard Harding Davis, this figure was chivalrous and yet also modern—the latter quality signaled by the absence of facial hair that had identified the ideal upper-class Victorian era man. "It was Gibson's pen which sent mustaches out of fashion and made the tailors pad the shoulders of well-cut coats," reported one early-twentieth-century newspaper. [12]

Together the Gibson Girl and the Gibson Man made a striking pair. Like the century, they were young, but their appearance was old stock;

they were superior to recent arrivals while also being models for upward mobility. "Next to their Anglo-Saxon attractiveness, their assurance was their most enviable quality," writes illustration historian Henry Pitz. "To many they seemed the superior creatures of a better, but not too remote, world. With effort and a bit of luck one might scramble up to their level." [13]

For such aspirants, the Gibson Girl image was widely available, moving quickly from the pages of magazines to a broad range of American material culture. Her "chiseled face and aristocratic bearing" were reproduced on china—including collectors' plates advertised in *Life* itself—as well as silverware, pillowcovers, chairs, tabletops, matchboxes, ashtrays, scarves, and wallpaper. She appeared on the covers of sheet music and advertising posters for songs and plays that were written about her. Her figure and garb inspired the manufacture and sale of Gibson Girl shirtwaists, skirts, corsets, shoes, and hats. [14] Richard Harding Davis reported meeting "countless young women" dressed and coiffed like Gibson Girls "from New York and Boston to Grand Rapids and Sioux City" and seeing his friend's artwork "pinned up in as far distant and various places as the dressing room of a theatre in Fort Worth, Tex., and in a students' club at Oxford." [15]

As a matter of clothing and hairdos, the Gibson Girl look enabled the "rising" classes to imitate upper-class style in their own appearances. And on tangible, ownable objects, her image enabled them to import that style into their homes. Both *Life* and *Collier's* made mail-order offers of Gibson coffee-table books and framable reprints. [16] Gibson heads on china plates and parlor walls functioned as a middle-class talisman, an outward sign of inward transformation.

While the Gibson Girl image was valued as a status symbol, it also contained specific ideas about gender. The profile shown in Figure 2.2 suggested that the female sex was an enigma. If the reader missed the message inscribed in her hair—which formed a question mark—the title was more direct: "The Eternal Question." [17] More sexual connotations characterized other Gibson Heads, which were drawn as peaches to be picked or woven together into a pattern for a "bachelor's wallpaper."

Gibson's version of the New Woman was one who came from wealth and who had no need or wish for political or financial independence. Even so, she often was shown (in drawings where she had a body) in some sort of conflict with men. The strong will of women was a recur-

The Eternal Question
CHARLES DANA GIBSON

*Figure 2.2. Charles Dana Gibson, "The Eternal Question" (ca. early 1900s).
Courtesy of the Alice Marshall Women's History Collection, Penn State Harrisburg;
photo by Georganne H. Hughes, Metrophoto.*

Figure 2.3. Charles Dana Gibson, "The Weaker Sex," publication unknown (ca. 1903). Reproduced from the Collections of the Library of Congress.

ring theme in Gibson's commentary on turn-of-the-century gender relations. He drew his Girls nearly causing a man a heart attack as they breezed by him on the street or turning away poutily from their exasperated boyfriends. They were difficult enough alone, and the banding-together of these self-assured young women could emasculate men, Gibson suggested in a 1903 illustration titled "The Weaker Sex" (Figure 2.3)—the title presumably referring to the tiny, pleading man being examined, under glass, by four beauties.

Similarly, a drawing titled "Summer Sports" showed Gibson Girls flying what at first seemed to be kites but actually were little men, suspended in air over the ocean's deep water. Gibson's cover for the 1903 Valentine's Day issue of *Life* featured a statuesque woman juggling small male escorts, whose acrobatic poses formed the magazine's title. These drawings were early examples of the many magazine illustrations (several of which appear in the following chapter) during the first wave of American feminism that showed women tormenting miniature men, a suggestion of the potential for sex-role reversal in the twentieth century.

The meaning of the Gibson Girl was contested in her own day. Gibson was, in the words of one of his contemporaries, the novelist Anthony

Hope, "a cheerful satirist," [18] and one can read in his drawings ridicule of *either* the New Woman herself *or* the overblown charges of her detractors. In her 1898 classic feminist argument, *Women and Economics*, Charlotte Perkins Gilman specifically cited Gibson Girls as "the new women . . . a noble type, indeed." [19] An article for the *Atlantic Monthly* also cast the type as a women's rights symbol but saw no cause for celebration: Americans, the writer implied, had misguidedly come to idealize a rude and overly athletic girl who disdained home life. [20]

In magazines, the Gibson Girl was bold, confident, and free to do as she pleased. But most often her freedom was superficial, a matter of style rather than substance. [21] When the Ziegfeld Follies debuted in 1907, it featured a showgirl number called "The Gibson Bathing Girl," in which beautiful young women musically begged the illustrator to let them show some leg and get in the water. [22] The artist had already complied by creating the first mass media bathing beauties. He placed his beautiful, idealized girls in precisely the spot that had prompted *Ladies' Home Journal* editor Edward Bok's dire warnings about the moral dangers of summertime. Yet at the seashore, the Gibson Girl's steely resolve melted away. If nature emboldened the True Woman, it softened the Gibson Girl, confirming Anthony Hope's summary of her appeal to men: "We perceive that there is something to conquer . . . [and] we believe that the hard-won victory will be complete." [23] In Figure 2.4, one bathing Gibson Girl (fully dressed, curiously) appeared to actually dissolve in the tide while wrapped in the arms of the Gibson Man.

Gibson's Girl did not last far beyond the end of the first decade of the century—by which time the illustrator, who wanted to take up "serious" art, had largely disassociated himself from her—but the notion of an ideal American Girl did. [24] The Gibson Girl's reign overlapped with, and was succeeded by, new "Girls" created by illustrators working much in the same vein. Two of the most successful, Harrison Fisher and Howard Chandler Christy, presided artistically over an era one contemporary social commentator called "The Day of the Girl." [25] The young women they drew for magazine covers were more modern than Gibson Girls, going to college and riding in cars, but they too were types.

In a 1910 newspaper article about illustration, a magazine editor of the day commented on the popularity of familiar visual images identifiable as signature work. He observed that "the man [26] with one type like Fisher is bound to turn out more work than the chap whose earnings depend largely on a diversity of ideas. . . . [T]here is a constant call

Figure 2.4. Charles Dana Gibson, "The Turning of the Tide," Life (1901). Reproduced from the Collections of the Library of Congress.

for work of their peculiar sort, and magazine editors tumble over one another to nail them down with long-term contracts."[27]

Such contracts (from book as well as magazine publishers) were lucrative for Fisher and Christy. It had taken Gibson more than fifteen years of drawing his Girls to reach an annual income of $65,000 by 1905; it took less than a decade for Fisher to do better. By 1910, Fisher's annual earnings were estimated to be $75,000, and Christy's (still rising) were $50,000.[28] Fisher was perfectly aware of the income potential of the "Fisher Girl," explaining to a reporter: "Here are a lot of girls' heads and full-length drawings . . . which have already been used for cover pages to a magazine. I do not sell them outright, and thus they are returned to me. Since their first use they have already appeared in a gift book and my calendar. Some of them have been used as the queens of card packs, and for postal cards. . . . They will [then] go first into a second edition of the gift book. . . . Then copies will be struck from them for poster and decorative designs, and finally originals themselves are sold."[29]

Christy considered girlhood the prime moment in a woman's life, the time when she was most interesting and meaningful to society as a whole. "To know her truly," he wrote in a book actually titled *The American Girl*, "we must look upon her just when all her beauties, her powers, her graces and her virtues are at their early maturity." [30] He claimed that the beauty of the American Girl was universal and eternal.

Fisher was more practical, aware of the fickleness of public taste. He knew that particular kinds of images of women went in and out of fashion. "The Fisher girl is sought to-day," he observed. "Will she be tomorrow, or who will say for how long!" [31] Fisher's Girl received enormous exposure while she was in vogue—for a decade or so, about 1905 to 1915—appearing on the covers of several mass circulation magazines. Two of them, the *Ladies' Home Journal* and the *Saturday Evening Post*, each sold more than a million copies a month during this period; two others, *Cosmopolitan* and the *Woman's Home Companion*, each reached about three-quarters of a million readers per month. [32]

The Fisher Girl had an upswept hairdo and a heart-shaped face similar to the Gibson Girl, though her features, like those of the subject of the *Saturday Evening Post* cover shown in Figure 2.5, were softer and rounder. Her expression was not her predecessor's haughtiness but rather a coquettishness. She was sexual yet also, somehow, wholesome; hers was the come-hither look of the girl next door who was just realizing her charms. Fisher's Girls, unlike Gibson's, appeared without titles, so their meaning was more open to interpretation and their beauty was less often undercut by sly puns.

Like the Gibson Girl, the Fisher Girl was well dressed and appeared genteel. Some of the material inside the magazines on which she appeared hinted that she might have started out in different circumstances. An early 1906 article in *Cosmopolitan* (then a general interest, not a women's, publication) titled "Poor Girls Who Marry Millions" told the stories of twenty young working women who had done just that. The author gushed: "[T]here is sufficient progress in the union of wealth and ease with poverty and toil to emphasize the fact that Cupid, even in these sordid times, reckons less than ever before, perhaps, with social inequalities." The women's tales were presented as modern-day Cinderella stories, continuing the Gibsonian theme that beauty was one path to upward social and economic mobility. [33]

Fisher's cover girls were more casually dressed than the Gibson Girl, and he gave them props that suggested specific outdoor activities; for instance, one girl posed with a horse and riding crop, another in a swim-

Figure 2.5. Harrison Fisher, The Saturday Evening Post *(Aug. 15, 1908).*
Reproduced from the Collections of the Library of Congress.

ming cap, a third with bird-watching binoculars in hand. These young women were what Martha Banta, in her analysis of women's imagery of this era, calls "The New Woman as Charmer and Outdoors Pal."[34] The *Ladies' Home Journal* cover in Figure 2.6, which showed girls actually participating in sports and hobbies, was almost parodic in its celebration of outdoor girlhood. Just as significant as their various activities was the fact that this was a *group* of girls wearing uniforms—these were schoolgirls, perhaps at college.

Throughout 1908, the *Journal* ran a series of illustrations collectively titled "Harrison Fisher's College Girls," paying tribute to the young women who comprised 40 percent of college students by the century's second decade.[35] Fisher's college scenes blended conventionally feminine activities with the newer pastimes of the outdoor girl. His Girls sang and cooked together, but also played basketball and rowed. In June 1913, Fisher celebrated their graduation on the cover of a "Girls' Number" of the *Journal* (Figure 2.7).

Howard Chandler Christy also approved of women going to college. His early drawings for *Scribner's* were Gibsonian, like the singer and scene in Figure 2.8, an illustration titled "Our Girl Graduate." Like Fisher, he imagined college as a place where girls formed friendships and took up sports that would make them better mothers and wives. What Christy approved of most of all was physical fitness in women. "[T]he American girl of to-day finds in outdoor life the true secret of health and the beauty that can have no other secure foundation," he wrote. "The hand that swings the tennis racquet is the hand that rocks the cradle."[36] Despite his emphasis on outdoor life, then, Christy's beliefs paralleled those of Edward Bok, who editorialized in the *Ladies' Home Journal* that "A truly educated girl . . . comes back to her home and friends broadened in heart as well as in mind. . . . Her greatest lessons are to be learned after she leaves college."[37]

Though he published in such magazines as the *Ladies' Home Journal, Cosmopolitan,* and *McClure's,* most of Christy's work appeared in *Scribner's, Leslie's Weekly,* and *Harper's Monthly.* Despite the smaller circulation of the latter titles, the Christy Girl outdistanced the Fisher Girl in national popularity thanks to the seven book collections of his drawings and his philosophies about young women, a subject on which the artist considered himself an expert.[38]

The Christy Girl, for whom hats, shoes, and gowns were named,[39] debuted in the late 1890s as "The Soldier's Dream," a picture illustrat-

Figure 2.6. Harrison Fisher, The Ladies' Home Journal *(Aug. 1912).*
Courtesy of the Alice Marshall Women's History Collection, Penn State Harrisburg;
photo by Georganne H. Hughes, Metrophoto.

Figure 2.7. Harrison Fisher, The Ladies' Home Journal *(June 1913)*.
Courtesy of the Alice Marshall Women's History Collection, Penn State Harrisburg;
photo by Georganne H. Hughes, Metrophoto.

OUR GIRL GRADUATE

Figure 2.8. Howard Chandler Christy, "Our Girl Graduate" (ca. early 1900s).
Reproduced from the Collections of the Library of Congress. From
The American Girl *(New York: Moffat, Yard, 1906).*

ing a short story in *Scribner's* about the Spanish-American War.[40] If she began as a man's dream, she soon became his friend as well. She was a good sport. She dressed for the weather and didn't worry if her hair was messed by the wind. She often looked directly outward at the viewer in a frank and upbeat way. Her sheer friendliness may be one reason she lasted longer than the other versions of the prewar American Girl; also, her haircut made her an early version of the 1920s "flapper," to be discussed in Chapter 6. Figure 2.9 is an example of his Girl's survival into that decade.

Illustration scholar Mimi Miley credits Fisher and Christy with "turning the demure Victorian girl into an athletic modern woman."[41] The cheerful girls Christy drew in military uniforms for World War I posters—his best-remembered work, shown in Chapter 5—were positively tomboyish. Such images were particularly intriguing in a college setting, a place where women were educated for careers and where same-sex friendships might grow into something more threatening to the heterosexual norm.

Figure 2.9. Howard Chandler Christy, Motor *(Nov. 1923).*
Reproduced from the Collections of the Library of Congress.

In one of his books, Christy actually addressed this fear, advising parents not to worry about intense attachments between girls in college: "[L]ike some other disorders, [it] will run its course without harm to the patient. . . . Just now both feel that they would go to the altar for one another; but it is not the sacrificial but the matrimonial altar that will put an end to this endless bond, when one is the other's bride's-maid." [42] His advice supports historian Lynn D. Gordon's charge that illustrators of this era "softened the disturbing image of educated women" by showing that " 'college girls' were attractive and feminine," that "higher education was 'safe' for women . . . [and that] it need not lead to social change." [43]

Nevertheless, the idealization of the American Girl as Outdoor Pal was representationally complex. Illustrators' placement of their subjects in nature and in sporting activities reflected a very real trend (among both women and men) toward health and physical fitness during the second decade of the century. Historian Donald Mrozek links this trend to a sexual openness inspired by Freudian psychology, while T. J. Jackson Lears contends that psychological and physical fitness came to replace moral virtue during this era. Yet for women, exercise and mobility offered new and tangible rewards, true liberation from the physical restraints of nineteenth-century clothing and behavioral norms.[44]

Women's health was a frequent editorial theme in media of the era. One article in the *Philadelphia Press* urged young women not to neglect exercise ("body culture") once they were out of school and into the work world (no less). The author advised her female reader to join a gymnasium where, after a long day at work, she could swim, play basketball — or box! [45] A *Good Housekeeping* feature described the "Girl of Today" as confidently athletic: "It is as much a source of shame to her to be sickly as it is for a man to be a weakling. Girls boast of their muscle and how they can play golf all day, dance or skate half the night, without turning a hair. The daughters of a house are quite as able-bodied as the sons, and a neurotic, hysterical young maiden lying about on a sofa, once a frequent and familiar sight, is now almost as uncommon a spectacle as a dodo." [46]

The *Good Housekeeping* article was not just a message *about* women's strength; it was delivered *to* them. It's impossible to discuss the meaning of the "girl" on magazine covers without considering her institutional setting. Compare, for instance, the demure, sideways glance of the girl on the cover of the *Saturday Evening Post* in Figure 2.5 — a picture image

to be *looked at* by that magazine's primarily male readership in 1908—
to the direct gazes connecting the college students in Fisher's two *Journal* covers (Figures 2.6 and 2.7) with the reader, who was female. This noticeable difference suggests the importance of the audience in the creation as well as the reception of cover images, and in the illustrator's anticipation of a "female gaze," whether or not the artist was female.

It also is remarkable that a popular illustrator showcased female college graduates—not just one pretty "head" but a stream of *seventeen* graduating young women—on the cover of a major magazine in 1913. Like Stephens's work for the same magazine sixteen years earlier, and like the colleges most women then attended, it was an entirely female space. Stephens's woman took one last look backward before ascending a staircase into Society; Fisher's Girl did the same before descending a staircase into, presumably, the World.

Whether or not she was portrayed as educated or athletic, the magazine cover girl of this era was almost always shown outside the home, a rhetorical shift that acknowledged real change in women's social roles. This change continued to prompt editorial fretting. Even while it published the drawings of Gibson, Fisher, and Christy, *Cosmopolitan* ran a three-part series in 1906 and 1907 on the snares that awaited to trap a young woman who left her parents' or husband's home without protection. Two of the installments told the tale of an attractive young woman who traveled alone by train and was alternately accosted by lecherous men and snubbed by married women traveling with their husbands. The third was about single women forced to earn a living, another path fraught with physical danger and reputation-tarnishing temptations.[47] A 1909 *Cosmopolitan* article warned career women that their marriage chances would quickly pass them by, that they would find themselves, in their thirties, desperately single when "the desirable men . . . are nearly all either married or dead."[48] In such an editorial climate, visual images of young women at sports and in college may have worked to challenge rather than confirm Victorian ideas about womanhood. Certainly textual and visual images were often inconsistent, and descriptions of women's and girls' lives in magazines were less uniform than they had been in the 1890s.

If magazine messages about a young woman's "place" (figurative and literal) in society were mixed during the first decade of the twentieth century, they were extremely complicated by the second. The same year that Harrison Fisher depicted College Girls going to commencement on the cover of the *Ladies' Home Journal,* the works of Sigmund Freud were widely popularized in the United States, and the press reported on "anti-vice" crusades taking place in cities across the country. As one newspaper editor put it, "sex o'clock" had struck in America.[49]

Journalistic commentary on sexuality obviously was an occasion to debate the New Woman's effect on men, but it also was a way of discussing the growing "dangers" of city life as the country became increasingly urban and populated with immigrants. Whereas the promise of uptown gentility and wealth had been represented in the figure of the Gibson Girl at the turn of the century, the dangers of the downtown world of the working classes were represented in popular media through the figures of women after 1910.

Dangerous Women and the Crisis of Masculinity

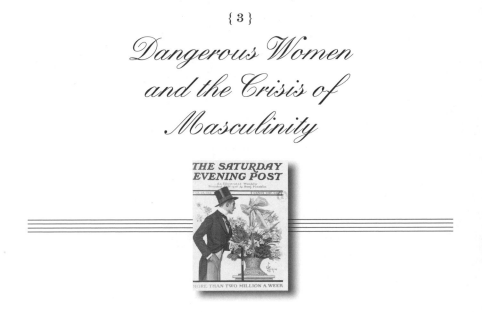

Long before there were mass media, artists and novelists depicted women as either "good" or "bad," a dichotomy in which good women made men stronger and bad women destroyed them. The opposition of the virgin and the vamp has been a theme of media, and media criticism, throughout the twentieth century.[1] In its second decade—the time when the word "vamp" was first applied to women—the image of the bad woman prevailed in American popular culture, emerging simultaneously in magazine art and the new medium of film.

At best this female character was what magazine historian Patricia Frantz Kery calls "the new, playful woman," a coy creature a man could enjoy but not trust.[2] Illustrator James Montgomery Flagg poured his version of the "Sweet Girl Graduate" (Figure 3.1) into a graduated chemistry beaker that bore a suspicious resemblance to a drinking glass; with not a foot to stand on (let alone commence), she was a potion ready to be consumed. But she was a dangerous brew, as suggested by the girls Flagg and fellow illustrator Coles Phillips drew for the covers of *Judge* and *Life*.

These titles were weekly humor magazines with readerships much smaller than those of circulation powerhouses such as the *Journal* and the *Post*. Still, the Day of the Girl, as one journalist dubbed this era, was

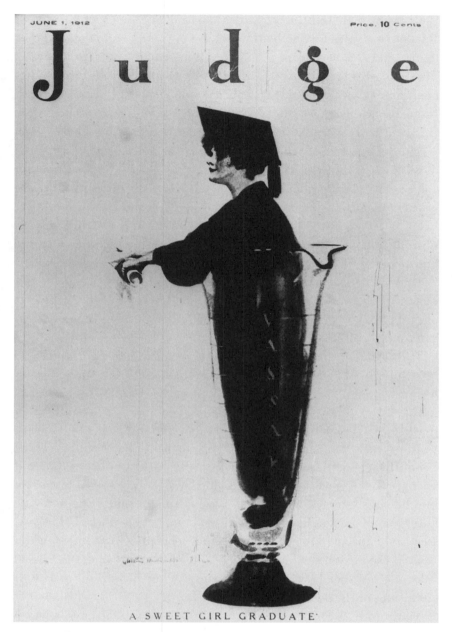

JUNE 1, 1912   Price. 10 Cents

Judge

A SWEET GIRL GRADUATE

Figure 3.1. James Montgomery Flagg, "A Sweet Girl Graduate," Judge
(June 1, 1912). Reproduced from the Collections of the Library of Congress.

their day as well.[3] In 1910, both titles had healthy circulations of around 100,000 readers per week; by the decade's end, *Judge* had doubled that figure, and *Life* was nearing half a million, which would be its peak.[4] Though never truly "mass," their audiences were "class"—predominantly male, predominantly urban, a combination of the already well-to-do and the "acquisitive, upward-bound, middle class."[5] These were the readers whom manufacturers of higher-ticket items, such as cars, fashion, china, tobacco, liquor, and other "lifestyle" products, wanted most to reach through advertising.

The new "playful woman" as imagined on the covers and inside pages of these magazines defined play as sin—whether in the form of alcohol or illicit sex, a temptation to men that seemed irresistible yet was ultimately destructive. In publications targeted toward upwardly mobile men, she was a complicated study in class relations, embracing not the ball-going glamour of the upper crust but rather the "cheap amusements" of the working class.[6] Her image was a reverse of the "aesthetic of imitation," a sort of class fluidity that created the illusion of *downward* social mobility.

It was in fact upper- and middle-class women, not men, who came into closest contact with working-class women in this era, for quite serious rather than playful purposes. Progressive reformers (whose ranks were, as Robyn Muncy puts it, a "female dominion")[7] literally went downtown to create settlement houses for immigrants and to join with working-class women in organizations such as the Women's Trade Union League.[8] These activities not only brought women of different backgrounds together, but also provided a socially acceptable way for middle-class married women and recent female college graduates to enter public life and have (albeit unpaid) important work to do there. In what historians now call the "social housekeeping" movement, white women used traditional notions about domesticity to claim the job of "cleaning up" society, which included improving the working and living conditions of the poor.

Kathryn Kish Sklar contends that this was a political move in which "gender served as a surrogate for class."[9] Such volunteer activity combined with the suffrage campaign (many of the same women were involved in both) increased women's presence in public, while bringing "good" and "bad" women together. These alliances disrupted the dichotomous ideas about working-class behavior and about womanhood that were nevertheless regular themes in mainstream magazines.

Ironically, some of the female reformers were involved in the antivice crusades of the decade that targeted the very working-class institutions that worried middle-class men. One concern was the urban dance hall, where young women and men were ostensibly ruined by alcohol and promiscuity.[10] The "dance craze" was a theme of magazine illustration, articles, and fiction featuring young women who flirted dangerously with the mysteries of ethnicity and city life—and who were themselves threats to men.

Though never so dangerous in actuality, the dance craze was real. In elite ballrooms and in middle-class social clubs, Americans did the slow drag, the tango, and the "animal dances"—the turkey trot, bunny hug, grizzly bear, fox trot, monkey glide, lame duck, camel walk, kangaroo dip, fish walk, and snake. These last were considered scandalous because they required close contact and thrusting or shimmying moves. Underlying the sexual tensions were racial as well as class fascinations. The animal dances, which had originated in working-class dance halls and brothels, were performed to syncopated rhythms of African American origin. As if to highlight the exoticism of their own behavior, white socialites employed all-black dance bands to play at society events.[11] Some tried to sanitize the dances by renaming them; when Helen Taft, the president's daughter, hosted a ball at the White House in 1911, the turkey trot was called the "Long Boston." [12]

New York City alone had more than 500 dance halls, including huge arenas such as the Grand Central Dance Palace and the Roseland Ballroom, plus 100,000 "dancing academies" where lessons were given.[13] Dancing enabled a shedding of restraint, figuratively through the illusion of class mobility ("slumming") and literally through physical mobility. It also required a shedding of clothing and a transformation in dress styles. Women's fashions became less constraining, more revealing yet also more girlish. The sleeveless, straight shift, ending around the knee, was popularized by dancer Irene Castle, who bobbed her hair and, with husband Vernon, fox-trotted at chic New York clubs and on cross-country tours.[14]

An article in the April 1914 issue of the *Delineator*, a fashion magazine, described the ideal dancing body as "the straight figure, with small hips, large waist and no bust," making it clear that, in real-life imitations of popular styles, the Gibson Girl had been replaced by an adolescent sister or daughter. "The face alone, no matter how pretty, counts for nothing unless the body is as straight and yielding as a very young girl's," the writer explained.[15] To show this new form, illustrators increasingly drew full-length portraits rather than "heads."

Young women did not actually have to turkey trot in order to adopt the new look, of course. And dancing was significant less as a pastime than as a metaphor for sexual experimentation. The "hitherto forbidden body movements" and "single standard of sexual conduct" on the dance floor represented only one aspect of changing behavior codes for young men and women.[16] The new practice of dating, which moved courtship from the home into public, similarly relaxed rules about physical contact.[17]

Debates about the morality of dating and dancing stressed their pitfalls for young women, echoing the prediction of one male observer of a college dance that "[t]his wriggling will soon lead to a nervous breakdown for innocent girls."[18] Yet much media imagery suggested just the opposite—that the endangered sex was not female but male.

On magazine covers and at the movies, the idea of a new, sexually free American woman was presented as a threat to men, and she was captured in at least three new visual "types" of the American woman. One was the party girl, such as the graduate poured into Flagg's glass. Another was Flagg's specialty, the vamp. A third was the scheming beauty, a gold-digging heartbreaker who emasculated men and who populated the illustrations of Coles Phillips. All of these female types were portrayed as dangerous to men in an era when social commentators worried publicly about men's virility and the survival of the white race.

The term "vamp" came from the title of a Rudyard Kipling poem— about a woman who sucks the spirit out of a man by refusing to return his love—that inspired a 1915 silent film starring the kohl-eyed actress Theda Bara. Bara, who assumed the vamp identity as her professional persona, called herself a "feministe." During the decade when the term "feminist" was first used by women's rights activists (some of whom advocated greater sexual freedom for women), this was a political statement. Yet, in Bara's celebrity image, "feministe" quite specifically meant revenge. The actress declared that men "take everything from women—love, devotion, beauty, youth—and give nothing in return! V stands for Vampire and it stands for Vengeance, too. The vampire that I play is the vengeance of my sex upon its exploiters."[19]

Such a character was quite a contrast to other types of film heroines of the day, the sweet young girls played by such actresses as Mary Pickford and Lillian Gish in movies with titles like *Hearts Adrift* and *Home, Sweet Home*.[20] In her study of women's characterization in early film, Serafina Bathrick confirms that in silent movies, the vamp was "posed as the True Woman's opposite. She is dark, she is sexual, she is volatile, she is mobile, and, above all, she lives alone, outside the sphere of home and family."[21] Bathrick further notes that the character of the vamp as a creature of public space served to preserve (not challenge) the nineteenth-century opposition between public and private life and to equate women's appearance in public with their desire to ruin men and the family. In this view, there was only a fine line between a vamp and a prostitute; so too was there only a fine line between prostitutes and all women who left the home, for any reason.[22]

The conflation of vamping and prostitution was accomplished on a 1914 cover of *Judge* (Figure 3.2) drawn by James Montgomery Flagg. His vamp's direct gaze was both a challenge and an invitation, as was the pose of her body, with hand on hip and one knee forward. She stood alone, the recipient of disapproving stares from a group of unattractive older women representing not just propriety, but also, in their dress and age, a previous era.[23] The girl's outfit was even more revealing than the slim shift popularized by the dance craze, and the title, "Passed by the Board of Censorship," suggested either that she was dressed in imitation of a movie star (efforts to censor films began as early as 1911)[24] or that she somehow had avoided the vice squad.

Flagg's sympathies were not with this girl's detractors; he approved of sexy young women. In his autobiography, Flagg explained his philosophy on this subject: "Women *should* be coquettes. How dull and unfeminine women are who are forthright, good-fellows, good pals, one of the boys, honest, take-it-or-leave-it creatures. Good God! I'd much rather be with men when I just want good company."[25] He also approved of movie stars, some of whom were his friends (John Barrymore and cowboy-hero William S. Hart) and his models (actresses Norma Shearer and Mabel Normand).[26]

Flagg himself was a celebrity, and the demand for his work was reflected in his earnings of more than $75,000 a year. His drawings appeared in books (including works of P. G. Wodehouse, Sinclair Lewis, and Booth Tarkington) as well as in magazines. The latter included, in addition to *Judge* and *Life*, the *American Magazine, Scribner's, Harper's*

Figure 3.2. James Montgomery Flagg, "Passed by the Board of Censorship," Judge
(June 13, 1914). Reproduced from the Collections of the Library of Congress.

Weekly, Leslie's Weekly, Cosmopolitan, Liberty, the Woman's Home Companion, and Good Housekeeping. He also wrote two dozen movie scripts
featuring the "Flagg Girl" he drew for magazines.[27]

Flagg did two different kinds of illustration work, cover images and
pen-and-ink drawings that were commissioned to accompany specific

subject matter of interior pages. His black-and-white, pen-and-ink women, who frequently illustrated romantic short stories, looked very much like Gibson Girls. But the Flagg Girl who appeared in color on his magazine covers was a different kind of woman. She was "saucy" rather than proper in the manner of a Gibson Girl or a pal in the manner of a Fisher or Christy Girl.[28]

Novelist Owen Johnson called this type the "Salamander" in his 1914 tale of the same name. He considered such behavior merely a stage in a young woman's life, ending around age twenty-five. But what a stage! He explained: ". . . she can meet what men she wishes, men of every station, men drawn to her by the lure of her laughter and tantalizing arts . . . hunters who . . . seek with a renewal of excitement this corruption of innocence. She has no fear of these last, matching her wits against their appetites, paying them back cruelly in snare and disillusion. . . . [S]he adores perilous adventures and somehow or other, miraculously, she never fails in saving her skirts from the contagion of the flames."[29]

The author's reference to men as "hunters" was a joke on them; they in fact were the creatures to be hunted and tamed. Flagg took this idea to an extreme in a 1912 *Life* cover portraying a man as a trained monkey on a rope (Figure 3.3), titled—for the magazine's predominantly male readership—"Has This Ever Happened to You?" This image also may have been a humorous reference to the animal dances, as was Flagg's 1914 *Judge* cover drawing of a woman dancing with a lobster who was all claws. In Flagg's artistic world, beautiful women seduced men and led them to ruin. Sometimes he conveyed this threat comically, as in one of his *Judge* covers showing a well-dressed man startled to find himself surrounded by women's shapely legs in dancing shoes. In a more ominous cover drawing, romance was compared to a hazardous game of chance, conjuring an unsmiling female "black widow" up from a card table.

A prettier but equally deadly spider appeared as a girl on the 1911 "Coquette's Number" of *Life,* a cover drawn by Coles Phillips (Figure 3.4). Titled "Net Results," the illustration showed four tiny men entangled in the coquette's web, along with a discarded "Engagements" book. The image seemed to ask, "Why should women marry men when they could devour them?"

Not all of Phillips's work was satirical, and he drew women for covers of *Collier's, Liberty, McCall's,* the *Ladies' Home Journal, Woman's Home Companion,* the *Saturday Evening Post,* and *Good Housekeeping,* doing

Life

PRICE 10 CENTS
Vol. 60, No. 1550. July 11, 1912
Copyright, 1912, Life Publishing Company

HAS THIS EVER HAPPENED TO YOU?

JAMES MONTGOMERY FLAGG

Figure 3.3. James Montgomery Flagg, "Has This Ever Happened to You?"
Life *(July 11, 1912). Reproduced from the Collections of the Library of Congress.*

more than five dozen covers for the last of those.[30] His signature image
was known as the "Fadeaway Girl," a slim young woman whose dress
and/or hair blended into the color or pattern of her background (as did
his girl-spider, who wore a red dress against a red backdrop).[31] Phillips
published book collections of his trademark beauties, and *Life* offered

The Crisis of Masculinity

{ 64 }

AUG 22 1911

Life

PRICE. 10 CENTS
VOL. LVIII, NO. 1504. AUGUST 24, 1911

NET RESULTS

Figure 3.4. Coles Phillips, "Net Results," Life *(Aug. 24, 1911).*
Reproduced from the Collections of the Library of Congress.

its readers reprints of his covers (for which the magazine paid him as
much as $2,000 apiece) as well as a Fadeaway Girl calendar.[32]

Phillips described his typical subject as "always alluring . . . a real
woman from the tip of her dainty boot to the soft glory of her hair . . .
a young man's fancy at its highest and best."[33] This compliment may

Figure 3.5. Coles Phillips, "The Time of Her Life," Life *(Aug. 5, 1909).*
Reproduced from the Collections of the Library of Congress.

have fit the women he drew for *Good Housekeeping* (aside from the fact
that they melted into the cover). But on *Life,* for which Phillips did most
of his work, his Fadeaway Girl was more like a young man's nightmare.
She was having, as noted by the title of one of his *Life* covers, "The Time
of Her Life" (Figure 3.5). Men were merely hours of the day; when one

was finished, another was coming around to have his moment. (Note that this is an *alarm* clock.)

This theme—a beauty deciding what to do with all the tiny men at her disposal—recurred in Phillips's cover work for *Life*. Several of these pictures, like the drawing of the clock-setter, showed a young woman trying to choose among suitors represented in multiple and small forms: as playing cards (titled "Discarding from Strength"); as faces on a wall calendar ("Dates"); as checkerboard spaces representing strategic options of money, love, royalty, and religion ("Her Move"); and as the gifts her various boyfriends had given her ("Know All Men by These Presents"). Another Phillips *Life* cover image, a counterpart to the girl-spider, depicted the woman as an elegant butterfly pursued by tiny men with nets (Figure 3.6), the joke being that this tall and cooly unconcerned beauty could easily swat them away.

Such images were common in other media of the 1910s as well. Popular songs portrayed women as heartless golddiggers, and their sheet-music covers showed beauties bossing little men around, flinging them about, and stepping on them.[34] Early comic movies about suffragists depicted "a brutal world in which women abused their husbands" or infantilized them (one showed women dressing men in diapers).[35] Even better known were the film characters played by Charlie Chaplin, whose "little tramp" and assorted other powerless men pined away for women who seemed out of their grasp.

Writing about the scenarios of early silent movies starring Chaplin and Buster Keaton, film critic Molly Haskell notes that their love interest "was never a 'realistic' partner, with defects like their own, but the most beautiful and exquisite of creatures. . . . [T]hey created a situation which could only lead to disappointment, and a woman who . . . could only reflect the shallowness and vanity of all women."[36] These befuddled romantics were updated versions of Gibson's pin-pricked man under the magnifying glass, and they lived in the same world as Coles Phillips's pleading suitors.

All of these images were commentaries on the New Woman in a decade of Freudian psychology and women's suffrage. Their heavy-handed point was that if women gained control in the bedroom or at the ballot box, American manhood would suffer. But they articulated other concerns as well. Chaplin's little tramp struggled for potency not only with women but also in a society that was increasingly urban,

Figure 3.6. Coles Phillips, "The Butterfly Chase," Life *(Mar. 10, 1910).*
Reproduced from the Collections of the Library of Congress.

corporate, and bureaucratic. The little men of the era's media articulated what historians have called the "crisis of masculinity" in early-twentieth-century America, a dilemma having to do with societal changes that included but went beyond male-female relations.

Joe Dubbert contends that nineteenth-century men "tended to see themselves successfully forcing their will on their environment," whereas for the man in the twentieth century "things happened to him as luck and fate would have it."[37] C. Wright Mills saw precisely this image in men's portrayals in literature: "The nineteenth-century farmer and businessman were generally thought to be stalwart individuals—their own men, men who could quickly grow to be almost as big as anyone else. The twentieth-century white-collar man . . . [was] the small creature who is acted upon but who does not act, who works along unnoticed in somebody's office or store, never talking loud, never talking back, never taking a stand."[38]

The twentieth-century white-collar man was the core reader of the country's largest-circulation magazine at the time, the *Saturday Evening Post*, which had a weekly audience of two million by the early 1910s. Building that man's confidence—and resolving the crisis of masculinity, a paradox in which the business world that supported the *Post* made its reader feel small—was the primary goal of editor George Horace Lorimer. Imagining his readers as "ambitious young men of the great middle-class American public," Lorimer created a magazine that glorified the business world while making the ordinary man the hero of that world. In this vision, the little (common) man controlled his own destiny and gained status and power through hard work. The magazine's articles and fiction were tales of "the romance of large fortunes and the rise of a young man from the bottom of the ladder to the topmost rung of millionaireship."[39] Lorimer's editorials honored "the desire of every man to be the architect of his own fortunes."[40] Norman Rockwell later described Lorimer's strategy as "building a success on success stories, for his theme was high-class Horatio Alger."[41]

The *Post*'s leading cover artist of these years was a living example of the editor's creed. A German immigrant and the son of a brewer, J. C. (Joseph Christian) Leyendecker worked his way through art schools in Chicago and Paris before moving to New York in the late 1890s. He preferred cover art—which, he claimed, "hits harder because it is a symbol; it is concentrated"—and excelled at it, taking assignments from the *Literary Digest, Century, Success, Collier's,* and the *Post*. During his fifty-year career, he drew more than 500 covers, some 320 of them for the *Post* alone, earning as much as $2,000 per cover.[42] Like Gibson before him, Leyendecker rose to the society his magazine celebrated, and with his newfound wealth he built a mansion in New Rochelle, New York, where Coles Phillips and, later, Rockwell were his neighbors.[43]

Leyendecker was one of the few illustrators who created men for magazine covers. Drawn in his distinctive style—as Michael Schau describes it, "the very wide, deliberate stroke done with authority and control"—his male figures depicted competing ideals of masculinity at the heart of the "crisis."[44]

One version, representing the social and financial improvement Lorimer's editorials encouraged, showed young men who were rising in the world or already at the top. This upscale ideal was characterized by the high-hatted gentleman dressed in tails on Leyendecker's Easter 1913 *Post* cover (Figure 3.7), posed almost painstakingly for inspection as a symbol of what readers might someday attain. The artist's cover girls had the well-heeled appearance and finely chiseled features of his men, and together the two characters symbolized a lifestyle, a world of "well-to-do, civilized people with self-confidence reinforced by breeding, education, position, and taste."[45]

The Easter cover man's jutting chin, broad shoulders, and slim waist also typified the advertising image for which Leyendecker was best known, the "Arrow Collar Man" (shown in Chapter 8). "Just as Charles Dana Gibson presented his public with the distinctive mark of the patrician American woman," writes illustration historian Susan Meyer, "so did J. C. Leyendecker establish the prototype of the fashionable American male . . . the symbol of what manhood should be."[46]

Actually, this fashionable man was only one of two notions of what manhood should be. During the preceding decade, then-president Theodore Roosevelt had advocated the "strenuous life" for young (white) men at a time when, he believed, the weakness of "the over-civilized man"—the man dominated by women—endangered the future of the race and the strength of the nation.[47] This was precisely the anxiety expressed through the figures of vamps and miniature men in popular culture.

Growing interest in physical fitness and in new organizations such as the Boy Scouts of America, founded in 1910, reflected Americans' real-life preoccupation with the second ideal for masculinity. The mission of the Boy Scouts "responded explicitly to adult sex-role concerns," writes historian Jeffrey Hantover. "It provided concerned men the opportunity to support 'an organized effort to make big men of little boys.'"[48] (Hantover is quoting a *Good Housekeeping* article whose author explained to mothers that it was "boy nature" for adolescent sons to need to find "a world in which petticoats are scorned.")[49] Sports also

Figure 3.7. J. C. Leyendecker, The Saturday Evening Post *(Mar. 22, 1913).*
Reproduced from the Collections of the Library of Congress.

were seen as a path to rugged manhood (through exercise) and upward mobility (through discipline), a means for young men to quite literally become "self-made."

Art historian Eric Segal divides the era's "competing versions of white, middle-class American masculinity" into "sartorial masculinity that is based on fashion and taste" and "corporal masculinity," a matter of "bodily fortitude."[50] Leyendecker gave pictorial form to both of these ideals. In addition to his suave society men, he drew athletes for his *Post* covers. He also created a series of posters depicting the sportsmen of Ivy League schools,[51] some of which were printed in the *Post*. Rockwell, who was greatly influenced by Leyendecker's work, remembered these images, "which had titles like 'Rushing the Line' and 'The Kickoff' and which college boys framed and hung about in their rooms."[52]

The artist's college football players (Figure 3.8), shown in strenuous competition and in forward motion, symbolized the success attainable by "the ambitious young men of the great middle-class American public." Football also initiated young men, as a group, into a particular style of masculinity: "The football field was an exclusively male world where the players could legitimately act out aggressions and win measurable victories," notes Peter Filene.[53] "Aggressions" may be an understatement in describing this new American sport that caused 113 fatalities between 1905 and 1910.[54] "Before World War I," writes Joe Dubbert, "many considered the football player to be the most manly of men because of the courage required to play the game—especially so in its early history when protective gear was primitive or nonexistent."[55]

Surviving such a trial was a way for young men to be heroes in a frontierless and corporate society. And in an era when—as magazines and books claimed—men were physically weakened by the feminizing domesticity of good women and morally weakened by the sexual temptations of bad women, sports "acted as a moral safety valve to a nation of people filled with energy to renew the race," writes Dubbert.[56] Like the activities of the Boy Scouts, the sports played by Leyendecker's characters were rituals through which men regained their stature, professionally, physically, morally, and racially.

Excluded from these rituals of mastery were not just women, but also African Americans and most recent immigrants—collectively, the forces that eugenicists believed threatened white male survival during the century's first two decades. Their challenge, like the crisis of

Figure 3.8. J. C. Leyendecker, The Saturday Evening Post *(Nov. 15, 1913).*
Reproduced from the Collections of the Library of Congress.

masculinity, would be largely resolved by the coming war. But in the prewar years, mass-circulation-magazine visions of rugged manhood were countered by other kinds of imagery in magazines outside the mainstream. Those periodicals would, briefly, offer alternative views of womanhood, manhood, and Americanness.

Alternative Visions

In 1909, *Cosmopolitan* magazine published a short story, "The Emancipation of Sarah," about a young Jewish woman named Sarah and her overbearing mother who believed that they had been successful in converting Sarah's immigrant suitor to feminism and socialism. Immediately after marrying her, however, the young man put his new wife in her place, and, with only a little resistance, Sarah happily assumed the role of a pious and prosperous merchant's wife.[1]

Appearing in a mass circulation magazine, this tale provided a catalog of what the mainstream press perceived as a series of threats to the American way of life during the first two decades of the twentieth century: feminism, socialism, and immigration. The fourth major social tension of the era, not directly addressed in this story, was that of deteriorating race relations, exacerbated by African Americans' migration from the rural South to northern cities.

All of these threats were underscored by the emergence of alternative magazines. While these publications called for significant societal change, they did so in familiar rhetoric. As with their mainstream counterparts, alternative periodicals of this era chose women—often an allegorical Woman—as their primary cover figures, using the female form to convey both resistance and reassurance. This chapter considers how such work was accomplished in magazines advocating women's suffrage, socialism, and the advancement of African Americans.

Suffrage publications reflected widely held views, yet they continued to provoke controversy. Since the 1848 Seneca Falls convention, female activists had published a number of periodicals advancing their cause. During the final decade of the drive for the vote—and the peak period for public discussion of the issue—suffrage magazines represented various factions of the movement. Beginning in 1913, Alice Paul's radical Congressional Union, which became the National Woman's Party, published the *Suffragist* and then *Equal Rights*. The more conservative National American Woman Suffrage Association published the *Woman's Journal*, founded by Lucy Stone in 1870; in 1917 it switched from newspaper to magazine format and became the *Woman Citizen*. Edited by Stone's daughter, Lucy Stone Blackwell, the *Woman Citizen* represented the mainstream of the movement, and its covers are analyzed here.

Artists working for women's rights periodicals did not invent new imagery to visualize the New Woman who was a suffragist; instead, they used familiar and comforting notions of womanhood to make suffrage seem right and natural. As both Alice Sheppard and Lisa Tickner have noted in their histories of American and British suffrage art, illustrators were forced to contend with stereotypes already in place in the surrounding culture, pervasive imagery collectively forming "a kind of iconographic shorthand" that defined womanhood. "Suffragists were engaged in skirmishes . . . around ideal, normative, and deviant types of femininity," Tickner explains. "Their artists were obliged to negotiate a set of inherited and interdependent categories." [2]

On the covers of the *Woman Citizen*, these inherited images often reappeared in the form of figures from Greek mythology or military iconology. Such symbols represented not actual women (or even necessarily womanhood) but nobler concepts conveyed by their expressions, bodies, and poses. [3] Part of their appeal was their irony: the invocation of "Justice" or "Liberty" on behalf of the suffrage cause suggested women's lack of these rights. On a 1917 *Woman Citizen* cover (Figure 4.1), a statue of Justice came to life in the face of injustice and, trailing her scales, angrily stalked with the suffrage banner through New York toward Washington. A cover published a month later showed a tall, classically clothed figure personifying Suffrage itself, who refused to be swayed by partisanship (two short men pulling from either side).

These were radical messages. The women they depicted were angry and refused to be influenced by men: one could not be stopped; the other would not budge. The latter illustration also utilized the big woman/little man motif popular in the era's graphic humor about suf-

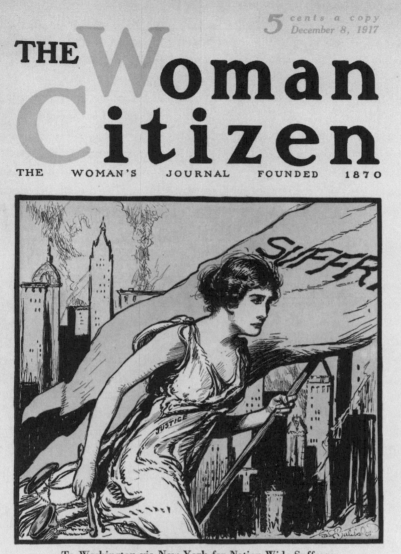

To Washington via New York for Nation-Wide Suffrage

Figure 4.1. C. D. Batchelor, The Woman Citizen *(Dec. 8, 1917)*.
Courtesy of the Alice Marshall Women's History Collection, Penn State Harrisburg;
photo by Georganne H. Hughes, Metrophoto.

fragists, though here it was not funny. This reversal of conventional size represented the threat that drove the plot of "The Emancipation of Sarah." Interestingly, these particular images were drawn by a male artist, C. D. Batchelor, though many suffrage artists were female (as were all three art directors of the publication at the time).[4]

Still, it was crucial to the broad communicative power of such images in 1917 and 1918 that the threat be tempered by the women's beauty, and these women bore a striking resemblance to Gibson Girls. Their impact was further softened by their depiction of universally approved concepts. The women's personification as, respectively, the pursuit of justice and the ideal of nonpartisanship placed the radical messages of these covers squarely within the democratic rhetoric that linked suffrage with patriotism. A more overt connection was made by another allegorical cover showing "the modern Betsy Ross" sewing onto the American flag a star for each state that had ratified the suffrage amendment. Here suffrage was also linked to conventional notions about women's role as the homemakers and menders of American society.

Patriotic rhetoric was consistently invoked in the editorial pages of the *Woman Citizen* during World War I. In "What We Are Fighting For," the publication's editors referred to the democratic "right of the individual who submits to authority to have a voice in his own government," arguing, "[t]hat being true, is it not also true that the struggle of American women for nation-wide suffrage is one and the same with the world struggle, part of it, integral? . . . The war is for democracy. Suffrage is very sign and seal of democracy." Once women were granted suffrage, the editors concluded, "the crack in America's democratic armor [would] be made whole."[5]

Other articles went further, pointing out the extent to which American women contributed to the war effort, at home and abroad, despite their lack of full citizenship. On the magazine's 1918 covers, this point was made by a series titled "Win-the-War Women," including "The Doctor" and "The [Railway] Conductor" (Figure 4.2), which highlighted not just women's war service but also their willingness and ability, if called, to perform men's jobs. They were beautiful and modern, with bobbed hair, but they wore sober and determined expressions; these were not Christy Girls delighted to find themselves wearing men's uniforms. Similarly serious, almost saintlike, were the patriotic twin sisters "Justice," a suffrage marcher, and "Mercy," a Red Cross nurse

Figure 4.2. C. D. Batchelor, The Woman Citizen *(May 18, 1918)*.
Courtesy of the Alice Marshall Women's History Collection, Penn State Harrisburg;
photo by Georganne H. Hughes, Metrophoto.

bound (the title explained) for France, where her own life would be in danger.[6]

Another type of wartime woman was the mother who sacrificed her son for democracy, a theme taken up in mainstream media by popular artists. In suffrage art, her sacrifice was doubly painful, as conveyed by one mother-and-son image that appeared on the cover of the *Woman Citizen* at the end of the war. Its long title asked readers: "With the Federal Suffrage Amendment Not Yet Ratified, Ain't It a Grand and Glorious Feeling to Have Your Son Return with Wound Stripes and Tell You of Seeing German Women Vote?" The implied shame that evil foreign women could vote, while good American mothers could not, was echoed in editorials such as "Antis Outdo Bolsheviki," which accused "antis" (women who opposed suffrage) of being worse than communists.[7]

In the final push for ratification of the Nineteenth Amendment, women's war service was frequently cited as a reason they deserved full citizenship. In 1919, the Texas state legislature passed a resolution that condemned antisuffrage agitation, declared that women had proven their patriotism in the war, and recommended that suffrage should be their reward. The *Woman Citizen* partly reprinted this document and its paternalistic language: "Along with the patriotic service rendered by these good mothers, wives, sisters and sweethearts of the boys of the great State of Texas, they suffered untold mental anguish while the boys were at the front. . . . [Therefore we] are standing unequivocally for the adoption of the woman's suffrage amendment."[8]

A parallel argument, borrowed from "maternalist" Progressive Era reformers, was that the vote would better equip women to perform their traditional maternal role. The motherhood envisioned by suffragists extended to all of America's children. A 1918 *Woman Citizen* cover (Figure 4.3) showed Suffrage ensuring the passage of labor laws that would protect the cowering youngsters from the "exploiters of children" whose claws threatened in the margin. On another issue published a year later, Justice protected Child Labor, who was "Small and Helpless." In this second image "Child Labor" was in shadow, suggesting the darker skin tones of Eastern European immigrants and African Americans whose children in fact comprised the underaged labor force.

Indeed, suffragists, many of whom were involved in broader Progressive reform, used maternal and patriotic rhetoric to justify their views on not only gender but also class. Articles in the *Woman Citizen* championed the causes of poor children (the children of "society"), as well as

Figure 4.3. C. D. Batchelor, The Woman Citizen *(Jan. 26, 1918).*
Courtesy of the Alice Marshall Women's History Collection, Penn State Harrisburg;
photo by Georganne H. Hughes, Metrophoto.

their literal mothers, working-class women. The child labor issue was closely connected to the "Americanization" work frequently described in the publication's pages. A 1919 feature, "Taking Uncle Sam's Foster Children into the Family," praised the YWCA's effort to find American homes for European children orphaned by the war. An editorial published the same year, titled "Americanize the Mother," claimed that suffrage would enlighten immigrant women who wanted to teach their children patriotism and the American way of life.[9]

Female activists' efforts to shape the lives of their less privileged "sisters" often contained elements of moralizing and patronization, as well as cultural chauvinism.[10] The upper-middle-class status of the *Woman Citizen*'s readers was revealed by the types of products advertised in its pages, from fine linens to "motoring" outfits, Fifth Avenue hat shops to summer resorts. Startling juxtapositions of editorial and ads—such as an article about the wages of female railroad workers next to a large promotion of "Furs of Superior Quality" in an issue published in 1919, a year of violent labor strikes through the United States—underscored the class tensions not only in the "Americanization" work of Progressive Era reformers but also in the suffrage movement itself.[11]

Similar tensions—and extremely similar imagery—could be seen in the *Masses*, a radical magazine read not so much by the working classes as by intellectuals who concerned themselves with labor problems and believed that socialism was the answer. The Socialist Party had reached unprecedented popularity in the United States, and when Eugene V. Debs ran for president as a Socialist in 1912, he won nearly a million votes. The *Masses* lasted only six years, from 1911 to 1917, and estimates of its peak circulation range from 12,000 to 40,000; whatever the actual figure, it had nothing like the reach of the *Saturday Evening Post* or *Cosmopolitan*.[12] Yet the audience it did have was loyal and influential in intellectual circles of the day. So were its editors and contributors, who worked without pay.[13] They included the writers Max Eastman, John Reed, Floyd Dell, and Mary Heaton Vorse and the painter John Sloan, who served as an illustrator and as art director.

One of the magazine's earliest major visual statements was not a cover but rather a frontispiece[14] drawn by Anton Otto Fischer, a German immigrant and the husband of the suffrage illustrator Mary Ellen Sigsbee.[15] Titled "The Cheapest Commodity on the Market," this illustration quite clearly depicted women—not allegorical figures, but lifelike representations of people—as commodities in a capitalist society.

The combination of the title and Fischer's drawing was a strong statement (especially during the reign of the *other* "Fisher Girl"), though the text on the adjacent page was paternalistic and similar to Progressive reformers' arguments about the value of women: "From these women will come the race of the future. According to their health and strength will be the health and strength of the next generation. . . . Rebuke the civilization that degrades its women; that sends forth the mothers of the next generation as the Cheapest Commodity on the Market." [16]

The earnestness of this picture, conveyed not only by the setting but also by the illustration's dark tones, characterized two other early *Masses* covers by artists who were husband and wife. Alice Beach Winter, who also drew for suffrage publications, used a different type of maternal (or paternal) appeal in her closely cropped face of a pathetic little girl, staring out at the reader and asking "Why Must I Work?" on the cover of the May 1912 issue. Though sentimental, this protest of child labor differed from the *Woman Citizen*'s handling of the theme in that the laborer herself, not her protector, was the main figure.

The familiar protector figure appeared in Charles Allen Winter's August 1913 cover (Figure 4.4). "The Militant" was a not a woman but a symbol, her removal from the real world suggested by the castle-in-the-air behind her. She was a cross between Joan of Arc and the Statue of Liberty: arm and determined face upraised, she marched forward into the future, protecting a less confident won   migrant-like shawl over her head) who cowered behi   title, this beautiful white woman, with a visible weddi   most a Progressive, not a militant, image in 1913.

More provocative messages about gender and class in the *Masses* were conveyed by the magazine's cartoonish "joke" covers. Perhaps the most famous of these was the cover shown in Figure 4.5, by Stuart Davis, which also appeared in 1913 and was much discussed in other periodicals. The *New York Globe* reported that the cover "shows two girls' heads, not Gibson Girls, nor Howard Chandler Christy girls, but girls from Eighth Avenue way. . . . Most cover designs don't mean anything. But this one does." [17]

This cover could be construed to mean many things. These women were drawn to be not only ugly but also unfeminine, as signified by their masculine Adam's apples and thick necks. Unattractive women appeared (usually as suffragists) inside popular magazines, but beady-eyed, thick-lipped creatures like these rarely adorned a *cover*, which

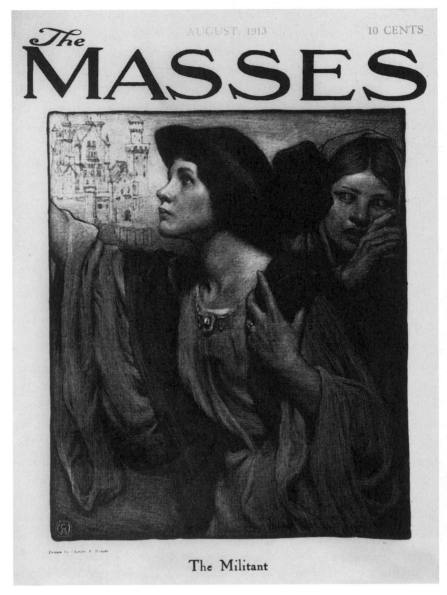

Figure 4.4. Charles Allen Winter, "The Militant," The Masses (Aug. 1913).
Photo courtesy of Helen Farr Sloan Library, Delaware Art Museum.

THE MASSES

JUNE, 1913   10 CENTS

"Gee, Mag, Think of Us Bein' on a Magazine Cover!"

Figure 4.5. Stuart Davis, "Gee, Mag, Think of Us Bein' on a Magazine Cover!"
The Masses (June 1913). Delaware Art Museum, Sloan Archive.

was meant to sell the magazine. The *Globe* writer implied that these
women were prostitutes ("from Eighth Avenue way"). The title below
it—"Gee, Mag, Think of Us Bein' on a Magazine Cover!"—turned it
into a send-up of mainstream magazines. While Davis did the drawing, the title was supplied by the art editor, John Sloan.[18] With its addition, the image could be seen as "a caustic response to the sickeningly

pretty cover girls" of mass circulation magazines. *Harper's Weekly* re-printed the illustration, calling it an "anti-dote" to the "plague of pink and white imbecility." [19]

The magazine's cover, which featured women three times as often as men,[20] frequently drew on conventional notions about femininity and working-class morality, intertwining the two concepts into political symbols. So did its editorial matter, which Leslie Fishbein defines as a mix of "strains of political radicalism, Freudianism, bohemianism, and feminism in an intriguing but generally unstable combination." [21]

In the *Masses*, feminism was defined more broadly than suffrage, including not just the campaign for the vote but also divorce, fashion reform, and equal pay for female workers. Some of the articles on these subjects were written by women themselves. A 1915 article by feminist anthropologist Elsie Clews Parsons criticized "the race-suicide croakers," and the magazine printed Emma Goldman's courtroom defense speech when she was convicted in 1916 for delivering a public lecture on birth control. Another female author advocated homemaking cooperatives as a way of "socializ[ing] the household industry," including childcare. In 1913, the year of a strike at silk mills in Paterson, New Jersey — for which the *Masses* staff staged a fundraising pageant in Madison Square Garden — the magazine published the first-person account of a fifteen-year-old girl who worked there.[22]

Editor Max Eastman (a cofounder of the Men's League for Woman Suffrage) believed that socialism and feminism were inextricably linked: "Almost from the first use of the word 'Socialism' the freedom of woman has been united with it," he wrote in a 1913 editorial.[23] Yet for many of his male contemporaries, "free love, not votes for women, was the burning question" of feminism.[24] Floyd Dell hoped that feminism would ease social constraints on extramarital sex and relieve men of the financial burden of supporting wives: "[T]hat is what feminism is going to do for men — give them back their souls, so that they can risk them fearlessly in the adventure of life," wrote the married Dell in 1914.[25]

A more complex vision emerged in the writing of women. While most preferred monogamy, they envisioned a similar utopia: in their view, which merged Freudian theory with maternalism, marriage was a sexually fulfilling union of uninhibited bodies, a psychologically satisfying meeting of minds, and a spiritually uplifting mingling of souls.[26] This matrimonial model was a glaring example of the discrepancies between the radical feminists' intellectual vision and the realities of working-class women, for whom marriage and motherhood largely remained a necessity and a duty.[27]

In 1916, Emma Goldman acknowledged in the *Masses* that "the question of birth control is . . . above all a workingwoman's question,"[28] and the magazine praised the birth-control advocacy of Margaret Sanger, which had been inspired by her involvement in labor union movements. Yet both Goldman and Sanger thought of sex as self-expression, and Sanger justified her activism in terms of "a mystique about womanliness, the successor to nineteenth-century feminist notions of the moral superiority of women," notes Linda Gordon.[29] In the view of many *Masses* contributors, male and female, women would thrive under socialism not because they would become independent, but because men would be able to earn enough money to enable their wives to turn their higher moral powers to caring for them and raising their children. This vision, notes Rebecca Zurier, "actually perpetuated Victorian sexual stereotypes."[30]

The *Masses* romanticized not only mothers but also their seeming social opposite, prostitutes. In fiction and nonfiction, male writers cast prostitutes alternately as nobly suffering victims, revolutionary heroines, and erotic adventurers.[31] James Henle wrote of the prostitute: "Sins?—she has none . . . she is as honest as the day is long. . . . She is satisfied with dry bread. . . . I doubt not that she prays more sincerely than most of our professed and obsessed reformers."[32] Thus while seeming to support the most vilified of working-class women, the magazine glossed over the realities of their lives by sanctifying them, much as it did mothers.

Prostitutes were a common subject in the illustration work of John Sloan.[33] In his own day and since, Sloan was best known as a painter who was a member of "the Eight" (which in 1910 staged the first "Independents" exhibition, a challenge to the conservative National Academy of Design) and of the Ashcan school of New York City realists.[34] His magazine illustration was a significant body of artistic work in itself. He drew for two Socialist magazines, the *Call* and the *Progressive Woman,* before joining the *Masses* in 1912.[35] Over four years, he contributed more than five dozen illustrations to the magazine.[36]

Sloan used the figures of women to point out double standards of both class and gender. The setting for "The Women's Night Court: Before Her Makers and Her Judges" was an actual place Sloan visited, the women's night court at Jefferson Market on Sixth Avenue.[37] In this illustration, he reversed stereotypes of criminality by drawing the prostitute as the only dignified person in the room, her reserve a sharp contrast to the leering spectators, overbearing judge, threatening court officers, and boyish policeman. Yet in doing so he placed the prostitute on a moral pedestal. A similar message was contained in another interior drawing titled "'Circumstances' Alter Cases," which showed middle-class women in transparent skirts glancing contemptuously at a woman in rags with her bare leg exposed—who looked so noble in poverty that she appeared almost biblical. The caption conveyed the pair's comments: "'Positively disgusting! It's an outrage to public decency to allow such exposure on the streets.'"

The latter image served to comment on class and public sexuality, concerns that were expressed more subtly in some of Sloan's other depictions of working-class women, even while they were key to their meaning and impact. His cover titled "At the Top of the Swing" (Figure 4.6) has been called "a poem of city youth" by one scholar, who sees it as an "affirmative statement that workers were not necessarily the pathetic stock figures of Socialist cartoons."[38] Certainly there was a positive feeling in this illustration, yet its content was not entirely "affirmative." The girl—truly a *girl* on the magazine cover—seemed happy and carefree. On second glance, though, the reader could not help noticing the three men sitting on a park bench behind her, staring at her. Here Sloan was acknowledging female youthful beauty and sexuality as public spectacle while also documenting the literal surveillance of young women in public. At the moment, the girl did not care; she was "at the top of the swing." But she, like the swing, could quickly fall.

As it had been for Edward Bok in 1897, the phenomenon of the woman in public was still profoundly troubling to many Americans twenty years later, especially when she was working-class. Robert Snyder and Rebecca Zurier note that "New Yorkers wondered not only how to maintain composure on the street and public transit but also how to reconcile immigrant street life, or the more athletic forms of working-class leisure, with a Victorian sense of privacy and decorum that shunned exposure and limited women's activities."[39] The constant presence of working-class women in public in the *Masses*—and in New York City itself—blurred gender and class boundaries.

The two young women in Sloan's November 1913 *Masses* cover titled "Innocent Girlish Prattle—Plus Environment" were definitely outside conventional boundaries. They were pretty, wearing pleasant expres-

MAY, 1913   10 CENTS

The MASSES

At The Top Of The Swing

Figure 4.6. John Sloan, "At the Top of the Swing," The Masses (May 1913).
Delaware Art Museum, Sloan Archive.

sions and modestly long skirts. Yet they were unconcernedly walking without a male escort at night through a bad neighborhood, signified by their "environment," trash on the street and a slovenly woman standing in a doorway. The caption revealed the girls' shocking vocabulary: " 'What! Him? The Little ———! He's Worse'n She Is, the ———!' " These were, perhaps, not ladies out for the evening, but ladies *of* the evening, streetwalkers in the common sense.

Of course, the contemporary viewer could not be *sure* that these were prostitutes, in this and other drawings of women in public by Sloan. This vagueness was the artist's most radical statement of all—not his matter-of-fact representation of prostitutes, whom antivice campaigners sought to isolate, but his suggestion that, given the right "environment," any woman on the street might be one. In her study of Sloan's depiction of the urban prostitute, Suzanne Kinser notes that "[d]uring the Progressive Era, prostitution became a master symbol, a code word for a range of anxieties engendered by the great social and cultural changes" of the period.[40]

One of Sloan's best-known depictions of working-class women, "The Return from Toil" (Figure 4.7), referred to these anxieties. Many scholars see this picture as another of Sloan's affirmations of happy comradery among working women. Robert Snyder offers a typical reading, contending that it "depicts young women looking fashionable, high spirited, and ready for fun after being liberated from work, perhaps in the garment industry. Work has not cowed them or turned them into wage slaves with broken spirits. The evening holds the promise of unfettered leisure, of visits to a movie theater, amusement park, or vaudeville house." [41]

The title suggested otherwise. If these women were coming home *from* work, not going out on the town, their attire suggested one particular occupation (a trade based just west of the garment district). Another clue was the presence of feathers in their hats, a symbol of prostitution in art of the era.[42] In this interpretation, the light casting their shadows may have been not evening streetlight, but morning sun.

While radical in their ambiguity—the reader could not *tell* what they had done or were about to do—Sloan's cover women were also emblematic of the tensions between feminism and socialism in the *Masses*. They acknowledged and affirmed the urban presence of bold and unrefined women, offering an alternative image to the "bedraggled sweatshop girls" described by *Masses* writers.[43] In bending over backward

The Return from Toil.

Figure 4.7. John Sloan, "The Return from Toil," The Masses (July 1913).
Delaware Art Museum, Sloan Archive.

to avoid labeling his subjects in one way, though, the artist labeled
them in another, relying on the dichotomies that have long been used
to understand women. His prostitutes were either dignified victims or
irreverent aggressors. He also sometimes used the stereotypical shorthand of beauty versus ugliness to criticize capitalism: his poor women

were often pretty, while he portrayed wealthy women as ugly and over-weight.[44]

When they wrote about or drew women, the editors and writers of the *Masses* surely meant to surprise and disturb readers. Yet in their attempts to do so, they ended up reiterating conventional notions about womanhood—an irony that suggests the true ideological power of the stereotypes already in place in American culture by the second decade of the century. What is more, the magazine used women as a cipher for class, as ways of characterizing the poor. Like their female symbols, these notions, from ignorance and shame to innocence and happy abandon, were stereotypes, too.

Despite its avowed commitment to the proletariat, the *Masses* paid little attention to a growing portion of the urban working class, African Americans. And the faces on its covers were quite similar in appearance to those of mainstream magazines. Whether her depiction was literal, idealized, comical, or allegorical, the American Girl or the American Woman in the century's early media (mass or otherwise) was almost unfailingly white.

The few exceptions appeared in publications written by and for African Americans, which were increasing in number. By 1910, at least nine such periodicals existed in the United States.[45] The most popular and influential was the *Crisis*, published by the newly founded National Association for the Advancement of Colored People. According to Charles Johnson, the *Crisis* "attained the highest circulation of any Negro magazine and became self-supporting" soon after its November 1910 founding. Its editors, W. E. B. Du Bois and Oswald Garrison Villard, declared that "this is a critical time in the history of the advancement of men." [46]

They meant "men" fairly literally, and the chief topics of the *Crisis* were racial problems primarily affecting men—lynching, public segregation, and disenfranchisement (of those who already legally had the vote). Du Bois imagined his primary reader as male, as suggested by the phrasing of his opening for a 1912 editorial on women's suffrage: "Why should the colored voter be interested in woman's suffrage?" [47]

The editor was in fact interested in women's enfranchisement, and he published several special issues on the topic. A September 1912 "Woman's Suffrage Number" contained articles by Fanny Garrison Villard (mother of assistant editor Villard and daughter of nineteenth-century abolitionist William Lloyd Garrison) and clubwoman Mary Church Terrell. Terrell argued in favor of women's suffrage on grounds of individual liberty under democracy: "The founders of this republic should be called a government of the people, for the people and by the people, and yet the elective franchise is withheld from one-half of its citizens . . . [T]he word 'people' has been turned and twisted to mean all who were shrewd and wise enough to have themselves born boys instead of girls, and white instead of black."[48]

Terrell voiced a similar argument in her contribution to the magazine's "Votes for Women" special issue three years later, which included prosuffrage testimony from twenty-five African American leaders, fourteen of them women.[49] Some of these writers believed that women deserved the vote because, as mothers and Christians, they would make moral political decisions. But most echoed the opinions expressed in Du Bois's ongoing editorials on the subject—that suffrage for African American women was more important for the advancement of the race than it was important for the progress of women themselves.[50]

This conflation of suffrage and racial concerns was reinforced by the covers of the magazine's "suffrage numbers," which featured not images of suffragists but rather symbolic figures signifying racial emancipation: on one, a drawing of Frederick Douglass, and on another, a pairing of Abraham Lincoln with Harriet Tubman.[51] The presumed commitment of African American women to "the race" rather than "the sex" was also conveyed in imagery such as the cover drawing for July 1914, of a sideways-glancing young woman on the arm of a man striding purposefully forward. The title of this cover, "Commencement," referred obliquely to another issue of great importance in the pages of the *Crisis*, education.

The magazine championed education, including advanced degrees, for women as well as men, featuring photographs of graduates on summer covers. Sadie Tanner Mossell appeared on the magazine's July 1921 cover after she had received her doctorate from the University of Pennsylvania.[52] Another female graduate, identified only as "A Master of Arts, University of California," appeared on the cover the following summer (Figure 4.8). Her stern expression presented a contrast to the "sweet girl graduates" of Harrison Fisher and Howard Chandler Christy.

Yet much cover imagery of the *Crisis* replicated the various "girls" of the era's white popular culture, acknowledging what were quickly becoming national standards for women's beauty. The magazine used women's heads, posed looking down or turned sideways, in the tradi-

The CRISIS

AUGUST, 1922   FIFTEEN CENTS A COPY

Figure 4.8. Photographer unknown, The Crisis *(Aug. 1922).*
Photo by Georganne H. Hughes, Metrophoto.

tion of Gibson. Figure 4.9 was the sort of framed head that would have adorned a locket, like the one the girl herself wore, or hung on a parlor wall—a representation (which was itself a status symbol) of a woman who was a status symbol.

The Fisher Girl was suggested in the dress and pose of a girl photographed for a 1916 cover (Figure 4.10), whose haircut and sailor-style blouse and tie mark her as the same type of modern girl who appeared on the cover of the *Saturday Evening Post*. Similarly, a 1915 *Crisis* cover photograph (Figure 4.11) showed a bare-shouldered woman who could have been one of James Montgomery Flagg's dangerous but beautiful vamps.

One important difference between the cover imagery of the *Crisis* and that of mainstream magazines was that it combined illustration and photography. Though common inside magazines by the 1910s, photographs rarely appeared on covers. To middle-class Americans in the late nineteenth century and the Progressive Era, illustrations implied ideals, whereas photographs connoted a realism that was even more real than that of urban painters like Sloan. A photograph was presumably not a representation of reality but reality itself, the "truth."[58] Therefore, the *Crisis*'s use of photos on its covers can be seen as a form of documentation.

The commencement cover photos offered *proof* that African Americans attended major universities and succeeded there. Such proof extended to more than just the pictured individual: along with photos of religious leaders, orators, and other prominent individuals, a photo of a college graduate offered visual testimony to the achievement of the race. When viewed as documentation, photography confounded racial stereotypes. The wholesome-looking, sailor-bloused girl in Figure 4.10 and the sultry beauty in Figure 4.11 seemed to be attractive models— yet because these images were photographs, they offered "proof" that actual African American women looked just like the era's ideal types of white women. As photographs, not artists' creations, both covers challenged white notions about the place of blacks in the larger American culture.

Martha Patterson considers African American magazines' use of girl "types" from white popular culture "a rebuttal to all of the popular racist images of the black buffoons, coons, mammies, lascivious wenches, and happy darkies" of the era's mainstream media. The representation of "the 'New Negro Women' [as] well-dressed and light-

Figure 4.9. Artist unknown, The Crisis *(Easter, 1915).*
Reproduced from the Collections of the Library of Congress.

The CRISIS

Vol. 12—No. 5   SEPTEMBER, 1916   Whole No. 71

ONE DOLLAR A YEAR   TEN CENTS A COPY

Figure 4.10. Photographer unknown, The Crisis *(Sept. 1916).*
Photo by Georganne H. Hughes, Metrophoto.

Figure 4.11. Photographer unknown, The Crisis *(Nov. 1915).*
Photo by Georganne H. Hughes, Metrophoto.

skinned with European facial characteristics," she believes, was a strategy by which African American media sought to "undermine the Gibson Girl's assurances of white racial supremacy by broadening the availability of 'womanhood' currency."[54] It is likely that, in this sense, the images of women in the *Crisis* were empowering for the magazine's audience. Here were faces recognizable as the Christy Girl, the vamp, the flapper—and they were black.

The "whiteness" of these figures, however, sent female readers a dis-empowering message as well, one that was repeated in advertisements inside the magazine. "Nile Queen Preparations" defined the range of African American skin tones as "Pink, Flesh, White, Brunette, and Cream Brown."[55] Madame C. J. Walker promised that her treatments would straighten readers' hair, bleach their skin, and whiten their teeth. Walker, who became the first African American millionaire, ironically claimed that her products promoted racial pride: "No greater force is working to glorify the womanhood of our Race . . . [by] softening and thickening short, stubborn, thin, unsightly hair . . . You too may learn how they can preserve and enhance your beauty, make you admired by men and the envy of women. . . . Madam [*sic*] C. J. Walker . . . has a message of hope, cheer, of the way she is glorifying our womanhood and how you too may have long, luxurious hair and beauty-kissed complex-ion."[56] This vision was not only a white one but also a middle-class one. And it was an ambition to be achieved through the acquisition of prod-ucts that would confer "style"—the same solution proposed by mass circulation magazines like the *Ladies' Home Journal*.

The covers of the *Crisis* offered a unique view of womanhood by providing the first major media forum for positive representations of African Americans. As Martha Patterson points out, the magazine broadened mainstream notions of womanhood by including African Americans within those visions, by inserting black faces into white ideals and therefore assuming part ownership of those ideals. Sarah J. Moore makes a similar point about suffrage imagery when she argues that its use of existing stereotypes had "the strategic value of counter-ing often virulent antisuffrage propaganda that relied heavily on . . . Victorian ideology."[57] In this view, "traditional pictorial rhetoric and iconology [were] a political instrument."[58]

As was the case with suffrage imagery, however, the very repetition in the *Crisis* of existing stereotypes reinforced the desirability of main-stream ideals. And, as with the socialist journalism of the *Masses*, discussion of women's issues in the *Crisis* was verbally and visually subsumed in its commitment to what it saw as a more compelling political problem.

Of the three periodicals discussed in this chapter, the *Masses* went the farthest in suggesting new ways of representing womanhood, and of discussing women's lives and opportunities, in American media. This magazine, whose editors were prosecuted under the Espionage Act of 1917 for their continuing pacifism, folded during World War I,[59] a time when mainstream gender stereotypes were further disseminated through war posters. During the decade following the war, both socialism and feminism would be labeled un-American, and African American advancement would be hindered by race hatred fueled by a rejuvenated Ku Klux Klan. The confluence of political forces that seemed so potent in the prewar years—political radicalism, feminism, and racial activism—would not again occur for another half-century.

Patriotic Images

Though suffrage and sex-role-reversal imagery continued to appear in American media through the end of women's drive for the vote, the more radical messages of the *Masses* disappeared when the magazine folded in 1917, the year the United States entered World War I. Throughout popular culture, the emergency of war prompted a return to more traditional images.

Irving Berlin, whose song "Whose Little Heart Are You Breaking Now?" was a hit in 1917, shifted his musical view of women after the United States entered the war (and he himself joined the army), penning "I'm Gonna Pin a Medal on the Girl I Left Behind" the following year. In film, the delicate Lillian Gish and Mary Pickford starred in war films such as *Hearts of the World* and *One Hundred Percent American*.[1] And muscular soldiers marched across the millions of war posters displayed throughout the country. These images of American manhood suggested that the crisis of masculinity was over. Their female poster counterparts, who played supporting roles in the stories these media told, were familiar images; they were drawn by the very same illustrators whose "signature" work dominated popular magazines. They were New Women who were strong and sexually glamorous, but they used those attributes for altruistic purposes.

World War I posters are well-traveled territory in media history research and in popular memory of twentieth-century visual communication. What is rarely discussed, however, is the extent to which their gender-specific messages (about both femininity and masculinity) were informed specifically by magazine art. These now-famous poster images were not born solely out of patriotic spirit; instead, they were the product of a stereotyping process that had begun in an established mass medium and that was played out against the historical backdrop of first-wave feminism. They were a powerful invocation of visual icons whose meaning was *already* in place.

For a brief period of time, they were everywhere, their distribution wider than that of the *Saturday Evening Post,* the *Ladies' Home Journal, Good Housekeeping,* and *McCall's* put together. During 1917 and 1918, the two years of American involvement in the war, more than twenty million copies of some 2,500 recruitment and homefront-fundraising posters were displayed in stores, at theaters, in train stations, and at post offices.[2] Though the other nations involved in the war also used posters as a form of public communication, none did so as aggressively as the United States.[3]

While the poster was the most visible and distinctive medium employed in the war-publicity effort, it was not the only one. Posters' patriotic prescriptions were echoed in films, songs, plays, magazines, and newspapers of the era. The mastermind behind this media campaign was George Creel, a journalist who headed the government's wartime Committee on Public Information. Creel called this work "a vast enterprise in salesmanship, the world's greatest adventure in advertising" and believed that such an undertaking was necessary to clarify Americans' emotions and opinions after two years of neutrality.[4]

Creel understood the immense ideological power of visual stereotypes. Consequently, for the poster component of the publicity campaign, he turned to the best-known producers of such images. The Creel Committee's "Division of Pictorial Publicity" was headed by none other than Charles Dana Gibson, and it commissioned posters from all of the mainstream magazine illustrators discussed in this book, with the exception of John Held Jr.[5] The prestige of these drawings was enhanced by their creators' fame and by the well-publicized fact that these normally highly paid artists had donated their time and talent,[6] a gesture implying their endorsement of America's involvement in the war.[7]

The wide recognition of these artists' work was crucial to the success of war propaganda (a word the illustrators themselves used). In his study of World War I posters, Walton Rawls states:

The purpose of these government-sponsored works of art was to communicate essential information rapidly and efficiently. . . . No less an authority than Adolf Hitler, a corporal in the First World War and a sometime artist, admired the simplicity of British and American posters and found them more popularly compelling than the sophisticated variety produced in Germany. Later he wrote in *Mein Kampf:* "All effective propaganda must be confined to a few bare essentials, and those must be expressed as far as possible in stereotyped formulas." [8]

Rather than an isolated message, each poster was part of a much larger campaign, its meaning influenced and reinforced by other recruitment and homefront efforts. Posters were created and received in the context of events such as pageants, flag days, fundraising evenings at movie theaters, and rallies at which celebrities appeared.[9] In his autobiography, James Montgomery Flagg—who did forty-six war posters for the federal government and was named state military artist for New York—wrote of painting poster designs on huge canvases set up in front of the New York Public Library, where publicity events were frequently held to sell Liberty Bonds.[10] He remembered that "Ginger Rogers later told me that either she or her mother posed on its steps for me, when she or her mother was a little girl, for a thousand-dollar Liberty Bond." [11] Howard Chandler Christy, who drew more than forty war posters (and was later named an honorary graduate of the U.S. Naval Academy because of his navy recruitment images), personally auctioned off the oil paintings from which his posters were printed. At one fundraiser, Christy and the popular actress Marie Dressler acted out one of his war bond posters, prompting a million-dollar bid for the original artwork, and in three hours Christy helped sell $7.4 million worth of bonds.[12]

Though Gibson headed the poster effort and contributed drawings himself, the best known of the wartime artists, then and now, was Flagg. In fact, today Flagg is rarely remembered as an illustrator of women because of the lasting popularity of a single war-poster image, his drawing of Uncle Sam, pointing toward the viewer over the phrase "I Want You for U.S. Army." This is the most famous of all war recruitment images and has been the most widely distributed: four million copies were in circulation during the First World War, and another 350,000 copies were printed during World War II.[13] (It is still used at U.S. military recruiting centers.) The illustration originally had appeared on the cover of *Leslie's Weekly,* and Flagg's rendition of Uncle Sam (for which he himself was the model) reinforced notions that magazines promoted about masculinity and progress in the new century.[14] "Formerly a benign old man in stars and stripes, Uncle Sam was transformed by Flagg into a compelling leader who meant business," notes illustration scholar Susan Meyer.[15]

Flagg's depiction of men in recruitment posters embodied what historian John Higham called the "muscular spirit" of the broader American culture in the World War I era.[16] These images further implied that physical fitness and willingness to fight blurred class distinctions, endowing men of all backgrounds with the same wartime status. In one such scene (Figure 5.1), a laborer linked arms with representatives of the army and navy, becoming part of a vision of patriotic progress. Its title, "Together We Win," portrayed America (or American men, at any rate) as a classless society while suggesting the opportunities for advancement that war offered working-class men. The latter message was even clearer in J. C. Leyendecker's navy recruitment poster (Figure 5.2) showing a long-legged, square-jawed sailor hailing his countrymen and promising travel and "trade-instruction" as benefits of military service.

In these drawings, American men at war were broad-chested, adventurous, proud to serve their country, and enraged by wartime atrocities. Woven into this vision of masculine strength were notions about vulnerable womanhood. One Flagg poster showed an angry man taking off his suit jacket (presumably to don a uniform) in response to a newspaper headline that read, "Huns Kill Women and Children." The poster's title played on a joke of the day that denigrated military competence: "Tell that to the Marines," one historian explains, was "a phrase that had previously implied the Marines would believe anything." Flagg "transformed this insulting phrase into a battle cry."[17]

Female symbols complemented wartime manhood in poster art. In a Leyendecker poster for war bonds, a member of the Boy Scouts—an organization meant to teach masculinity to American boys—handed a sword representing preparation and victory to a flag-clad, shield-bearing Statue of Liberty. For a recruitment poster, Leyendecker again drew Liberty shaking hands with one of his rugged sailors. On war posters, the figures of both men and women were meant to stand for ideas, for larger concepts and values that made war seem noble and necessary. Visual theorist W. J. T. Mitchell calls such symbols "hiero-

Figure 5.1. James Montgomery Flagg, "Together We Win," World War I poster.
Reproduced from the Collections of the Library of Congress.

Figure 5.2. J. C. Leyendecker, "Hailing You for U.S. Navy," World War I poster.
Reproduced from the Collections of the Library of Congress.

glyphs," explaining, for example, that "the image of an eagle may depict a feathered predator, but it expresses the idea of wisdom." [18]

Women in particular represented cherished virtues that might be lost—a reinterpretation of the era's popular culture preoccupation with "fallen" women. They represented mercy, compassion, and nobility as well as the broader ideals of justice, democracy, and freedom. Harrison Fisher's Red Cross nurse was a somewhat heavy-handed example, wrapped in the American flag and standing in front of the Capitol building as she called out her "summons" (Figure 5.3). A woman frequently symbolized the nation itself, as in Leyendecker's Liberty figures and Flagg's poster urging "America"—a sleeping, defenseless woman dressed in the American flag—to "Wake Up."

Flag-clad women also appeared as Britannia and Marianne, symbols of America's allies. Like the avenging angels he drew, Flagg's ferocious Marianne (Figure 5.4) brandished a sword and appeared particularly bloodthirsty. Though such women were to be seen as dangerous, they delivered a very different type of threat than his saucy vamps did on magazine covers. Similarly, Charles Dana Gibson put his oversized Girl to new use, recruiting female ambulance drivers, in a poster showing an amazonlike woman, dressed in the flag, choking a ghoulish death figure who tried to claim a wounded soldier. During the war, *Life* printed several similar images by Gibson, which the artist's biographer, Fairfax Downey, called "[t]he noblest types of Gibson Girl . . . martial, yet seldom unfeminine; they are never Valkyrie." [19]

These were examples of one of the two opposing female stereotypes Martha Banta identifies in World War I poster art: "Militant Victory," she argues, "was an acceptable version of the New Woman, now caparisoned as Warrior and Conqueror." The other stereotype could be seen in depictions of women as altruistic nurses and angels, symbols Banta has characterized as "The Protecting Angel" who embodied conventionally feminine values of purity and nurturance.[20] Thus ideas about womanhood were invoked to serve contradictory symbolic purposes—to glorify both destruction and healing, danger and safety, war and peace.

Howard Chandler Christy's war-poster women embodied a different set of tensions. The flag-wielding woman on his poster titled "Fight or Buy Bonds" (Figure 5.5) was dressed classically in white and yet was overtly sexual, her bound dress emphasizing her breasts, crotch, and thighs. On another Christy poster, "Your Angel of Mercy" (Figure 5.6)

Figure 5.3. Harrison Fisher, "I Summon You to Comradeship in the Red Cross,"
World War I poster. Reproduced from the Collections of the Library of Congress.

Figure 5.4. James Montgomery Flagg, "Vive La France!" World War I poster. Photo by Georganne H. Hughes, Metrophoto.

Figure 5.5. Howard Chandler Christy, "Fight or Buy Bonds," World War I poster. Photo by Georganne H. Hughes, Metrophoto.

Figure 5.6. Howard Chandler Christy, "Your Angel of Mercy," World War I poster. Photo by Georganne H. Hughes, Metrophoto.

Figure 5.7. Neysa McMein, "One of the Thousand Y.M.C.A. Girls in France,"
World War I poster. Reproduced from the Collections of the Library of Congress.

beckoned with outspread arms, bedroom eyes, and parted lips. The
seductive appeal of these women was sanitized by their ethereality
and their otherworldly dress—Christy's poster women wore clothing
from Greek mythology, while his "Angel of Mercy" nurse actually had
feathered wings. The woman in "Fight or Buy Bonds" was surrounded
by soldiers and yet not actually part of the battle herself; instead, she
hovered overhead. On most war posters, women were shown on the
battlefield only as ghosts and angels. One field nurse on a Flagg poster
was actually transparent, revealing soldiers marching behind her (a different type of "fadeaway girl").

The notion of combat as a supremely masculine arena removed
women from "the front" in the public imagination as shaped by mass
media, despite the presence in battle areas of thousands of flesh-and-
blood nurses and women who served as volunteer drivers or entertainers
in Europe. Though nurses and other female war workers were frequent
subjects of war posters (including those meant to recruit young women
into service), they were usually rendered with visual cues that removed
them from the harsh realities of war.

One exception was the poster of a YMCA volunteer shown in Figure
5.7. Though she too was unconnected with violent action, she looked

like an actual woman: far from angelic, she looked mortal and even weary. This contrast was even more significant given the fact that the image was drawn by a female illustrator—Nesya McMein, the *McCall's* cover artist whose work is discussed in Chapter 7—and was a self-portrait. Of all the illustrators discussed here, McMein was the only one to come under fire during the war, while she was a musical entertainer with the YMCA.[21] A 1918 magazine writer described such volunteers as a truly new kind of American girl who "may still be young in years when the war ends but to whom life will have brought such experiences that youth will have been replaced by age in its wisdom of the world and its people."[22]

On Christy's war posters, girls could only *wish* they might be involved in the war, as in "Gee!! I Wish I Were a Man" (Figure 5.8). In his posters meant to recruit male volunteers, Christy dressed his signature Girl in a navy uniform, giving her a seductive pose and expression. A similar figure on another recruitment poster gave new meaning to the by-then-familiar title "I Want You" (Figure 5.9). By putting young women into men's clothes, the artist *suggested* the boldness of the modern woman, while also making reference to the gender-identity anxieties in popular culture of the years just before the war. Yet these images did nothing to contradict the wartime norms that placed women in inspirational or supporting roles.

Martha Banta has described the Christy Girl as "the sister who becomes the American male's dream-wife" and who also "becomes the mother of the nation's future."[23] This important transition in female imagery occurred during World War I, when mothers and wives re-entered popular culture in significant ways. Though Gibson had frequently used the figure of an older mother as a joke in his magazine sketches, in wartime she became heroic. One of his recruiting posters—which also ran as a cover of *Life* during the war—featured a careworn but proud older woman who offered her son to Uncle Sam, saying, "Here he is, Sir." Extending this theme for the same magazine was Norman Rockwell, whose 1917 cover titled "The Lord Loveth a Cheerful Giver" (Figure 5.10) showed an older woman quite happily giving *two* sons away to the army and the navy.

The latter cover appeared on a "Woman-in-the-War Number" of *Life,* and the inside pages featured several visual and verbal representations of the proper role of the American woman in wartime. In an ad, she was shown doing "her bit" at a mimeograph machine; in illustra-

Figure 5.8. Howard Chandler Christy, "Gee!! I Wish I Were a Man," World War I poster. Reproduced from the Collections of the Library of Congress.

Figure 5.9. Howard Chandler Christy, "I Want You for the Navy," World War I poster. Reproduced from the Collections of the Library of Congress.

Life

WOMAN-IN-THE-WAR NUMBER

THE LORD LOVETH A CHEERFUL GIVER

Figure 5.10. Norman Rockwell, "The Lord Loveth a Cheerful Giver," Life
*(Nov. 8, 1917). Courtesy of the Alice Marshall Women's History Collection,
Penn State Harrisburg; photo by Georganne H. Hughes, Metrophoto. Works by
Norman Rockwell reproduced courtesy of the Norman Rockwell Family Trust.*

tions, she handed out cigarettes and chocolate to departing soldiers; in articles, she knitted, gardened, did canteen work, and sold Liberty Bonds.[24] Articles in women's magazines reinforced these prescriptions. *Good Housekeeping* praised the "army of women employed" in typically male occupations, including factory workers, bank clerks, and farmers. One 1918 issue of that publication ran a page-long tribute titled "To the American Woman! An Appreciation," in which the editors applauded readers for assuming civic and financial responsibilities at home.[25]

In many ways, these editorial messages pushed the boundaries of typical gender roles; for instance, *Good Housekeeping* noted that "college-bred girls" who worked at manual labor during the war grew physically fit and deserved as much pay as their male colleagues.[26] Yet magazines of the day made clear that a woman's noblest wartime calling was that of mother, whether her children were young adults serving their country or youngsters who represented the future of democracy. On war posters, maternity served as a central metaphor that united the hundreds of images of women as guardian angels and healing nurses.

Perhaps the most striking mothering image of the war was "The Greatest Mother in the World" (Figure 5.11). Though its artist, Alonzo Earl Foringer, did little magazine work, with this Red Cross poster he reconciled two contradictory gender images: the comforting mother figure, and the tiny man in the control of a giant woman. Like Christy's uniformed girl—whose wearing of man's clothes only underscored *his* right to them—this image reversed representational norms without challenging them. Indeed, as a version of the *pietá*, this tableau represented nursing as mothering and mothering as Christian, noble, and selfless.

The assignment of maternal motives to the female figures of war-poster art blunted the implications in popular culture imagery about women's strength, their capability, and their "newness." When the war ended, magazine covers extended the "return to normalcy" of gender roles in American society. A Norman Rockwell cover for *Life* showed the nation "Carrying On" (Figure 5.12) after the war. In this image—a preview of the artist's more famous work for the *Saturday Evening Post*—a typical family represented America itself, a representational shift that is the subject of Chapter 7. Though the silhouette of a running soldier in the background recalled the disruption of war, the veteran (now a member of the American Legion, whose seal formed a circular frame) looked confidently forward, holding a baby that symbolized the future.

Figure 5.11. Alonzo Earl Foringer, "The Greatest Mother in the World," World War I poster. Reproduced from the Collections of the Library of Congress.

American Legion Number **Life** PRICE 15 CENTS
Vol. 76, No. 1965   July 1, 1920
Copyright, 1920, Life Publishing Company

CARRYING ON

Figure 5.12. Norman Rockwell, "Carrying On," Life *(July 1, 1920). Photo courtesy of the Norman Rockwell Museum at Stockbridge. Works by Norman Rockwell reproduced courtesy of the Norman Rockwell Family Trust.*

The woman who was a homefront heroine a few years earlier gazed up at her husband. In the postwar years, she would channel her modern sensibilities, Progressive education, and newfound political agency into her marriage and her family, the future of her country.

World War I poster imagery presented a rejuvenated American

masculinity while naturalizing various ideals for womanhood through exaggerations of them: beckoning beauty, angelic healer, avenging warrior, sacrificing mother, supportive wife. The idealized woman on American war posters was a summary of the girl on the American magazine cover; moreover, she blended several different images in ways that resolved many of their tensions. Key to that resolution was a new ideal having to do with postwar family life, a vision that would be defined in mass circulation magazines in terms of both masculinity and femininity. Modern ideas about marriage also would unite the two seemingly opposite popular culture images of the 1920s New Woman: the flapper and the suburban mother.

The Flapper

The playful woman of the teens had one last, brief moment in the media spotlight—in slightly altered form. In movies, magazines, and new mass market novels of the 1920s, the "flapper" was another fearless, dancing, sex-crazed girl. Yet she was not terribly dangerous (she *liked* men), and she was much more fun than the vamp. Not an exotic creature, she was "recognizable as the girl next door, or down the block, or at the office" who simply wanted "to raise a little hell before she settled down to married life," writes Patricia Erens.[1] The flapper was an ordinary woman having an extraordinary moment, one that was made possible by the new morality of a postwar youth culture and by leisure products.

One artist in particular popularized the flapper on the American magazine cover. A humorist of the era claimed that "Fitzgerald christened it the Jazz Age, but John Held Jr. set its styles and manners. His angular and scantily clad flapper was . . . the symbol of our moral revolution."[2] Held's typical girl was a tall, thin, cartoonish young woman preoccupied with dancing, drinking, and necking. She appeared—usually accompanied by a gawky boy or a squat older man—in periodicals including *Judge, Puck, Liberty, Cosmopolitan, Smart Set, Vanity Fair,* and the *New Yorker,* but her main showcase was the cover of *Life.*[3]

A Mormon from Salt Lake City, John Held Jr. seemed an unlikely candidate to create one of the best-known symbols of sexual play, urbanity, and modernism in the 1920s. Equally unlikely to promote such a construct was the owner of *Life* at the time, Charles Dana Gibson, whose own version of femininity was the antithesis of Held's girls. But Gibson, concerned by *Life*'s falling circulation after the war (between 1920 and 1922, it lost half of its 500,000 readers), was anxious to capture the spirit of the times in an effort to keep the humor magazine afloat.[4] Gibson's own illustration work was at that point considered "history," noted the older artist's biographer Fairfax Downey: by the third decade of the twentieth century, "the Gibson Girl resigned herself to retirement as the mother of flappers."[5]

The symbol of the flapper represented the real life experience of only some American youth, yet the *idea* of her spread quickly across the country. In the decade that began with the passage of the Nineteenth Amendment, she redefined American women's freedom as sexual rather than political. As had been the case with the Gibson Girl, her style — hair, dress, stockings, makeup, jewelry — was marketed aggressively by national advertisers, and young women in cities and towns across the United States dressed and acted in imitation of this new media image.

As a visual icon, the flapper was, most of all, vertical. Her shape, defined by height and almost no width, was a stark contrast to the Gibson Girl's upright hourglass figure or the sexy curves of the Flagg Girl. Held's flapper was a cartoon, a caricature of the New Woman who was neither sophisticated nor smart; instead, she was self-absorbed and silly. She was flat-chested and skinny, made up mainly of arms and legs, and sometimes she had an equally ridiculous-looking male in tow. She wore a sleeveless, short dress and roll-top stockings that were often falling down. She was a joke, which, on most covers, was punctuated by a title, a pun Held drew into the illustration. When *Life* used women's images to poke fun at social change — in the work of Gibson, Flagg, and Coles Phillips as well as that of Held — the magazine's cover titles served as "anchorage" that underscored or redirected the likely impact of the pictures; they sharpened the wit and delivered the punch line.[6]

Held's flapper lived for leisure and never seemed to lack for money. She was a visualization of the typical flapper described in a 1925 issue of the *New Republic* — a nineteen-year-old girl with short hair, wearing a "brief" dress but a great deal of makeup, who "strolls across the lawn of her parents' suburban home, having just put the car away after driving sixty miles in two hours." This breezily confident young woman was triumphantly (if superficially) "free," making daring choices about clothing and behavior "while from the sidelines to which he has been relegated mere man is vouchsafed permission only to pipe a feeble Hurrah!"[7]

Some of Held's cover girls were college students who cheered at football games and whose boyfriends wore coonskin coats and carried hip flasks. Illustrators' frequent depictions of young women in college reflected an actual upward trend in women's enrollment, which peaked at 47 percent in 1920 (a level it would not reach again until 1980).[8] But Held's campus flapper, whom he sometimes called "Betty Co-Ed," was not the studious type. Jack Shuttlesworth, a contemporary of Held, described her as a "girl [with] fingers snapping, feet jumping, troubled by nothing very much except yesterday's hangover and tomorrow's heavy date."[9] Nor was she the "sweet girl graduate" of Fisher and Christy, a type Held parodied on a *Life* cover drawing (Figure 6.1) of a rouged flapper, displaying her long, bare legs, smoking a cigarette—and using it to set her diploma on fire!

Betty Co-Ed was loud, like the cheering flapper on a *Life* cover titled "Hold 'Em," a phrase that suggested both the football game in progress and the girl's sagging stockings (Figure 6.2). She was immodest, like a girl shown lowering her bathing strap to check for sunburn in front of her snickering boyfriend on another *Life* cover titled "The Girl Who Gave Him the Cold Shoulder." She dominated her dating relationships. One Held flapper proposed to her shorter boyfriend in a 1926 *Life* barnyard scene with the title, "The Laughing Stock," describing both the braying animals in the background and the gulping young man in the foreground. Another girl, on a 1923 *Judge* cover, actually punched her boyfriend in a scene with a musical-pun title, "Where the Blue Begins," describing the mark beneath the young man's eye.

Other Held flappers were young society women who fit F. Scott's Fitzgerald's description of his own female characters—"lovely and expensive and about nineteen."[10] They remained appealing despite shocking behavior, such as swigging whiskey from a bottle ("The Lass Who Loved a Sailor"), smoking ("She Left Home Under a Cloud"), and bobbing their hair ("The Long and the Short of It"). Though such acts were flirtations with "low-class" life, they were merely teenage rebellions, not rejections of the moneyed life from which these jazz-baby debutantes came. The only behavior that could truly upset a society flapper's boyfriend was letting her appearance go. Held's *Life* cover titled "A Heavy Date," picturing an obese young woman in formal wear sitting

Figure 6.1. John Held Jr., "The Sweet Girl Graduate," Life *(June 3, 1926).*
Courtesy of the Alice Marshall Women's History Collection, Penn State Harrisburg;
photo by Georganne H. Hughes, Metrophoto.

on the lap of a crushed man, showed how unthinkable an overweight flapper was.

Some of Held's socialites, like the one in Figure 6.3, were posed in sexually suggestive though awkward ways. (The title of this illustration, "Sitting Pretty," also made an unflattering comparison between the

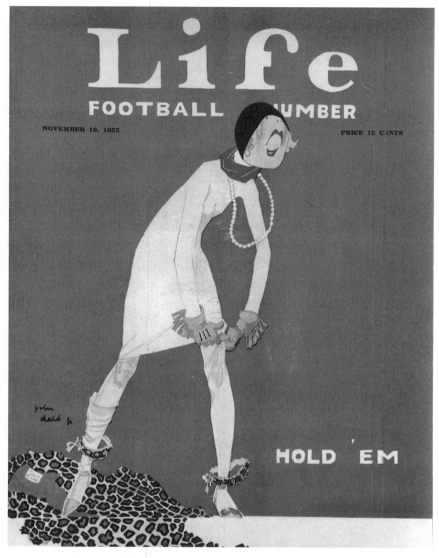

*Figure 6.2. John Held Jr., "Hold 'Em," Life (Nov. 19, 1925).
Courtesy of the Alice Marshall Women's History Collection, Penn State Harrisburg;
photo by Georganne H. Hughes, Metrophoto.*

young woman and her dog.) Like their schoolgirl counterparts, these women could be physically abusive to men, as in a *Life* cover titled "She Missed the Boat," in which a young woman smashed her older, shorter, bald date with a champagne bottle as their ship pulled away from the dock. In the cartoonish style of Held, such violence was comical, an

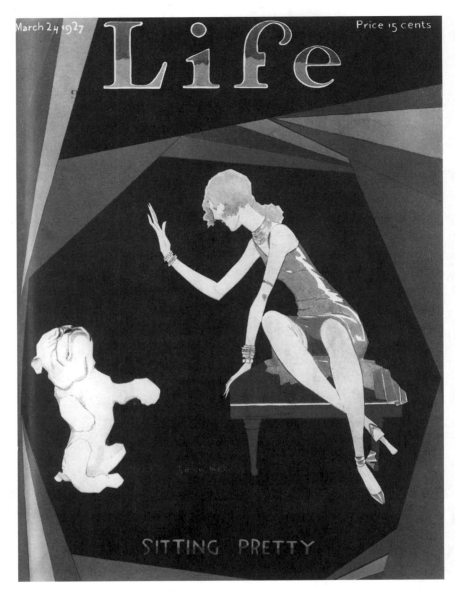

Figure 6.3. John Held Jr., "Sitting Pretty," Life *(Mar. 24, 1927).*
Reproduced from the Collections of the Library of Congress.

act of slapstick that revealed the woman's selfishness and immaturity. While the vamp of the previous decade had threatened to suck the life out of a man, the flapper merely bruised him in a passing fit of petulance.

She did want something from men, though, and it was money. "Missing the boat" provoked the champagne flapper's disgust at her sugar-

Figure 6.4. John Held Jr., "Teaching Old Dogs New Tricks," Life (Feb. 18, 1928).
Reproduced from the Collections of the Library of Congress.

daddy escort. The same depiction of the flapper as a golddigger could
be seen in Held's 1928 dancing cover for *Life* titled "Teaching Old Dogs
New Tricks" (Figure 6.4). Here again was the little man, though now he
was not so much a victim of scheming beauty as he was the appropriate
mate for an equally substanceless woman. If American men of the 1920s

were thwarted and made small by corporate progress, Held seemed to be saying, so too were American women by their own insistence on political and social freedom. So too, perhaps (as not only Held but also his literary contemporaries alleged), was the generation of young adults of the modern era "lost" in their quest for self-gratification.

Such an interpretation is one of several ways Held's flapper can be seen as symbolic of change in the larger American culture. Film historian Sumiko Higashi, writing about movies of the 1920s, argues that "the image of womanhood upheld by society is a cultural byproduct of its mores and profoundly resistant to change"; therefore, "whenever change [in the image] occurs, society is experiencing certain transformations, as it was during World War I and its aftermath." [11]

Two images of women bracketed this transition—the Gibson Girl and the flapper. The remarkable contrast between these emblems of different eras was the theme of a drawing, appearing inside a 1926 issue of *Life*, that combined Gibson's Girl and Held's flapper (Figure 6.5). Historian Kenneth Yellis similarly compared these images in his assessment of a major cultural shift in America: "The Gibson girl was the embodiment of stability. The flapper's aesthetic ideal was motion, [and] her characteristics were intensity, energy, volatility. . . . She refused to recognize the traditional moral code of American civilization, while the Gibson girl had been its guardian." [12]

Held's flapper signaled a change in national mood after World War I. Describing American men's reaction to the war's end, one writer remembered, "[W]e all got drunk. We had come through, we were still alive. . . . We danced in the streets . . . with bottles of champagne, fell asleep somewhere. On the next day, after we got over our hangovers, we didn't know what to do, so we got drunk." [13] As they danced, smoked, and drank bootleg gin, Held's flappers offered comic versions of the dissipation that characterized such reactions, as well as much American literature of the period.

Held's flapper further symbolized modernity in that she embodied several characteristics of modern art, as explained by Roland Marchand. One was "the license [modern art] gave to 'expressive distortion,' to exaggeration even to the point of caricature." The flapper was not only pencil-thin but also unrealistically tall. [14] In advertising, the modern woman "was immediately recognizable in her elongated neck, stiletto fingers, and towering height. . . . The proportions of some women . . . suggested a height of over nine feet. . . . Their pointed feet and toes

Figure 6.5. John Held Jr. and Charles Dana Gibson, "Thirty Years of Progress, 1896–1926," Life (1926). Photo by Georganne H. Hughes, Metrophoto.

appeared to have emerged fresh from a pencil sharpener." Though in real life fewer than one in five American women were thin and over five feet three inches, the tall twentieth-century woman was as much a symbol of modernity as the skyscraper.[15]

The second characteristic of modern art evident in Held's character was the "stylistic elimination of details," a technique that became a way of "respond[ing] to the demands of the age for a fast tempo of reading based on 'effortless simplicity' in the type." [16] The girl's facial features were indistinct, her expression was blank, and her height and angular thinness made her seem two- rather than three-dimensional. The "fast reading" this simplified image allowed was not only modern, but also conducive to stereotyping.

Finally, Held conveyed motion through the use of diagonal lines, a third quality of modern art. Movement was suggested by the flapper's frequently leaning body, by her bent legs and arms ("flapping" out), by her slimness, and by the jagged hem or swaying skirt of her outfit. [17] These visual cues "fostered the image of the woman in actual or impending motion—the woman on the move." [18] So did her activities, such as cheering, fighting, and dancing. The angular pose of the flappers in Figures 6.3 and 6.5, contrasted with the prim, straight posture of the Gibson Girl, was an example of this technique.

Part of the kinetic nature of modern images was an illusion of newness and novelty, a feeling of constant change. On magazine covers of the early twentieth century, the concept of change was strongly gendered female, and the flapper was the "newest" of all versions of the New Woman. Whether she was a negative or positive representation of women was a matter of debate among women of the 1920s—and remains contested among historians.

In her history of beauty, Lois Banner notes that the flapper image conveyed multiple and conflicting "behavior messages" for women. [19] Ann Douglas argues that the flapper's boyish looks and careless attitude were expressions not of self-assertion but of self-hatred, an attempt to escape from herself, from her mother, from anything that marked her as female. [20] Other scholars, however, have admired the flapper's irreverence and seen her as a revolutionary figure, the first media depiction of woman as man's sexual and social equal. [21]

The latter interpretation is, to some extent, supported by evidence left by women of the 1920s who chose the flapper label as a way of rejecting social conventions. One self-identified flapper, Ruth Hooper, explained in a 1922 *New York Times* article that "a flapper is proud of her nerve. . . . She is shameless, selfish and honest." Speaking directly to young men, Hooper warned that girls like her "will never make you a hatband or knit a necktie, but she'll drive you from the station hot summer nights in her own little sport car. She'll don knickers and go skiing with you; or if it happens to be summer time [*sic*], swimming; she'll dive as well as you, perhaps better; she'll dance as long as you care to, and she'll take everything you say the way you mean it." [22]

Here indeed was a description of an independent, confident young woman. Yet the New Woman who became a flapper was depicted—by Hooper as well as by Held—as an equal with men only in the world of youthful leisure. Another *New York Times* piece, a tongue-in-cheek essay published in 1929, claimed that the flapper had earned "the feminine right to equal representation in such hitherto masculine fields of endeavor as smoking and drinking, swearing, petting and disturbing the community peace." [23]

Held's flapper had no adult responsibilities at all; she was never shown caring for children or working at a job. Her counterparts in film sometimes did have jobs, yet they were temporary types of employment designed to advance the plots toward romance and marriage. Underlying these plots was a strong message about class as well as gender. It wasn't that women didn't *need* money; it was just that employment wasn't the best way to get it. Upward mobility was to be achieved not through education and work, the screen flappers' stories suggested, but through sexual charms that would snare the right man. The typical character played by the well-known actress Clara Bow, for instance, "was usually lower or lower-middle class, often . . . [in] roles which allowed the average American girl to identify with her and to dream. In her films she played a manicurist, usherette, waitress, cigarette girl, taxi driver, swimming instructor, and salesgirl. Interestingly, her jobs always brought her into contact with men. As a manicurist in *Mantrap* (1926), she worked in a barber shop. Even as a salesgirl in the lingerie department, she was visited by more men than women buyers. Also, these jobs provided ample opportunities for touching members of the opposite sex." [24]

Through the flapper image, the new freedom of American women was symbolically reduced to flirting and touching, to exhibitionistic fun. With its end goal of a traditional relationship with a man, this behavior stopped short of any real sexual or social danger. By the 1920s, public displays of sexuality were far from shocking; they were, in fact, expected behavior among middle-class youth. [25] And in films of the decade, the flapper behaved outrageously but only hinted at promiscuity. She "was not as naughty as she seemed, but rather a disturber of the peace, redeemable by marriage," writes critic Molly Haskell. [26] This characterization was confirmed by Colleen Moore, a 1920s actress who chuckled over the fuss created by her headstrong "jazz baby" role: "Actually all she did was drink a cocktail and smoke a cigarette in public. Underneath she was a good girl."[27]

According to social historian Kevin White's study of "the flapper's boyfriend," men still wanted "good girls." The young man who dated flappers considered sexual experimentation healthy and gave at least lip service to supporting women's rights, yet ultimately he sought a monogamous marriage that would enable him to have a family and leave his youth behind.[28]

Fortunately for him, his girlfriend's naughtiness was portrayed as a passing phase. Not only was a flapper's brazenness a sign of immaturity, a prank she played on men; she herself was childish. Her sexual daring was comical because her figure itself was essentially asexual. Flat-chested, hipless, and skinny, Held's flapper was not a woman at all, but an adolescent, as her name suggested. "The term 'flapper,'" explains Kenneth Yellis, "originated in England as a description of girls of the awkward age . . . meant literally . . . a girl who flapped had not yet reached mature, dignified womanhood."[29] Communication scholars Margaret Hawkins and Thomas Nakayama see this representational shift as a symbol of backlash against women after the achievement of suffrage, "a crucial weapon in disempowering women by idealizing the body of a girl."[30]

In Held's cover work for *Life* (which was read primarily by upper-middle- and middle-class men), the flapper was certainly a form of political backlash, a way of making fun of assertive women by showing them as immature and vapid. In movies and the broader culture, though, the flapper was less a dismissal of the New Woman than a commercialization of her. Paradoxically, the girlish body became central to the selling of women's sexuality. Because of the *absence* of heavy breasts and hips, media producers could display the body, even clad only in underwear (movie flappers often wore lingerie), with little scandal.[31]

In the flapper, the New Woman became the New Girl who was a new product, "a new arrangement of the elements of sex and fashion."[32] She was a cultural ideal who proved the point made by scholars Rayna Rapp and Ellen Ross that, during the 1920s, "themes of female independence" disappeared from the political sphere but "resurfac[ed] in advertising" and other popular media that contained advertising.[33]

What the flapper sold was not sex but sex *appeal,* the "it" quality of the screen heroine who got her man. Therefore, she was of great interest to women as well as men. The flapper image—not just her look but also her activities shown and described in magazines, movies, and popular fiction—helped women in the growing American middle class imagine how they might spend their discretionary income. She promoted a range of consumer products and services, but her main work was selling fashion. So closely was her fashion style associated with Held's magazine art that F. Scott Fitzgerald called them "John Held Clothes."[34] The flapper uniform included not only the short dress but also a girdle-bra that bound the breasts and minimized the hips; roll-top silk stockings; a handbag (the streamlined shift could not contain functional pockets); and makeup.

The sales of hose and cosmetics alone between 1923 and 1925 prompted the advertising firm N. W. Ayer to take flappers seriously. In an industry ad, Ayer executives noted that "tomorrow these young women will be home executives. . . . They will buy enormous quantities of every conceivable kind of staple merchandise."[35] In *Middletown*, their 1929 study of a representative American town, sociologists Robert Lynd and Helen Lynd found evidence that flapper imagery had spurred national consumption. Since the turn of the century, they reported, women's "skirts have shortened from the ground to the knee and the lower limbs have been emphasized by sheer silk stockings; more of the arms and neck are habitually exposed."[36]

Thanks to the new ready-to-wear clothing industry, this outfit, which began as a costume for urban elites, became affordable to middle-class women all across the country. Flapper-style dresses were available through the Sears, Roebuck mail-order catalog beginning in 1923, and stores sold them in the fashion industry's first standardized sizes.[37] The vertical dress style and the new sizing system bolstered two other growing industries, the weight-loss business and the tobacco industry. (Then as now, smoking was advertised as a gesture of independence and touted as a diet aid—as a Lucky Strike ad put it, a "new-day and common-sense way to keep a slender, fashionable figure.")[38]

For women who took their cues from movies and magazines, the correct combination of purchased products produced a "look" that was a matter not just of style but of status. Silent-movie flapper Blanche Sweet promoted a "Bobbed Hair Club," and theaters held contests among their female patrons for "Most Beautiful Bobbed Head" and "Most Beautiful Legs."[39] At the same time that it recast womanhood as girlhood, the image of the flapper showed American women what

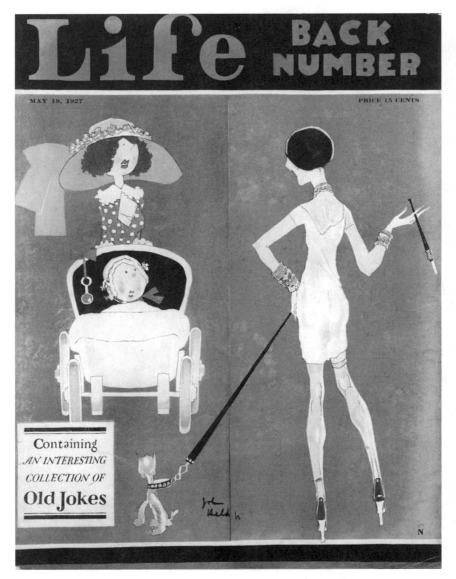

Figure 6.6. John Held Jr., Life *(May 19, 1927). Courtesy of the*
Alice Marshall Women's History Collection, Penn State Harrisburg;
photo by Georganne H. Hughes, Metrophoto.

to buy and how to put themselves together, piece by piece, in order to be modern and "liberated." In both senses, this construct reveals how first-wave feminist notions about progress, freedom, and choice were coopted by commercial culture, and how the New Woman in the new century became more profitable than political.

But the flapper was not the only female stereotype involved in this transformation. A 1927 cover drawn by Held (Figure 6.6) showed the pair of female images that together expressed cultural notions about the New Woman and about modern American life in the 1920s, the flapper and the mother. As their confrontation on this *Life* cover suggested, they seemed to be opposite ideas, yet they were in fact (as the illustration also conveyed) two parts of the same idea. Marriage was the end goal of the flapper's brief fling, and she would carry her brand of freedom into her new role; even as a wife, she would continue to be a material girl. It was the latter construct of the New Mother—who built a modern, suburban "lifestyle" with a new kind of husband and their children—that would have the greatest staying power in twentieth-century commercial media.

The Modern
American Family

In the postwar era, most middle-class girls, however carefree in their youth, did grow up to marry and have children and to make home-making their primary role.[1] In popular culture and in real life, though, the American wife of the 1920s was cut of a somewhat different cloth than the Victorian era True Woman. She had not forgotten the novelties of her girlhood, and she expected certain freedoms in marriage. Like the vamp, she expected sexual satisfaction;[2] like the flapper, she wore the latest styles and shopped for status in "a world organized by brand names and made coherent by patterns of consumption."[3]

The modern couple brought higher expectations to the institution of marriage, looking to each other for companionship.[4] They also brought higher expectations to parenthood, in an era when middle-class children were valued "almost [as] a commodity, a kind of consumer good that symbolized family completion and marital success."[5] This new model for the American family in the twentieth century was played out in a new type of living space: the suburb, an outgrowth of swelling urban populations and of advances in transportation that enabled middle-class men to commute to their jobs.

Beginning around 1916 and continuing throughout the 1920s, the imagery of mass circulation magazines reflected these changes. The three "family magazines" discussed in this chapter did so in different visual ways, each through the work of a cover illustrator with "signature" imagery associated specifically with that magazine. In the work of Neysa McMein for *McCall's,* the modern American wife and mother was still shown as the subject of the picture and depicted as a stylish New Woman. In the work of Jessie Willcox Smith for *Good Housekeeping* and Norman Rockwell for the *Saturday Evening Post,* the woman was rarely the focus of the picture, instead shown as a mother within a family. Children dominated the imagery of the latter two magazines, and on the covers of the *Post* fathers would play a significant role for the first time.

Neysa McMein first made a name for herself as a cover artist in the *Saturday Evening Post*—she did five dozen of its covers in the late 1910s and early 1920s—while also working for *Woman's Home Companion* and the *Ladies' World.*[6] In 1923 she became the exclusive cover artist for *McCall's,* which paid her $1,000 a cover every month for the next fourteen years.[7] Like the other magazines, *McCall's* was edited for a broad, middle-class audience during the 1920s.[8] Given the magazine's circulation of two million,[9] its statisticians proclaimed that "readers might occupy houses every twenty-five feet on both sides of a street from Boston to San Diego," an imaginary place its editors called "McCall Street."[10] Teamed with a pattern company, the magazine had been devoted to fashion from its founding in 1873 to the turn of the century, though by the 1920s it had an editorial mix similar to its competitors, the *Ladies' Home Journal, Woman's Home Companion,* and *Good Housekeeping:* home-care advice, beauty and fashion, fiction, and articles about well-known people.[11]

McMein was one of the first artists to draw celebrities for magazine covers. She herself was a celebrity, a member of F. Scott Fitzgerald's Long Island North Shore summer community and of the famed Algonquin Roundtable of Manhattan writers and actors. McMein was socially central to this crowd, holding weekly salons at her Fifty-seventh Street studio where she hosted, in addition to the Algonquin circle, figures from the worlds of music (Irving Berlin, George M. Cohan), theater (Helen Hayes, Charlie MacArthur, Fanny Brice), and the movies (Charlie Chaplin, Tallulah Bankhead, Harpo Marx).[12] Noël Coward recalled that McMein would set up a gin still in the bathtub and then "paid little or no attention to anyone except when they arrived or left, when . . . she would ram a paint-brush into her mouth and shake hands with a kind of dishevelled politeness."[13]

The artist's working style belied how seriously she took her career.

She explained to an interviewer in 1926 that the key to her success was being "a good saleswoman . . . studying out just what would fit into this magazine or that—and then going and telling them so!" [14] McMein, who cared for her invalid mother and raised a daughter while continuing to work,[15] featured other glamorous but real career women of the stage and screen on some of her *McCall's* covers. She also joined the Lucy Stone League (an organization of women who kept their maiden names after marriage) [16] and campaigned for women's suffrage.[17] Five months before the passage of the Nineteenth Amendment, she drew a voting woman for a cover of the *Saturday Evening Post.* Like several of Coles Phillips's *Life* covers, this scene showed a woman thoughtfully choosing between little pictures of men, though here they were political candidates rather than suitors.

Most of her covers were relatively apolitical, however, featuring confident, well-dressed women who projected neither coolness nor cuteness. McMein's friend Alexander Woollcott once observed that "[e]ach girl of hers was a real girl, salty with actuality." [18] Her biographer, Brian Gallagher, writes of the artist's typical cover subject, "[w]hile she was strikingly pretty, her beauty was at least of the possible type. And her smart, casual air was something young women could attain, even if they were not pretty." [19] McMein used few props or outfits that signified social standing or income. Her cover subjects were images in which her readers could have seen themselves.

In her cover work, the artist mixed recognizable faces with representations of the ordinary woman, and both types appeared in thematic, yearlong series during the 1920s. McMein depicted the "Twelve Most Beautiful Women in America," a series that began in 1923 and included Mary Pickford, Irene Castle, and Ethel Barrymore.[20] Throughout 1925, her covers portrayed anonymous subjects enacting the "Twelve Milestones in a Woman's Life."

Seventy years later, the editors of *McCall's* printed a reminiscent summary of the latter series, which included "Her First Birthday" (a baby), "Her First Dance," "The Engagement Ring," "Her Bridal Day," and "Her First Born" (another baby).[21] Not mentioned but among these images were two drawings of schoolgirls, reminiscent of Harrison Fisher's College Girls for the *Ladies' Home Journal* more than a decade earlier. One was an athlete with bobbed hair, holding a basketball and gazing sternly outward. The other (Figure 7.1) was her own version of

McCALL'S

JUNE 1925   TEN CENTS

VE NOVELS   HAROLD BELL WRIGHT   IN THIS ISSUE
             GENE STRATTON-PORTER

Figure 7.1. Neysa McMein, McCall's *(June 1925)*. *Courtesy of the Alice Marshall Women's History Collection, Penn State Harrisburg; photo by Georganne H. Hughes, Metrophoto.*

the "sweet girl graduate," looking upward with just a trace of a smile, on the magazine's June 1925 cover.

Here were alternatives to the seemingly dichotomized images of charming gal-pal versus destructive vamp or devoted mother versus silly flapper, a significant option if in fact the female readers of *McCall's* saw her cover portraits of femininity as "something [they] could attain." Of course, her series on the stages of womanhood did conform to conventional expectations for women, and its backdrop, the cover of a family magazine, implied that the subjects were wives and mothers (indeed, its final installment suggested that the stages of a woman's life *ended* with motherhood). McMein sometimes created domestic cover scenes featuring children or homemaking props.[22] Yet she drew most of her cover women alone, as individuals, and they retained the calm reserve and the nerve of her younger subjects.

Her June 1928 cover featured a beautiful woman at the beach—a standard summer image in the repertoire of nearly all illustrators of the era—who looked with delighted fascination not at the reader but at a crab that had crawled up onto her hand. The following summer she drew another common cover subject, a woman in a bathing suit (Figure 7.2), though hers looked out frankly at the reader and had the sense to wear a bathing cap (note the artist's own initials on her bathing-suit top).

In contrast to Phillips's girls who faded into background patterns, McMein's cover women stood out boldly, usually set against a plain color or white space. This contrast was clear in all the images shown here, including Figure 7.3. In this 1929 cover, the upward glance and turn of the woman's shoulders directed the reader's attention skyward, toward the little airplanes (and the magazine's logo). The subtext here was a third theme common in 1920s magazine illustration—progress through technology—and the horizon-scanning woman was herself progressively modern. Like McMein's college graduate in 1925, this adult woman looked upward into the future.

During the previous decade, *Good Housekeeping* had published an article (titled "With a College Education" and written by a female professor of English at Smith College) containing a scene that could have been the caption to Neysa McMein's graduating cover girl on *McCall's*. What at first seemed to be a wedding-day description turned out to be something else:

Figure 7.2. Neysa McMein, McCall's *(Aug. 1929)*. *Courtesy of the Alice Marshall Women's History Collection, Penn State Harrisburg; photo by Georganne H. Hughes, Metrophoto.*

Figure 7.3. Neysa McMein, McCall's (July 1929). Courtesy of the Alice Marshall Women's History Collection, Penn State Harrisburg; photo by Georganne H. Hughes, Metrophoto.

One cannot help wondering a little whether the rose, through the winter cold, with the snow whirling and drifting about it, has been making ready in color and fragrance and form for the one day of its life—to be carried in a girl's hand. The eyes above it look out, fearless. There is not anything she cannot do or be. I think it is that look that brings a tightening of the throat to the tall, gray-haired man looking on. It is *his* daughter who is walking with her head held high and the rose in her hand and the twentieth century in her eyes. The long double-file of girls passes slowly in front of the president . . ." [23]

Good Housekeeping had cautiously embraced the American women's rights movement, publishing prosuffrage opinions, and had chronicled the more radical activities of British suffragists.[24] When women gained the vote, it encouraged readers' informed participation in the electoral process.[25] But its editorial focus turned increasingly toward home care and motherhood.

By the 1920s, motherhood was championed in the pages of *Good Housekeeping* by none other than Mrs. Charles Dana Gibson (then heading a foster-child-placement agency), who urged readers to adopt if they were unable to have children. Mrs. Gibson told of "a cultured, well-to-do woman—the kind of woman about whom one says, 'She has everything in the world'" but who in fact "was bored and lonely and purposeless." Her husband, "a busy executive," thought he did not want children but reluctantly consented to adopt a daughter. The little girl charmed him and made them a complete family. "She's just what we have wanted for years, and we didn't know it," he exclaimed, speaking of his daughter as if she were a well-chosen gift.[26]

As Mrs. Gibson's article suggested, childless couples were stigmatized in the modern era. Because of the increasing availability of birth control, which lessened concerns about overwhelmingly large families, the children middle-class Americans did bear took on new status. Infertile couples sought medical help or adoption, and experts warned fertile women that refusal to have children would prevent them from experiencing sexual pleasure or would lead to marital stress and eventual divorce.[27]

Just as working-class children had been the focus of Progressive reform in the prewar era, middle-class children became public property in the postwar years.[28] Membership in the National Congress of Mothers, a network of local Mother's Clubs, more than tripled between 1915 and

1920, and in 1924 this organization became the Parent-Teacher Association.[29] The advice of medical and psychological experts, who advocated "educated motherhood,"[30] filled the pages of popular magazines, in which proper parenting was linked with the use of new products. An advertisement in a 1916 issue of *Good Housekeeping* explained that a child's health was "a question of food, hygiene and exercise. The food problem is easily solved with Shredded Wheat."[31] Articles in the magazine had similar themes. One installment in the regular "Mother and Child" column provided five pages of detailed advice from physicians on what children should eat so that they would not grow up to be "delicate or neurotic."[32]

The article on children's food was illustrated by Jessie Willcox Smith, and the treasured children of the 1920s romped through her cover art for *Good Housekeeping* every month. Its new emphasis on childhood was well received by readers. This decade was a turning point for the magazine: its circulation, which had been only 300,000 in 1912, passed the million mark and reached two million in the 1930s.[33] The nearly 200 covers Smith drew between 1918 and 1933 were a large part of the publication's editorial identity and success, and *Good Housekeeping* marketed reproductions of her drawings on postcards and china. Through these collectibles—such as her Madonna-and-Child plate series, offered through the magazine by mail order—her cover imagery was saved and displayed in readers' homes.[34]

By the time she became *Good Housekeeping*'s primary cover artist, Smith already was nationally known as an illustrator of children. Her advertising work for Ivory Soap in the 1890s had led to assignments in the early 1900s from *Scribner's, Collier's,* and *Century,* as well as covers for the *Ladies' Home Journal, McClure's,* and the *Woman's Home Companion.*[35] Though she never had children, she echoed the rhetoric of "maternalist" Progressive Era reformers, calling marriage and motherhood "the ideal life for a woman."[36] Unlike Neysa McMein, who was twenty-six years younger, she did not believe that a woman could have it all. "If she elects to be a housewife and mother, that is her sphere, and no other," she told an interviewer in 1927.[37]

The presence of children in almost all of Smith's cover illustrations was a clear sign that the woman accompanying them was (by virtue of having borne a child) a woman, not a girl. Smith's women were serious, rarely smiling, yet calm and pleasant-looking. She usually drew them in the process of doing something with their children, as though captured spontaneously in daily life rather than posed for a picture. The fact that her cover subjects were not smiling portraits linked them with those of McMein, a similarity that might be explained by the "female gaze" of their audiences. Both artists drew women in a way that would gain the identification and empathy, rather than the admiration and desire, of readers. Though the styles and settings of their work were quite different, both McMein and Smith drew cover women whom their magazines' readers could imagine *being*.

Smith's cover women were also as modern as McMein's. One example is Figure 7.4, a 1925 *Good Housekeeping* cover showing a mother reading to her daughter. No longer a Victorian matron, the Jazz Age mother was slim and pretty, a youthful woman urged to follow the advice of a 1927 Palmolive Soap ad in the magazine that reminded readers of the need to "Keep That Schoolgirl Complexion" long "after school days."[38] She was fashionable as well, with loosely gathered (or bobbed) hair, a flowing dress, long beads, a patterned shawl, and pointed, open shoes, all popular styles of the 1920s. This was the new suburban mother, as suggested by the outdoor backdrop.

As telling as her setting was the woman's body position. Smith's cover mothers were typically shown bending down or leaning over to comfort or help their children, and their attitudes directed readers' eyes toward the youngsters. In Smith's vision, maternity was more about the child than the mother. In fact, most of Smith's covers were of children only, shown usually in action and frequently in wholesome outdoor activities such as apple-gathering.

In many of these pictures, female children replicated the poses of Smith's women, as if preparing for their future roles as wives and mothers. Her covers showed girls leaning forward to feed a younger child, turning sideways to help a little brother learn how to ice-skate, and following a little boy in a waltz, as in Figure 7.5. The expression on this girl's face was typical of Smith's children, who often seemed perplexed or surprised.

One *Good Housekeeping* reader wrote to the editors that Smith's cover subjects "really look like children," and some mothers believed that Smith had actually, somehow, drawn *their* children.[39] Smith saved a letter sent in 1926 to the magazine by a mother in Beverly, Massachusetts, who wrote: "I was very much thrilled on seeing the November cover of *Good Housekeeping* [Figure 7.5], to find that my two darling children were portrayed thereon. . . . Little Freddie's every characteristic

Figure 7.4. Jessie Willcox Smith, Good Housekeeping (June 1925).
Reproduced from the Collections of the Library of Congress.

Figure 7.5. Jessie Willcox Smith, Good Housekeeping *(Nov. 1926).*
Courtesy of the Alice Marshall Women's History Collection, Penn State Harrisburg;
photo by Georganne H. Hughes, Metrophoto.

line and pose is so perfect, and Pamela's timid and wistful expression. . . . Where and when did you see the children?"[40]

The fact that Smith drew cherubic toddlers increased her subjects' typicality and the likelihood that any *Good Housekeeping* reader could imagine herself in, or just beyond the frame of, the picture. The seeming universality of Smith's cover children was a generalized representation of motherhood in the 1920s. In her work, "the girl on the magazine cover" was implied in the figure of a child who stood for the country in the new century, like the towheaded toddler building his future with ABCs in Figure 7.6.

Of course, her signature subject could not really have been *any* woman's son or daughter. Smith's cover children were white and usually fair-haired, and they frolicked in pastoral surroundings atypical of urban life. Their ubiquity on the cover of a mass circulation "family" magazine helped idealize American childhood as a white, middle-class, suburban experience, while also revealing the likely nature of the audiences of such magazines and naturalizing the typicality of those families as "American."

At the time, notes Mary Ellen Zuckerman, audience surveys rarely reported race, "the assumption being that readers were white." *Good Housekeeping* did rank highest of all major women's titles in a 1922 study done by advertising firm J. Walter Thompson that rated the "quality" of readership by (husband's) occupation. And publishing companies were able to target white (and white-collar) readers through their business practices as well as their editorial choices. The Curtis Publishing Company, which published the *Ladies' Home Journal* and the *Saturday Evening Post,* required its subscription salesmen to work according to "control maps" that identified "the better residential areas," and the company forbade them to visit black and immigrant neighborhoods.[41] The migration of white, middle-class families to "the better residential areas" outlying cities in the early twentieth century coincided with "the emergence of residential covenants that prohibited Jews, blacks, and in the West, Asians, from living in certain suburbs," notes Margaret Marsh.[42]

In this pastoral world, homes were built for family life. Architects noted "the decline of the parlor [and] . . . the 'return' of the living room," writes Marsh; "the arrangement of closets, bathrooms, and even the laundry area was planned with children in mind."[43] And the magazines that targeted these households focused on family life. Children were

Figure 7.6. Jessie Willcox Smith, Good Housekeeping *(Mar. 1929)*.
Reproduced from the Collections of the Library of Congress.

the subjects not only of Smith's cover work for *Good Housekeeping* but also of 90 percent of the covers Norman Rockwell drew for the *Saturday Evening Post* between 1916 and 1919 and half of all his covers for that magazine during the 1920s.[44]

Though Rockwell is now best remembered for his *Post* covers of the mid-twentieth century, his affiliation with the magazine dates to 1916 (the same year Smith's association with *Good Housekeeping* began), when he was just twenty-two years old. During the first two decades of his career, he also worked for *Boy's Life* (where he was briefly art director), the *Youth's Companion, American Boy, St. Nicholas,* the *Country Gentleman, American Farm and Fireside,* the *Popular Monthly,* the *Literary Digest, Life, Judge, Leslie's,* the *American Magazine,* and *Collier's.*[45]

Rockwell described the world of his artwork as "life as I would like it to be."[46] His vision coincided with that of *Post* editor George Horace Lorimer, who hoped to create "a sense of nationalism strong enough to override America's regional differences."[47] The magazine's cover scenes helped accomplish this: "Rockwell made America home, a comfortable sort of place where Main Street and Fifth Avenue exist in an easy truce and the great and the small have equal-sized emotions, pleasures and pains," noted one admirer.[48]

At the same time he tried to smooth over regional and class differences, Lorimer continued to appeal to his readers' ambition by telling them how they could rise in the world. Whereas in the century's early years the *Post* told success stories of young businessmen, in the 1920s it discussed upward mobility in terms of family life. A 1923 ad—addressing not the man but the woman of the household—showed two little girls and proclaimed, "In 10 years, Mother, one of these children will be enjoying social advantages which the other can never hope to attain." The ad copy, promoting a series of phonograph records, explained that "home musical training is all-important, inviting that subtle advantage of personality which enables some persons to advance so much further, in the keen struggle of life . . . [to] take their places, without embarrassment, among people of broad culture."[49]

These sorts of appeals in the *Post* of the 1920s reached an enormous audience, over two million at the decade's start and nearly three million at its end. Part of that growth can be attributed to its editorial repositioning as a family magazine rather than one targeted primarily toward men. Publisher Cyrus Curtis wanted the magazine to "speak to and symbolize the whole of American mainstream society."[50] Lorimer broadened the magazine's content to include more fiction and romance, as well as articles written specifically for women. Its advertising client base, previously dominated by automobile companies, now included manufacturers of kitchen appliances, cleansers, soaps, and silverware, and food companies such as Quaker Oats and Campbell's Soup.[51] By 1926, annual advertising revenue passed $50 million.[52] Each of the *Post*'s weekly issues, which cost only five cents, ran to over 200 pages and included political commentary, humor, human interest features, celebrity profiles, fiction, and instructional articles—an editorial mix with something for every member of the family.[53] And every member of the family was represented, at one time or another, on Norman Rockwell's covers.

Rockwell's young female figures were a far cry from the Flagg Girl or John Held's flapper; as he himself put it, "I paint the kind of girls your mother would want you to marry."[54] His cover mothers differed considerably from Smith's modern madonnas. In Rockwell's world, the figure of the mother was often something to be resisted or escaped by the child, who was usually a boy. This smothering mother embodied the contradictory rhetoric of parenting experts of the day, physicians and psychologists who urged women to make motherhood their first priority and yet to be careful not to overwhelm their children with too much attention. (Such mixed messages produced uncertainty that itself became a problem to be solved by experts. Promotional material for *Parents* magazine, launched in 1926, explained: "Many of us cringe at the revelation of our inadequacies. . . . [E]ducators, psychiatrists, writers and social workers are turning their searchlights on Parents . . . [who] realize that instinct and tradition are not sufficient equipment for their highly important job."[55])

Figure 7.7, a 1918 *Post* cover, is an early example of this postwar theme, a scene in which Rockwell "enables the observer to see the boy's glee at his shearing, suggesting that his life has moved on a niche, leaving his mother behind while he enters the world of men, symbolized by the debonair barber."[56] In the work of both Rockwell and J. C. Leyendecker, though, the debonair man's hold on the public imagination was weakening, and increasingly he was replaced by a more rugged ideal, a winning-out of "corporal" over "sartorial" ideals for masculinity.[57] These conflicting ideals presented a dilemma for the frowning boy in Figure 7.8, who suffered the taunts of his baseball-player friends not only because of his fancy dress but also because he was saddled with his

THE SATURDAY
EVENING POST

An Illustrated Weekly
...nded A° D! 1728 by Benj. Franklin

5c.

AUG. 10, 1918

Norman
Rockwell

Gerald Stanley Lee — Edward N. Hurley — Wallace Irwin — Arthur Train
Sinclair Lewis — Neville Taylor Gherardi — Frederick Orin Bartlett

Figure 7.7. Norman Rockwell, The Saturday Evening Post *(Aug. 10, 1918).*
Photo courtesy of the Norman Rockwell Museum at Stockbridge. Works by
Norman Rockwell reproduced courtesy of the Norman Rockwell Family Trust.

lace-capped baby sister. "The best part of the gag was the baby's bottle in the boy's pocket," the artist recalled. "I received lots of letters about his humiliation."[58]

Rockwell placed boys in the outdoors and in play and sports. Though his football players in Figure 7.9 appeared more ragged than rugged,

Figure 7.8. Norman Rockwell, The Saturday Evening Post *(May 20, 1916). Photo courtesy of the Curtis Publishing Company. Works by Norman Rockwell reproduced courtesy of the Norman Rockwell Family Trust.*

they led the "strenuous life"; what is more, they led it somewhere out-side the city, as signaled by the artist's frequent use of grass, ponds, and other nature cues. (One popular 1921 Rockwell cover, for instance, showed three half-dressed, wild boys and their dog running from a pond where they had evidently ignored the "No Swimming" sign.) The art-ist gave form to this muscular ideal while gently poking fun at it. The tackled boy in Figure 7.9 appeared stunned at what he had gotten him-self into; in Figure 7.10, a dumbbell-lifting "champ" looked longingly at the picture of a strongman showing him how to "be a man" ("it's easy" the poster proclaimed).

In the early twentieth century, these images had as much to do with adults as they did with children. Psychologists of the day saw athletic boyhood as a solution to diminished manhood in the modern era, con-vinced that "it was the innate primitive savagery of young boys that could point the way to the resolution of the crisis of masculinity" and that adult males "should learn to be more like boys and less like over-civilized men," notes Michael Kimmel. In this view, "the savage child could be father to the man and reinstill manly behavior." [59]

Rockwell's world of outdoor boyhood was replicated in organizations such as the new Boy Scouts of America (whose annual calendar Rock-well illustrated for fifty-three years), which enabled suburban boys to experience the fantasy of wilderness survival. While the Scouts repre-sented a rebellion against the feminizing influence of mothers, they also provided a safe channel for that rebellion and a way of socializing boys to work together toward common goals, as the work world later would require them to do. "If boys were provided a place away from the city, from women, and from culture—where they 'could be boys'—then they would surely become the 'real men' required by early-twentieth-century industrial capitalism," explains Kimmel.[60]

By the time he grew up, Rockwell's boy had indeed become a "real man" who, in the pages of the *Post,* was both a businessman and a hus-band who had made his way in the world and safely found his way home. On a *Literary Digest* cover drawn by Rockwell (Figure 7.11), he appeared in a picture of the 1920s American dream, examining home-building blueprints with his stylishly modern wife while their baby played at their feet. This image could easily have been on the *Post:* the husband was its typical reader, a businessman in the world but a family man at home—as Jan Cohn describes him, "an informed and responsible citi-zen, a balanced man who exercised thrift toward a self-reliant old age on

Figure 7.9. Norman Rockwell, The Saturday Evening Post *(Nov. 21, 1925).*
Photo courtesy of the Norman Rockwell Museum at Stockbridge. Works by
Norman Rockwell reproduced courtesy of the Norman Rockwell Family Trust.

Figure 7.10. Norman Rockwell, The Saturday Evening Post *(Apr. 29, 1922).*
Photo courtesy of the Norman Rockwell Museum at Stockbridge. Works by
Norman Rockwell reproduced courtesy of the Norman Rockwell Family Trust.

Figure 7.11. Norman Rockwell, "Planning the Home," The Literary Digest (May 8, 1920). Photo courtesy of the Norman Rockwell Museum at Stockbridge. Works by Norman Rockwell reproduced courtesy of the Norman Rockwell Family Trust.

THE SATURDAY EVENING POST

An Illustrated Weekly
Founded A.º D.! 1728 *by* Benj. Franklin

JULY 31, 1920

5c. THE COPY
10c. in Canada

EXCUSE MY DUST

Norman Rockwell

Helen Topping Miller—Don Marquis—William J. Neidig—Grace Lovell Bryan
Henry Payson Dowst—Admiral Smirnoff—Jay E. House—Jefferson Winter

Figure 7.12. Norman Rockwell, The Saturday Evening Post *(July 31, 1920).*
Photo courtesy of the Norman Rockwell Museum at Stockbridge. Works by
Norman Rockwell reproduced courtesy of the Norman Rockwell Family Trust.

the one hand and on the other, consumed, with moderation, the newly
available signs and tokens of upward mobility." [61]

This man was among the first fathers to appear on magazine covers
in a major role. Such a figure appeared simultaneously in advertising,
sometimes in the *Post* itself. A 1923 ad in the magazine showed a busi-

nessman leaning back in a rocking chair and holding a bowl of soapy water from which a toddler on his knees blew bubbles; the discarded newspaper on the floor was turned to the comic strip "Bringing Up Father." The copy proclaimed Palm Beach Suits the perfect attire for "A Summer Sunday morning when you drop your paper for a romp on the porch with the kids; during a heat-prophesying and heat-generating sermon; [or] a week-day business engagement in a stuffy office." [62]

The fact that the businessman-father was discussed in a clothing ad was significant. In his study of how American magazines articulated and reshaped masculinity, Tom Pendergast notes that during the 1920s "the path to success in business—always the true marker of masculine success in a capitalist society—began to be portrayed as resulting from a man's personality, his attention to the details of his appearance, his salesmanship. Masculinity came to be constructed in terms of how men presented themselves, not who they were." [63] Just as the seemingly oppositional images of the flapper and the mother had been reconciled through commerce, so too were the flapper and the man she married. The new ideal for masculinity suggested that readers could attain manhood by making the right purchases.

The ultimate commercial and social construct of the era was the family itself. According to the suburban domestic ideal, Americans were organized into *units* that negotiated the world together and advanced their lot by making smart decisions about "lifestyle"—where they lived, what they ate, what they wore, what they did together. This message was underscored in Figure 7.12, a *Post* cover, by the vehicle in which Rockwell's family moved forward—the automobile, the mass-produced status symbol that was also the era's primary symbol of progress.[64] In 1920s magazine imagery, the typical American family became a unifying metaphor for twentieth-century American life.

The Advertising Connection

Since the first national advertising campaigns more than a century ago, American manufacturers have promised that their products offered a "new" way of adhering to old values. Advertising is especially persuasive when it offers the new through familiar imagery.[1] In the earliest mass market ad campaigns, which appeared in magazines beginning in the 1890s, many images were more than familiar—they were in fact the same as those that adorned covers and illustrated editorial features.

Almost all of the artists whose editorial work is surveyed in this book worked for advertisers, many of them to a considerable extent. This chapter surveys the advertising art of J. C. Leyendecker, Coles Phillips, Jessie Willcox Smith, Norman Rockwell, and Neysa McMein. All five of these artists, and most of their peers in illustration, considered advertising work a side career, as well as the aesthetic stepchild of editorial art. Yet one cannot assume that early-twentieth-century audiences made such a distinction. Many readers could not tell the difference between editorial and advertising pages: when the *Ladies' Home Journal* asked its readers to select their favorite editorial illustrations from 1902, the majority chose a drawing by Alice Barber Stephens that had been an ad.[2] Other readers simply recognized the artists' "characters" wherever they appeared.

It was not a coincidence that the golden age of magazine illustration coincided with the birth of successful national advertising campaigns based on visual icons. The cherublike children of early Ivory Soap ads did not merely resemble Smith's *Good Housekeeping* cover children; they *were* these youngsters, drawn in the same form by the same hand. Leyendecker's debonair cover man for the *Saturday Evening Post* was widely recognized as "the Arrow Collar Man." And when modern companies such as Orange Crush (sodas) and Edison Mazda (electrical lighting) wanted to build brand loyalty by appealing to 1920s Americans' nostalgia for a simpler way of life, they chose work by Rockwell, the same illustrator who created that feeling for *Post* covers.

Thus the messages of editorial and advertising art in magazines were blurred. Not only did the same "signature" images appear in both aspects of mass media; they frequently appeared in, or on the back cover of, some of the very same issues that carried the illustrators' cover drawings. Their creators' celebrity status enhanced the credibility of an advertiser's product and suggested the approval of the illustrator. Some artists provided testimonials. Old Gold cigarettes put James Montgomery Flagg to a taste test and then ran his enthusiastic response in their ads: ". . . it suited me best even blindfolded. In fact, the man who said, *'not a cough in a carload'* knew whereof he spoke."[3] In turn, the broad exposure of national advertising campaigns offered illustrators even greater fame, while ensuring the repeated distribution of their imagery. A Procter & Gamble executive explained to Stephens: "[W]e give your work a wide circulation and probably ten times the opportunity for it to be seen and appreciated by the public than you get on the average from your pictures that are made for a single publication or book."[4]

Advertising also offered compelling financial incentives in an era when magazine publishers signed illustrators to exclusive contracts that prohibited them from doing editorial work for other magazines. Rockwell doubled his editorial fees when he worked for advertisers; in the early 1920s, one ad agency offered him an annual salary of $25,000 if he would devote himself full time to advertising (he declined).[5] Leyendecker and Phillips were so prolific in their "side" careers that they were as well known for their advertising work as they were for their cover art.

Leyendecker's most popular creation was the Arrow Collar Man, who appeared in the shirt company's ads from 1905 to 1930,[6] and today this is his best-remembered contribution to illustration history. This character, writes Michael Schau, "defined the ideal of the American male: a dignified, clear-eyed man of taste, manners, and quality. . . . The term 'Arrow Collar Man' became a common epithet for any handsome, nattily dressed gent, and the Arrow Man was the subject of admiring poems,

Figure 8.1. J. C. Leyendecker, Advertisement for Arrow Collars and Shirts (ca. 1910). By permission of, and photo courtesy of, the Arrow Company, a Division of Cluett, Peabody & Co., Inc.

songs, and even a Broadway play." [7] Many women thought he *was* real. Cluett, Peabody & Company, the firm that made Arrow Collars, received on average **17,000** letters per month from women writing to the Arrow Collar Man, some of them proposing marriage. This amount of fan mail made him more popular than silent-film star Rudolph Valentino.[8]

The "taste, manners, and quality" of the Arrow Collar Man was a matter of clothing, a choice most middle-class men could and should make, the ads suggested. "Manliness here does not reside in or on the body, but is purchased and applied to it under the sign of the brand name," Eric Segal notes of the clothing ads in the *Saturday Evening Post* of this era, many of them drawn by Leyendecker and Norman Rockwell in the years when their art was appearing on the covers of the publication.[9]

The Arrow Man set corporal as well as sartorial standards for masculinity. He was clean-shaven, square-jawed and broad-shouldered, worldly and serious-minded, as suggested by the men in the Arrow Collar ad shown in Figure 8.1. During World War I, it was not hard to make the connection between the businessman in the reading room and Leyendecker's Chesterfield-smoking flying "ace" or infantryman.[10]

Yet his predominant characteristic was *class*. In society, the Arrow

Man appeared with a sophisticated female partner with similarly long body lines and chiseled nose and chin, like the woman dancing with him in Figure 8.2. Just as her escort was a blend of notions about masculinity, the Leyendecker woman was a blend of notions about femininity during this era, a combination of sleek modernity with delicate prettiness and deference, signaled by her downturned gaze and lower positioning. As a couple, they embodied elitism and affluence, conveyed by their facial expressions, their formal poses (these were not the animal dances), and their setting. And of course these attributes were conveyed by their clothing. In that sense, "class" was not a rigid set of social categories but rather something that was for sale, available to people who did not have it but could afford to buy it.

Kent Steine and Frederic Taraba argue that Leyendecker's "impact on advertising and 'product identification' can only be considered monumental, even by today's standards."[11] Though he was most closely associated with Arrow Collars, Leyendecker's man reappeared in ads for other companies, wearing Interwoven socks and Kuppenheimer suits. In an ad for the latter company, the actor John Barrymore—probably the next-best-known American romantic icon of the 1920s, after the Arrow Collar Man and Rudolph Valentino—posed for Leyendecker's drawing and gave his personal endorsement, claiming, "This is my idea of a clean-cut town and business suit."[12] More often, however, the Kuppenheimer man, like the Arrow Man, was an anonymous figure into which male magazine readers could wishfully project themselves, the visual strategy of the artist's *Post* covers. The ads showed him hunting outdoors and traveling abroad, and the text of one claimed that the purchase of expensive clothing—"an investment in good appearance"—was an investment in oneself and one's future, eventually paying literal dividends.[13]

The same appeal to readers' desires for status and leisure appeared in the elegant advertising characters of Coles Phillips. One of his steady clients was Community Plate silverware, whose motto was "Silverware of Quality." In a 1924 ad for this company (Figure 8.3), Phillips used the female figure as a design element, a technique he had perfected on his covers for *Good Housekeeping* and *Life,* by posing a modernly dressed and coiffed woman in the midst of "The Magic Hour—Afternoon Tea" (an "exquisite setting for silver," the ad copy notes). This was the artist's trademark Fadeaway Girl, her striped top and checked stockings blend-

*Figure 8.2. J. C. Leyendecker, Advertisement for Arrow Collars and Shirts
(ca. 1923). By permission of, and photo courtesy of, the Arrow Company,
a Division of Cluett, Peabody & Co., Inc.*

Figure 8.3. Coles Phillips, Advertisement for Community Plate Silverware (n.d.).
Courtesy of the Alice Marshall Women's History Collection, Penn State Harrisburg;
photo by Georganne H. Hughes, Metrophoto.

ing with the yellow background. Definition in this image was provided not by its human subject but by things, the chair, the tea tables, and, most noticeably, the large silver knives gleaming against their black backdrop and bracketing the scene. In a similar ad that Phillips drew for Community Plate, a woman inspected a gravy ladle in which, the reader could have imagined, she saw her own reflection. Her "quality" possessions reflected well on her.

Like Leyendecker, Phillips would have been successful even without his editorial work. At the start of his career, he briefly owned his own advertising agency, and the list of clients for which he drew ads (before and during his years as a cover artist) was long, including Vitralite paint, Scranton lace, Unguentine suntanning oil, National Mazda Lamps, Blabon linoleum floors, Palmolive Soap, Jell-O, Watkins shampoo, and Oneida plateware. The Fadeaway Girl sold most of these products, though she was put to best use in ads for women's clothing, where she appeared wearing L'Aiglon dresses, Holeproof Hosiery, Luxite Hosiery, and Jantzen Swimsuits.[14]

In one Holeproof Hosiery ad, the outline of her body was blurred by the patterns of her semitransparent robe—patterns that, on closer inspection, created a spiderweb. This image is thematically very similar to Phillips's *Life* cover titled "Net Results" (Figure 3.4 in Chapter 3), in which little men were caught in the pretty girl-spider's web. If the sexual appeal of the image was lost on readers, the text below helped them out: "Trim ankles, demurely alluring. How they fascinate, captivate . . ."

In the ad shown in Figure 8.4, Phillips's girl, wearing a sheer-black, knee-length slip and transparent stockings, appeared against the background image of a feathered peacock. (This was one of several drawings Phillips made, for both ads and magazine covers, juxtaposing women and birds.)[15] The woman's downward glance directed the readers' attention to her legs, though they may have been distracted by the fact that she was, somewhat astonishingly, lifting her slip up in the air behind her, as a bird might spread feathers.

Though Phillips's advertising women were as alluring as his manipulative cover beauties, they were often shown as mothers (not surprisingly, given that mothers bought lots of products). Their elegance conveyed the aspirational messages of magazine articles about family life. One example is Figure 8.5, another Holeproof Hosiery ad, in which Phillips drew a seated woman lifting a baby into the air on one of her legs; while her skirt faded into the background, her black-stockinged

DEC 1?

Holeproof   *Hosiery*

COLES PHILLIPS

HOLEPROOF is the hosiery of lustrous beauty and fine texture that wears so well. It is not surprising, therefore, that it is selected by many people who can afford to pay far more for their hose, but who prefer the Holeproof combination of style and serviceability at such reasonable prices.

Obtainable in Pure Silk, Silk Faced, and Lusterized Lisle

HOLEPROOF HOSIERY COMPANY, Milwaukee, Wisconsin
Holeproof Hosiery Company of Canada, Limited, London, Ont.   © H. H. Co.

Figure 8.4. Coles Phillips, Advertisement for Holeproof Hosiery (ca. 1922).
Courtesy of the D'Arcy Collection of the Communications Library of the University
of Illinois at Urbana-Champaign.

legs stood out. These stockings were practical (they not only made her ankles shapely, but were durable enough to bounce an infant on them) and affordable. "Reasonable prices place this superior hosiery within reach of all," the text explained. This ad appeared in a 1922 issue of the *Literary Digest*, at a time when Norman Rockwell's young families

Holeproof Hosiery

© H. H. Co.

Sheer Elegant Hosiery Now an Everyday Economy

YOU can wear beautiful shapely hosiery every day as well as on dress occasions, without increasing your hosiery expense, if you buy Holeproof.

For back of Holeproof's exquisite beauty is a fine-spun strength that withstands long wear and repeated launderings.   Reasonable prices place this superior hosiery within reach of all.

Offered in Pure Silk, Silk Faced, and Lusterized Lisle, for men, women and children. If your dealer cannot supply you, write for illustrated booklet and price list.

HOLEPROOF HOSIERY COMPANY
MILWAUKEE, WISCONSIN
Holeproof Hosiery Company of Canada, Limited, London, Ontario

Figure 8.5. Coles Phillips, Advertisement for Holeproof Hosiery (ca. 1922). Courtesy of the D'Arcy Collection of the Communications Library of the University of Illinois at Urbana-Champaign.

were on its cover. In another domestic scene, this one for Jell-O pudding, Phillips drew a woman bowing down to serve two clapping little boys.

As she would for the covers of *Good Housekeeping,* Jessie Willcox Smith created advertising tableaux in which mothers were shown bending down to help children or in which children were themselves the focus. Her earliest advertising work appeared inside the pages of *Good Housekeeping*'s competitor the *Ladies' Home Journal.* For several years during the 1890s while she was studying art, she worked as a staff artist in the *Journal*'s advertising department.[16] This job led to major commercial assignments. She drew "delicate studies of ordinary families with new cameras" for Kodak, which at first used the more familiar medium of illustration to depict the act of amateur photography.[17] (During this era photography was used to document ideas, people, and products, while illustration was used to idealize them. Smith's work for Kodak was evidence of this tactic—even when the idealized product was a camera!)

Another important early client was Ivory Soap, for which she drew a series of ads that appeared in magazines from the late 1890s to the 1920s. The small print underneath the two ads shown here suggested the importance of Smith's role in the company's appeal to mothers. One (Figure 8.6) noted that the image had been created as "art" rather than as an advertisement, proclaiming that "The drawing by Jessie Willcox Smith, reproduced above, was awarded first prize of Six Hundred Dollars in an artists' competition conducted by The Procter & Gamble Co."[18] The other (Figure 8.7) promised readers that if they sent in ten Ivory Soap wrappers, "we will send a copy (without printing) on enamel plate paper, 14 × 17 inches, a suitable size for framing." The phrase "without printing" was telling: the removal of the advertising copy would return the status of this image to that of elevating "art" for home display. In another Smith-drawn ad, the company offered readers the premium of a wall calendar "especially for nurseries, playrooms, schoolrooms, etc.," featuring drawings of children by Smith and other artists of the day.

Smith's children were innocent and pure, just as Procter & Gamble wanted mothers to think Ivory Soap was. Figure 8.6, featuring Smith's picture of an adorable little girl standing on a stool to reach the sink where she washed her hands, visually referred to two themes that domi-

COPYRIGHT 1902 BY THE PROCTER & GAMBLE CO. CINCINNATI

The sweetest thing on earth is the face of a little child. Its skin is exquisitely delicate, like the bloom of a ripe peach. Imagine washing a peach with colored and perfumed soap! Next to pure water, Ivory Soap is the purest and most innocent thing for a child's skin. No chemicals! No free alkali! Just a soft, snow-white puff of down, which vanishes instantly when water is applied. It floats.

The drawing by Jessie Willcox Smith, reproduced above, was awarded first prize of Six Hundred Dollars in an artists' competition conducted by The Procter & Gamble Co.

Figure 8.6. Jessie Willcox Smith, Advertisement for Ivory Soap (1902).
Courtesy of the Alice Marshall Women's History Collection, Penn State Harrisburg;
photo by Georganne H. Hughes, Metrophoto.

Figure 8.7. Jessie Willcox Smith, Advertisement for Ivory Soap (1899).
Courtesy of the Alice Marshall Women's History Collection, Penn State Harrisburg;
photo by Georganne H. Hughes, Metrophoto.

nated the editorial content of magazines in this era. One was the importance of female sexual purity in the era of the New Woman, a theme that preoccupied editors from Edward Bok onward. The other was that of public health as entrusted to "civic housekeepers." The ad copy addressed mothers directly and stressed their responsibility as consumers, implying that their purchase of the wrong product would harm their children:

> The sweetest thing on earth is the face of a little child. Its skin is exquisitely delicate, like the bloom of a ripe peach. Imagine washing a peach with colored and perfumed soap! Next to pure water, Ivory Soap is the purest and most innocent thing for a child's skin. No chemicals! No free alkali! Just a soft, snow-white puff of down, which vanishes instantly when water is applied. It floats.[19]

More subtly inscribed in Smith's Ivory Soap ads was a third theme in popular discourse in the new century—racial purity. Anne McClintock has connected the turn-of-the-century advertising rhetoric of British soap manufacturers with that nation's imperialism, arguing that soap symbolized not just the purity of the white race but also the belief that the "dark countries" could be "cleansed" through colonization.[20] Smith's work for Ivory Soap appeared during the Spanish-American War, a time of American imperialism under Rough Rider and soon-to-be-president Theodore Roosevelt. Roosevelt first sounded the alarm about "race suicide" in an 1899 speech in which he equated manliness with mastery through global economic and military domination. Only "the man who embodies victorious effort," he said, would fulfill America's mission "to play a great part in the world" and to bring "order out of chaos." [21]

The themes of American naval imperialism and global eugenics might have been read into the image of an Ivory Soap ad (Figure 8.7) published the same year Roosevelt made his speech. In Smith's drawing, a sailor-suited boy stood in a military pose, guarding and overseeing a subservient little girl as she built an entirely "white house." The ad copy below it commented on the roles of gender and domesticity in "the future of the race," while conveying the increasingly familiar idea that readers could become "the best" by making the right shopping choices: "A careful builder insures the permanency and strength of his building by laying the foundations of the best materials. The good housewife lays a foundation of Ivory Soap and rests upon it the cleanliness and comfort of the family. It pays to use the best materials and the [*sic*] Ivory is the best Soap."

Children also dominated the advertising art of Norman Rockwell, who took assignments from more than 150 companies during his five decades as an illustrator. Much of this work was done early in his career. His clients included Black Cat [boys'] Reinforced Hosiery, Edison Mazda lighting, Orange Crush soda, Perfection Oil Heaters, Romance Chocolates, Coca-Cola, Montgomery Ward, Old Gold cigarettes, *Encyclopaedia Britannica,* and Arrow Collars (his Arrow Collar ads focused on the company's line of boys' dress shirts). During the 1920s, Rockwell's signature family tableaux appeared on the covers of the Sears, Roebuck catalog as well as the covers of the *Saturday Evening Post.*[22] Often his advertising work appeared in the same issues of the *Post* that carried his cover art.

Playing on the word "crush," Rockwell drew sweet and sometimes comical boy-girl images for Orange Crush soda, including the adolescents in Figure 8.8, whose act of sipping out of the same glass sent an old man into a huff. These were wholesome, likeable characters reminiscent of Victorian era values, yet they were shown living in an idealized post–World War I America—the world described in the articles, fiction, and cover art of the *Post.*

Rockwell's advertising imagery also employed his favorite visual subject, the rugged but suburban boy of the twentieth century. One scene he created for Edison Mazda Lamps showed a boy reading in bed by lamplight in his own bedroom, his run-down sneakers on the floor, his loyal dog curled up at his feet, his play sword stuck behind a painting on the wall—all clues proving that he was a "real boy," energetic and rambunctious.

"Real Boys!" was actually the title of a Rockwell ad for Black Cat Reinforced Hosiery that ran in the *Post* (Figure 8.9). It showed a young female schoolteacher, her back to the viewer, patiently sitting through either a recital or a song delivered by boys so distracted or uncomfortable that none of them could look at her. The ad's copywriter excused them, explaining that this was what women should expect from a real boy:

—Not the soulful child martyrs of the movie screen.
—Not the Little Lord Fauntleroys you read about in storybooks.

Figure 8.8. Norman Rockwell, Advertisement for Orange Crush (ca. 1921).
Photo courtesy of the Norman Rockwell Museum at Stockbridge. Works by
Norman Rockwell reproduced courtesy of the Norman Rockwell Family Trust.

But *real* Boys! The genuine—tree climbing—marble playing—
tousle-headed—made-in-America BOY!

He's his dad's double—ready for fight, frolic or foot-race. He's his
mother's manly little man—generous, noble-minded, cheerful, quick
to forgive.

He's the Emblem of Energy. He's the Personification of Progress.
He's the biggest asset of the richest race on earth. And—he's the
problem that produced

The Advertising Connection

Figure 8.9. Norman Rockwell, Advertisement for Black Cat Reinforced Hosiery
(ca. 1917). Photo courtesy of the Norman Rockwell Museum at Stockbridge. Works by
Norman Rockwell reproduced courtesy of the Norman Rockwell Family Trust.

Black Cat Reinforced Hosiery

Extra threads, knit into knee and heel and toe, give many weeks of wear before mother has to darn.

Black Cat triple reinforced knees were made for marble games. Black Cat heels for hop, step and jump. Black Cat toes for can-kicking and mileage. Black Cat legs for fence-climbing and football.

Black Cats fit snugly but have such stretch and give that it takes a mighty tug to tear them. Dragged on legs dripping wet at the swimming hole, they neither rip nor run. And Towser can help him take them off at night.

Accompanied by Rockwell's adorably uncivilized boys, this text was an extraordinary list of cultural concerns in 1917, the year it appeared in the *Saturday Evening Post*. Such a "real boy" resisted the feminizing influences of the faceless female teacher and the mother who fretted over all of the outdoor activities mentioned here, several of which ("fence-climbing," "the swimming hole," even the presence of "Towser") suggested a life outside the city. In his readiness for fight or frolic, the boy described in this ad reflected well on adult men ("He's his dad's double") during the crisis of masculinity. Praised the very year the United States entered World War I, this "made-in-America BOY!" and "biggest asset of the richest race on earth" was destined for the kind of rugged, heterosexual ("Not the Little Lord Fauntleroys") manhood that would ensure the future of "the race" within America and of American values across the globe.[23]

It is also significant that this ad addressed mothers at a time when the *Post* was making a transition from being a men's magazine to being a "family magazine." Writing about popular literature of the early twentieth century, Joe Dubbert has detected "a latent tension . . . between the naturally free, primitive instincts of boyhood and the moral governance of stern parents, especially mothers, who failed to understand the importance of allowing adolescent males to follow their natural instincts." [24] The same theme, which ran through much of Rockwell's cover art, was common in advertising.

The mother's desire to control her son, implied in the Black Cat ad, was more openly addressed in a clothing ad that ran in a 1920 issue of the *Post*. Underneath Rockwell's drawing of two falling-down roller skaters, the ad copy lectured women who overprotected their sons: "Mothers: Don't make your boy afraid-of-his-clothes by constantly telling him

'Be careful!' Don't worry him out of his boyish spirits, which demand healthy, rough-and-tumble fun. Put him in Dubbelbilt Clothes . . . your common sense will show you the thrift of buying these clothes of *guaranteed* dependability. Teach the boy thrift *by example.*" [25]

Like the Black Cat ad ("it takes a mighty tug to tear them . . . they neither rip nor run"), the Dubbelbilt ad ended with a promise to mothers that the product was durable and long-lasting—the same appeal to thrift and practicality made in the Holeproof Hosiery ads. Historian Daniel Horowitz notes that the financial instability and inflation of the immediate postwar period prompted a resurgence of middle-class concerns about saving money. [26] This concern was expressed in popular magazines within the context of upward mobility, a paradox especially present in the *Post,* whose editor, George Horace Lorimer, frequently editorialized on the virtues of thrift. The message of the Dubbelbilt ad and other ads like it was that postwar parents should spend money wisely ("the thrift of buying"). And it was a lesson addressed specifically to mothers, who made the decisions about what to buy.

Though there were no "real girls" whose durable clothing allowed them to climb fences and shoot marbles in popular culture of this era, the New Woman frequently was shown as an outdoor sportswoman. This was true in advertising as well as editorial imagery, and one example is Figure 8.10, an ad drawn by Neysa McMein. As in the many bicycle ads in the *Ladies' Home Journal* of the 1890s, women's physical activity in later ads had less to do with their free spirits than with their waistlines. Though the serious expression and turned head of McMein's golfer suggested that she was concentrating on something other than fashion, this ad, which ran in a 1924 issue of *Vogue,* promoted girdles— the last thing this young woman needed. The ad copy was actually written for older women: "No matter what her age, or the style of the moment, if a woman would be graceful, she must have that youth-line which Gossards give and preserve."

The close relationship between magazine advertising and cover images worked against the progressive messages about womanhood in McMein's editorial art, especially when one of her covers appeared on the same issue that contained her advertising work. [27] Brian Gallagher writes about the June 1924 issue of *McCall's,* which carried McMein's signature woman on both the front cover and the back cover advertisement for Colgate toothpaste: "In the years she drew for it, *McCall's* was filled with dozens of advertisements for products that promised

Figure 8.10. Neysa McMein, Advertisement for Gossard corsets (1924).
Courtesy of the Alice Marshall Women's History Collection, Penn State Harrisburg;
photo by Georganne H. Hughes, Metrophoto.

healthier skin, whiter teeth, shinier hair. . . . In short, much of the magazine's advertising 'text' was a lesson on how to become like the fetchingly attractive . . . young woman on its cover. The McMein girl was, from the point of view *McCall's* established, a unifying image."[28]

Her roles as a cover artist and an advertising artist were similarly blurred by an ad for Woodbury's Soap, which included her portrait of a beautiful woman posed much the same way as her Gossard golfer, except with a man rather than golf clubs at her side. While the text discussed how using the soap resulted in "the skin you love to touch," the title of the ad was "Given away—This beautiful picture for framing." Readers who bought a bar of soap, it promised, also would receive a copy of the drawing. Providing instructions for framing the print, the ad attributed the prestige of owning it to McMein's fame as an *editorial* artist, explaining that "this beautiful picture" had been "painted by Neysa McMein, *the popular artist, whose lovely women you see every month on the covers of your favorite magazines*" (emphasis added).[29] Just as Procter & Gamble had resold images of the adorable children drawn by Jessie Willcox Smith, the Jergens Company sold both the image of the New Woman in illustration and the New Woman who was her creator. And in both cases, soap manufacturers offered status objects (framable art), created by female artists, as a way of marketing the notions of purity and cleanliness.

Purity was the key word of a 1919 advertisement whose framed image, drawn by McMein, was the head of a nurse (Figure 8.11). As suggested by the opening phrase of the ad copy—"High ideals and cheerful service"—this image referred not just to the nursing profession but also to women's work in the recent war. In a postwar ad for Society Brand Clothes, McMein (who herself had been stationed in France as a YMCA volunteer) drew a female veteran disembarking from a ship along with male soldiers returning from the war.[30] But by 1919, the wartime nurse had been relegated to the drugstore window, where she promoted hygiene products.

McMein's portrait of this former national heroine, dignified and serene, was advertised as "the sign of the San-Tox druggist, and also the beautiful *symbol of purity* that identifies for you the many splendid San-Tox Preparations."[31] She was a saleswoman in a cameo, a helper for shoppers. "Look for her before you buy," read the text. As a symbol, she was no longer a "nurse" (a woman) but rather a "nurse-face." Not even her purity was her own; like Smith's toddlers, she had become a symbol

Look for this Nurse-Face
in the Drug Store Window

High ideals and cheerful service—Preparations of a purity to satisfy the
most exacting standards. These are the things the San-Tox nurse stands
for when you see her gracious face in the drug store window. ¶ Look for
her before you buy. She is the sign of the San-Tox druggist, and also the
beautiful *symbol of purity* that identifies for you the many splendid San-Tox
Preparations. ¶ There is a wide, wide range of these San-Tox Preparations,
all of perfect purity, and each for some definite need of toilet or hygiene.

SAN-TOX FOR PURITY
DePree   Chicago

San-Tox

Figure 8.11. Neysa McMein, Advertisement for San-Tox Preparations,
The American Magazine *(1919). Courtesy of the Alice Marshall Women's History*
Collection, Penn State Harrisburg; photo by Georganne H. Hughes, Metrophoto.

of *product* purity. This was a remarkable commercial transformation of the meaning of McMein's New Woman who appeared on the covers of *McCall's*.

Viewed collectively and in hindsight, the advertising art created by the era's major illustrators underscores the importance of commercial context in analyzing media imagery. While each of the artists discussed in this book created a particular "type" for a particular magazine, those types—as preceding chapters have shown—become more meaningful when seen in relation to each other. This chapter adds to that argument by suggesting that the historical importance of "the girl on the magazine cover" of this era (as well as the men and boys on magazine covers) lies partly in the fact that these images traveled off that cover and into the broader commercial culture. Sometimes their editorial meaning remained intact, and sometimes it was transformed. In either event, their move from editorial to advertising art was a leap, not a sidestep.

Both cover art and advertising are "commercial" texts, and, as previous chapters have noted, their imagery interacts in important ways. Within a magazine, they make meaning together rather than separately. Even so, they are too often collapsed into a single phenomenon in analyses of popular culture. When they appeared on covers of magazines, the famous characters of the era's top illustrators "sold" the magazine and created large audiences for the advertisers who bought space on inside pages. But in ads, they actually enjoyed, endorsed, and sold the advertisers' products. As the setting for this move, the early-twentieth-century mass circulation magazine created a blueprint for the routine blurring of editorial and advertising messages in mass media and for the commercial cooptation of ideas, and ideals, about femininity, masculinity, and upward class mobility.

Cover imagery of this era expressed—for the first time in media that were truly national—ideas about gender and about class, gradually diffusing those identity tensions by blending them into a larger notion about what it meant to be a "typical American" in the modern era. The broader editorial ideal in turn sold products through which a middle-class American lifestyle could be pursued and attained. This symbiotic representational process would characterize the cultural work of mass media imagery into the twenty-first century.

Epilogue and Discussion

The artwork in the preceding chapters offers a larger picture of how the New Woman, a political concept in the 1890s, became commercialized and diffused by the 1920s, a process that played out in the first American mass media and against the cultural backdrops of the suffrage movement and a modern consumer society. These images also collectively trace how a broader ideal of a middle-class family lifestyle —which seemed to be the answer to questions about womanhood, manhood, and who was "American"—emerged in mass media during the same decades.

This book has taken the shape of a narrative that unfolds in a seemingly logical way. This story is, of course, selective. During the thirty-five-year period it covers, hundreds of American magazines disseminated millions of visual and verbal images, and only a handful of the most popular types are analyzed here. Even with regard to that dominant art, much has been omitted. The examples of the illustrators' work were chosen based on what they were best known for drawing, though some of them drew other subjects that were quite different than the artwork shown here. (For instance, J. C. Leyendecker's "New Year's Baby" was an annual favorite of *Saturday Evening Post* readers.[1])

The progression of these images also was not as neat as it seems in my survey. Some of the visual ideas that are explained here in the context of specific years actually were around for decades. While their cultural resonance was strongest in the 1920s, Jessie Willcox Smith's babies appeared in magazines from the turn of the century to the early 1930s; Leyendecker's dapper man had a similarly long life. And from 1910 to 1920, the "signature" images of nearly all of the artists discussed in this book were in circulation. Their collision in popular culture of that era makes sense in retrospect, since these were years of enormous potential for change in gender and class relations and a time of diverse political ideas. But it is hard to argue that media imagery "unfolded" during these years. Indeed, the messy representational contradictions of this decade are as significant—historically and as a model for understanding current media—as the broader trajectory I describe.

Even so, the goal of this book has been to search for cultural patterns that have lasting meaning, to find in the past a lesson for the future. This is a necessarily selective and interpretive process (as is culture itself), and its outcome is a story. Though my study ends in 1930, the story it tells did not. In this chapter, I will try to bring that narrative up to the present day, and to consider what the media of the early twentieth century may tell us about media, and American life, in the twenty-first century.

By the late 1920s, the rhetoric of the women's rights movement still held currency in popular culture, but a woman's "freedom" was defined as a matter of the many ways she could be a better wife, mother, and shopper. A 1928 issue of the *Saturday Evening Post* featured a grocery-store-chain advertisement that explained "the new woman" to male readers: "How different is the new order that has been ushered in. Today, your wife finds opportunity to vary her interests . . . to be a companion to your children . . . to study closer your welfare. She has won a new freedom in her daily life." [2]

Articles inside mass circulation magazines reinforced this notion of feminism as a daily and private matter. As early as 1920, a female writer for the *Ladies' Home Journal* applauded readers' "free woman will" and claimed that their dedication to homemaking was "the result of intelligent choice." She concluded that "the most modern expression of feminism" was marriage and motherhood, explaining, "The newest new woman deifies not herself, but through her new freedom elects to serve others." [3] For women who elected to work and have a family, the issue of childcare was also a private issue. "The fact that a small number of women are already successfully combining both shows that it can be done," claimed an expert in a 1928 issue of *Independent Woman,* the magazine of the National Federation of Business and Professional Women's Clubs. "Those who have solved their problem thus happily must pass on their knowledge to other women." [4]

The "freedom" of the New Woman of the 1920s was presented as a matter of discriminating choice, the ability to select the "best" goods and services. In her choice of a suburban home, of the latest appliances, of cars—even her decision to have children and to raise them in a certain way—the modern woman appeared to be different than women of previous generations. [5] This domesticated flapper wore her newness on her body as well, in her slimness, hairdo, makeup, and clothing. [6]

The class continuum represented in 1890s magazines had similarly been collapsed into one central ideal by the 1920s—the white, suburban, nuclear family. A middle-class lifestyle seemed to be the birthright of *Good Housekeeping*'s toddling Everychild and the reward for the "real boy" who grew up to read the *Saturday Evening Post*. The visual and verbal imagery of that decade's media seemed to mark a "return to normalcy" after a culturally and politically intense, if brief, period of suffragism, socialism, and potentially emasculating sexology. The magazines' message was less a rejection than a dismissal of feminist and class-based political radicalism: the success and happiness of the individual, they proposed, had made collective action and group-based identities unnecessary.

This conclusion was classist (even if there was a "typical" lifestyle by the 1920s, not everyone could afford to live it) and explicitly postfeminist. The label of "feminist" had become "a term of opprobrium to the modern young woman," one such second-generation female wrote in a 1927 issue of *Harper's Monthly Magazine*. The word invoked "either the old school of fighting feminists who wore flat heels and had very little feminine charm, or the current species who antagonize men with the constant clamor about maiden names [and] equal rights." This writer could not understand why the generation of women before hers failed to realize that "the worst of the fight is over," why they were "still throwing hand grenades," why they "rant[ed] about equality when they might better prove their ability." In contrast, a "new-style" feminist, she explained, "professes no loyalty to women *en masse,* although she staunchly believes in individual women." [7]

To women living at the beginning of the twenty-first century, such remarks are startlingly familiar. Indeed, what is most remarkable about the current "backlash" against feminism is how very old it is and with what strength the old rhetoric has survived.

It was employed in the century's middle decades as well, when ideal womanhood continued to vary according to cultural circumstances. "During the Second World War the propaganda machine got women to work by celebrating the 'new woman' as one who could labour [*sic*] and love in perfect unison," writes Janet Lee. "And when the war was over, that very same 'new woman' was the one who preferred housework to paid work. Similarly in the sixties . . . [t]he advent of 'the Pill' meant that women were suddenly being encouraged from almost every direction to have more sex. It seems that whenever someone has something to sell to women—be it clothes, careers or contraception—we are urged to change ourselves into the 'new woman' of the moment."[8]

Lee is right that consumption was a major factor in which versions of womanhood were "new" in different eras, but these ideals also were connected to political tensions in society. As was true of the image of sexually bold "girls" during the second decade of the twentieth century, the image of a sexually free New Woman in the 1960s coincided not only with the availability of the Pill but also with race and class tensions (the civil rights movement, the "War on Poverty") and a youth culture fueled by U.S. involvement in an unpopular foreign war. Then, as in the earlier era, sex (symbolized by young women) was a cultural cipher for political turmoil.

Between the 1930s and 1960s, the old stereotypes—the "true" domestic woman, the all-American girl-pal, the sexually dangerous schemer, the vapid party girl, the modern madonna—resurfaced fairly intact. During the Great Depression, when men lost their jobs (and there was again labor radicalism throughout the country), and World War II, when women again entered the work force in significant numbers, media imagery of women was dichotomized into good and bad. Overtly sexualized imagery made a comeback on the covers of magazines targeted toward upscale American men (the Petty and Varga Girls on *Esquire*), and "the exotic bad girl" appeared in film in the characters of actresses such as Rita Hayworth.[9] During the politically conservative 1950s, women's sexuality was still a media theme, but it was seductively sweet in gal-pals such as the film characters of Doris Day or golddiggingly ditzy in the characters of Marilyn Monroe.

By the 1960s, the ideal female body was once again that of a preadolescent girl. Looking back on this image, novelist Susan Cheever writes about the media icon who embodied the new look: "Twiggy was the anti-woman: she had no breasts, she wore white lipstick, her nails were bitten, her shoulders were bony and her hair was cut like a boy's. . . . She was so skinny it was hard to tell she was a woman at all. Instead of a shirtwaist, she wore a skirt no bigger than a proper lady's pocket handkerchief. Instead of standing as if she were balancing a book on her head, she was knock-kneed and coltishly awkward. She was everything unfeminine in a way that seemed, mysteriously, totally girlish."[10] This is almost a perfect description of John Held's knock-kneed and coltishly awkward flapper on the covers of *Life* four decades earlier, and

Cheever's comparison of Twiggy with the "proper lady" made the same comment as the combined drawing of the flapper and the Gibson Girl (Figure 6.5).

Although a real woman, Twiggy was nevertheless a type, and this British model became known to Americans in the pages of fashion magazines. Magazine imagery was the focus of Betty Friedan's bestselling 1963 feminist critique of media, *The Feminine Mystique*,[11] and, during the second wave of the women's movement, magazines were still a site for conveying ideals about womanhood. But such notions were even more broadly distributed on television, which had usurped magazines' role as the most influential and pervasive national medium in America.

The advent of color television in particular had prompted a migration of audiences and advertisers from one medium to the other, causing the death or downfall of the great mass circulation magazines such as the *Saturday Evening Post* and forcing other magazines to compete by specializing their subject matter and changing their cover philosophies. When *Life* was resurrected in 1936 as a photo-feature magazine that put photographs of celebrities on its cover,[12] some magazines followed suit, but it was television that completed the celebrification of American media at midcentury. Women's magazines were still using cover illustrations in the 1950s, but by the following decade they had switched to cover photos of movie and, later, television stars—in a sense, still idealized images in which readers could wishfully project themselves, yet specific people who were doing specific things.[13] While articles inside magazines continued to portray the "typical" lifestyle, in terms of visual imagery, Americans in the second half of the twentieth century were more likely to "see themselves" on television.

The evolution of women's imagery in fictional television shows has been traced by two scholars, Susan Douglas and Bonnie Dow, and the following brief survey draws heavily on their analyses.[14] In the earliest television sitcoms, women were portrayed—in shows like *Leave It to Beaver* or *The Donna Reed Show*—as home-centered mothers who occasionally went out to shop or socialize, but whose "sphere" was private rather than public. Soon, however, a "new girl" appeared in characters such as Gidget, Patty Duke, and *That Girl*'s Ann Marie. These girl-pals were adorable, "like boys yet still very much a girl," a type for whom "perkiness [was] a temporary compromise" between conflicting gender-role identities.[15] (A *New York Times* reporter noted that *That*

Girl's star, Marlo Thomas, "made feminism approachable and almost, well, cute.") [16]

This perky innocence was countered in other 1960s shows by female characters with magical and potentially destructive powers. The lovely but spooky Morticia on *The Addams Family* and Lily on *The Munsters* were actual vampires who wore the black-widow, spiderweb outfits. A genie (*I Dream of Jeannie*) and a witch (*Bewitched*) struggled against the temptation to make mischief, which they could do with a nod of the head or a twitch of the nose. Yet all of these shows were comedies. "Since viewers had been socialized to regard female sexuality as monstrous," Douglas explains, "TV producers addressed the anxieties about letting it loose by domesticating the monster, by making her pretty and . . . by playing the situation for laughs." [17]

During the 1970s, some television shows did engage with the real goals of the women's movement. Dow cites the feminist heroines and plotlines of *Maude, One Day at a Time,* and *The Mary Tyler Moore Show.* Yet she questions the political messages of the third show, which was by far the most popular of the three. Mary's feminism was a decision she had made on her own, not a shared conviction of the show's other female characters (who pined for, clung to, or devoured men), and she found her own (unfailingly nice) solutions to her dilemmas. [18] What's more, notes Dow, "Mary's ability to choose the life she does is a function of her status as an educated, middle-class, white woman," a definition of feminism that was limited and was linked to trends in consumption. "The transformation of women's liberation into a lifestyle or set of attitudes was aided by the growth of the single-woman market and by the appearance of pop culture heroines who could symbolize the meaning of liberation. Mary Richards was just such a heroine, and she had her real-life counterpart in Gloria Steinem." [19]

In the 1980s, single heroines such as Mary Richards and the working-class Ann Romano were replaced by middle-class mothers who put a liberal gloss on domesticity. [20] Susan Faludi points to the popular television drama *thirtysomething,* based on Americans' (especially American women's) supposed "nesting" instincts during this decade. The smug heroine, Hope Steadman, had given up a career to be a full-time mother, and the wisdom of her decision was underscored by the problems of her unmarried, work-obsessed friends who grew increasingly neurotic about their ticking biological clocks. [21] Because her husband worked in advertising (fittingly), Hope could afford "to elect to serve others" in their suburban home. "The 'commodification' of feminism implicit in viewing it as a lifestyle rather than an ideology carries obvious class implications," argues Dow.[22] (Flora Davis further notes that the backlash against feminism in the Reagan era coincided with a widening of the income gap between the richest and poorest Americans and a deterioration of U.S. race relations, as it had in the 1920s.)[23]

The working-woman heroine returned in the form of *Murphy Brown*, offered as proof in a 1989 *Newsweek* article that "TV women have come a long, *long* way since Mrs. Cleaver whipped up her last breakfast for the Beav." The show was further touted as an example of "the presence of a revolutionary new force in prime-time television . . . womanpower." Yet the writers were quick to explain that "[t]he feminization of television has surprisingly little to do with feminism" and that it merely reflected the changing *choices* of female viewers.[24]

Just as Hope Steadman recalled the "free-woman will" of the 1920s homemaker, the character of Murphy Brown was reminiscent of the 1920s flapper. Played by pencil-thin actress Candace Bergen, Murphy was a brash, sarcastic woman whose selfishness was the joke on which many plotlines turned. *Newsweek* assured its readers that Bergen, in contrast to the abrasive Murphy, had "[f]inally . . . found contentment as a wife and mother." Three years later, Murphy would do the same, becoming a mother as absorbed in her child as she had been in herself.[25] Thus Murphy Brown and Candace Bergen were collapsed into one symbolic woman, the 1990s combination of the flapper and the "new" mother.

Murphy Brown was presented as a second-wave feminist who had "come a long way from Mrs. Cleaver" and who became a mother on "her own" terms. She was the New Woman of 1990. Or was she? There was, in fact, another kind of New Woman on the show. Murphy's foil was the younger character of Corky, the former beauty-pageant winner and anchorwoman who embraced her femininity. This divisive portrayal of American women was not limited to fictional media characters. In 1989, *Time* described women in their teens and twenties as a "'No, but . . .' generation" who refuse to accept the feminist label," noting that "[t]he long, ill-fated battle for the Equal Rights Amendment means nothing to young women who already assume they will be treated as equals."[26] In her 1993 bestselling book *Fire with Fire*, Naomi Wolf complained about the "sixties hangover" and urged women in the 1990s to use their "*new* female power [emphasis added]" to achieve individual success and to choose "power feminism" (getting what you want) rather than "victim feminism" (whining about the system).[27]

The new "power feminism"—what some have called the "third wave" of feminism—was encoded in new uses of the word "girl." This term was appropriated ironically by teenage feminist rock bands in the early 1990s. By the end of the decade, though, their concept of "girl power" had been reappropriated by advertisers. In 1998, one media reporter noted that "the use of 'girl' to describe a woman made stronger when she embraces her lacy, sex-kittenish side has made its way from the underground to mainstream commercial products."[28] This was the transformation that *Time* saw as evidence of feminism's demise at the end of the century.

A historical perspective on media imagery suggests that these most recent developments—among real women and as "reflected" and constructed by popular culture—mark neither the death of feminism nor a third wave. What they most likely do represent is a continuation of the cycle of gender imagery that has played out at least three times in twentieth-century mass media, most noticeably during periods of feminist activism but also during the middle decades of the century— supporting the notion that first-wave feminism did not die either (and challenging even the distinction between "first" and "second" waves).[29]

By the time this book was being written in the closing years of the twentieth century, both *thirtysomething* and *Murphy Brown* were off the air. So was the popular 1990s television madonna of the Old West, *Dr. Quinn, Medicine Woman,* a show Bonnie Dow interprets as a modern-day "legitimation of a maternal feminism."[30] Skinny and neurotic young-single-urban-dwellers like Ally McBeal and the female characters of *Friends* were back in style, and one popular new show actually was titled *Sex in the City.* Following the examples of Fox and Warner Brothers, television networks competed to attract audiences of teenagers with shows featuring young female characters. Some of these beauties were portrayed as having supernatural powers, such as the title characters of *Sabrina the Teen-Age Witch* and *Buffy the Vampire Slayer* and the coven of stars of *Charmed;* all of them also had commercial power at a time when advertisers targeted the "youth market."

Even more striking were images of men in American media. Like the female stereotypes, early masculine media ideals had retained their currency in popular culture throughout the twentieth century. The rugged manhood of World War I resurfaced in popular culture (including war posters) during World War II and survived through the century's middle decades—in ways that symbolized the strength and character of America as well as of its men—in, for instance, the movie characters played by John Wayne.[31] The suburban father was part of the prototypical middle-class family ideal in the 1950s and the 1980s, as he had been in the 1920s. But until quite recently there was no recurrence of the "crisis of masculinity."

A set of media messages emerging in the late 1980s and the 1990s suggested that modern life had deprived American men of the masculine identity they had once considered their birthright. The most popular suburban father on television was *Home Improvement*'s Tim Taylor, who was portrayed as being not at all in charge of his fate or his daily life (despite his thinking otherwise) and whose preoccupation with larger and larger power tools symbolized men's anxieties. The "new" notion of endangered masculinity during a period of corporate downsizing was articulated through the "men's movement," in which men retreated into the woods to reconnect with their primitive natures, and the rise of militia groups (some of them affiliated with white-supremacist organizations). Susan Faludi's 1999 book, *Stiffed*, chronicled American men's diminishment and anger.

The fiftieth anniversary of World War II prompted newsmagazine special issues and books (notably journalist Tom Brokaw's 1998 *The Greatest Generation*) glorifying masculine wartime heroism in a celebration that had not characterized media treatment of the Korean, Vietnam, or Gulf Wars. The 1990s also saw the American launch of two new men's magazines, *Men's Health* and *Maxim*, which envisioned masculinity as vain and misogynistic.[32] While *Men's Health* promoted "corporal" masculinity through physical strength, *Maxim* celebrated young men's undisciplined "boyishness." This same "hypermasculinity"[33] could be seen in television shows such as *Walker, Texas Ranger*, which in the 1990s replaced the "maternal feminism" of *Dr. Quinn, Medicine Woman* in the CBS Saturday night prime-time lineup.

These male images (and trends among actual men) emerged at the end of the twentieth century—as they had at its beginning—in an era of significant changes in America, a time of increasing attention to issues of race and multiculturalism, of corporate restructuring, and of a "new economy" based on an information and high technology. One could therefore argue that the newer form of the "crisis" (like the older one) had to do with broader societal trends and with questions about the status of the white male in the new century. Yet in media imagery, these ideas—fears about change—were again articulated in terms of gender roles and discussed in popular culture as reactions to feminism.

There are surely many other examples of current feminine and masculine stereotypes, images that (especially given the profusion of media today) exist simultaneously and seem to respond to each other, and to the culture itself, in complicated ways. The above discussion is meant as a speculative rather than comprehensive survey and as an effort to identify representational parallels rather than analyze individual television shows, magazines, or films. The goal of this chapter has been to consider twentieth-century American media imagery as a continuing iconology, as a growing web of related icons in which cultural ideas and ideals are gendered, communicated, and preserved.

Many scholars have offered a materialist explanation for media backlashes against both waves of feminism in the last century, contending that commercial culture coopts notions of change and uses their idea of "newness" to sell products. I have made that argument here (and I would extend it also to the idea of "youth culture"—in the period from 1910 to 1930, in the 1960s, and at the current moment). Yet behind the recurring media images discussed in this book is something more than an economic imperative.

Mass media exist not only to make money but also to make meaning. For a century, they have disseminated a particular group of visual stereotypes of womanhood and manhood (though mainly womanhood) that stand for not just gender ideals but also issues of what it means to be "typically" American and what it takes to have status in American culture. Many of these ideals have such resonance with audiences that we talk about them as if they were real: the Gibson Girl was as real to many Americans in the year 1900 as Ally McBeal is in the year 2001. They have become cultural icons whose names symbolize the zeitgeist of particular eras and, in an ongoing sense, what it means to be "modern." Provocative and yet reassuringly familiar, they are our way of making sense of societal change.

This book is a study in the cultural work of mass media, particularly through visual iconology, and the ways that media create and maintain ideals over time. Its conclusion underscores Catherine Covert's call for communication scholars to "study the implications of repeated messages over time, of repetitive forms, of reiterated values" in American culture.[34] In both scholarly work and public memory, an Enlightenment narrative has been the traditional model used to explain media history, the history of the women's rights movement, and the history of class in the United States (that is, "democracy"). This project suggests that we might use a more cyclical model to reconsider all three of these phenomena, a model revealing cultural climates we seem destined to recreate and revisit while particular tensions remain in American society.

The girl on the magazine cover is not a quaint historical phenomenon. She was the first mass-media stereotype, and in that role she has a long list of successors. She has now moved into other media as well, yet she remains recognizable. If the past informs the future, she will continue to tell us much about media and about American life in the twenty-first century.

Notes

INTRODUCTION

1. *Time,* June 29, 1998, cover, table of contents page (3), and Bellfante, "Feminism," 57–58.
2. *Time,* "The American Woman"; *Time,* "Women of the Year."
3. *Time,* Feb. 22, 1982, cover; Meyers, "A Letter from the Publisher"; and J. D. Reed, "The New Baby Bloom," 3, 52.
4. Wallis, "Onward, Women!," 81.
5. *Time,* "The Road Ahead."
6. Faludi, *Backlash.*
7. Gibbs, "The War against Feminism," 50–55.
8. Bellfante, "Feminism," 54–60; Labi, "Girl Power," 60–62.
9. Tuchman, "Introduction: The Symbolic Annihilation of Women by the Mass Media," 7.
10. Ryan, *Womanhood in America,* 10.
11. Williams, *The Long Revolution,* 53.
12. Tebbel and Zuckerman, *The Magazine in America,* 57, 68; Ohmann, *Selling Culture,* 29; Damon-Moore, *Magazines for the Millions,* 2. These figures are estimates based on publishers' claims; circulations were unaudited until the Audit Bureau of Circulations began in 1914 (Tebbel and Zuckerman, 68).
13. Illustrations had appeared *inside* magazines for half a century, however. Beginning in the 1840s, *Godey's Lady's Book,* an upscale women's fashion magazine, regularly ran interior illustrations, made by a steel-engraving process and hand-colored. Other magazines to use illustrations during the mid-nineteenth century included *Harper's New Monthly, Frank Leslie's Popular Monthly, Putnam's Monthly Magazine,* and *Scribner's* (Janello and Jones, *The American Magazine,* 165; Meyer, *America's Great Illustrators*). Michael Brown similarly argues that the magazine of this era was "a significant site for the early introduction of images into American culture" ("The Popular Art of American Magazine Illustration," 95).
14. *Cosmopolitan* was then a general-interest magazine and, in the early years of the century, among the foremost "muckraking" periodicals.
15. By 1907, advertising accounted for half of all pages in mass market magazines (Tebbel and Zuckerman, *The Magazine in America,* 141).
16. Other factors contributed to the growth of magazine publishing as a national industry during the late nineteenth century: a national economy after the Civil War, important to advertisers as well as magazine publishers; a national railroad system, enabling publishers to deliver magazines to

newsstands nationwide; increasing literacy; an 1885 postal law reducing the rate for second-class mail (to subscribers); the institution of a rural free delivery system in 1897; and the birth of the news distribution industry in the 1860s. In *American Popular Illustration*, James J. Best more fully explains how these changes affected the business of illustration.

17. Hale, "Hints to Young but Ambitious Artists."
18. Tebbel and Zuckerman, *The Magazine in America*, 72.
19. Perkins, "Rethinking Stereotypes," 141.
20. Quoted in Gregg, Introduction, *Salute to Norman Rockwell*, n.p.
21. Meyer, *America's Great Illustrators*, 21.
22. In its first incarnation, *Life* was a general-interest and humor periodical, very different from the photo-feature magazine launched in 1936 by *Time* founder Henry Luce.
23. Meyer, *America's Great Illustrators*, 24.
24. Lears, *Fables of Abundance*, 297.
25. Kimmel, "The Contemporary Crisis of Masculinity," 122–23.
26. Warner, *Monuments and Maidens*, 331.
27. Fleming, "The American Image as Indian Princess," 65–81, and "From Indian Princess to Greek Goddess," 37–66.
28. Ryan, *Womanhood in America*, 10. She places these archetypes within three basic historical models of American womanhood: (1) "Adam's Rib," colonial femininity, woman as helpmeet to her male partner in an agrarian economy; (2) "Mother of Civilization," Victorian femininity, woman as domestic goddess in an age of industrialization and separate spheres; and (3) "Sexy Saleslady," modern femininity, woman as both low-paid service worker and the ultimate consumer.
29. Banta, *Imaging American Women*, xxviii, xxxi.
30. Meyer, *Norman Rockwell's People*, 20.
31. In the early years of mass circulation magazines, market research was not done in any systematic way. In 1911, the Curtis Publishing Company, owner of the *Journal* and the *Post*, established a Division of Commercial Research that tracked consumer behavior. Cyrus Curtis was among the first to see that "readers were more than just an audience; they were a product in themselves," writes Douglas B. Ward in "Tracking the Culture of Consumption," 204. In the 1920s and 1930s (as discussed more fully in Chapter 7), the major magazines would increasingly target "quality" (higher-income) readers in response to "pressure on publishers to carve out of the American populace an audience with traits pleasing to advertisers" (Zuckerman, *A History of Popular Women's Magazines in the United States*, 69, 132).
32. Orvell, *The Real Thing*, 49–50.
33. Ohmann, *Selling Culture*, 174, 244.
34. Gombrich, *Art and Illusion*, 9; also see Panofsky, *Meaning in the Visual Arts*.
35. Women comprised 35 percent of all college students in 1890 and nearly half in 1920; the percentage of professionals who were female rose from 35 to 44

percent between 1900 and 1920 (Cott, *The Grounding of Modern Feminism*, 148, 350 n. 4).

36. Young, "What Is Feminism?," 679.
37. Sklar, "The Historical Foundations of Women's Power," 77.
38. Muncy, *Creating a Female Dominion in American Reform*.
39. Cott, *The Grounding of Modern Feminism*, 87.
40. Smith-Rosenberg, *Disorderly Conduct*, 264.
41. Welter, *Dimity Convictions*, 21.
42. Cott, Introduction, *Root of Bitterness*, 26.
43. Roosevelt, "The Strenuous Life." Roosevelt actually first made this argument in an 1899 speech, two years before he became president.
44. Ladd-Taylor, *Mother-Work*, 5.
45. Dubbert, *A Man's Place*; Filene, *Him/Her/Self*.
46. Kimmel, *Manhood in America*, 121. Kimmel notes the rise in the proportion of female schoolteachers (from 66 percent in 1870 to 80 percent in 1910) and quotes a report in which educators worried about the effect of the "feminization" of the schoolroom: "[T]he boy in America is not being brought up to punch another boy's head; or to stand having his own punched in an [*sic*] healthy and proper manner." Kimmel's book provides a comprehensive overview of changing masculine ideals.
47. Marsh, *Suburban Lives*, 129.
48. May, *Great Expectations*.
49. Vanek, "Time Spent in Housework," 503.
50. Cowan, "Two Washes in the Morning," 177.
51. Among these scholars are Muncy, *Creating a Female Dominion*; Cott, *The Grounding of Modern Feminism*; Lemons, *The Woman Citizen*; Ware, *Still Missing*; Sklar, "The Historical Foundations"; and Bonard, "The Women's Movement in the 1920s," 231–40.
52. Ryan, *Womanhood in America*, 256–57.
53. Lears, *Fables of Abundance*, 13.
54. In my own broader historiographic survey of how scholars in all of these fields have interpreted women's imagery (Kitch, "Changing Theoretical Perspectives"), I divide historical work in this area into four (albeit overlapping) categories: the stereotypes approach, the search for alternative images, the examination of imagery as ideology, and the "reading" of images as polysemic texts. The analysis in this book combines the first and third approaches, though it acknowledges the presence of alternative imagery during my time period (Chapter 4) and considers the role of the audience in creating the meaning of popular culture images (especially Chapters 1, 2, and 7).
55. Marzolf, "American Studies," 15.
56. Dix, "The Girl of Today," 288.
57. Covert, "Journalism History and Women's Experience," 6.
58. Williams, *The Long Revolution*, 47.

1. Hale, "Hints to Young but Ambitious Artists."
2. Untitled promotional page inside front cover, *Ladies' Home Journal*, Dec. 1896, n.p. Hereafter in notes, the magazine's title will be abbreviated *LHJ*.
3. The 850,000 figure is my own conservative estimate based on information from Tebbel and Zuckerman, who listed the *Journal*'s circulation at 800,000 in 1900 and 900,000 in 1902; it would reach a million in 1903 (*The Magazine in America*, 96).
4. Strasser, *Satisfaction Guaranteed*, 91; Janello and Jones, *The American Magazine*, 232. *Godey's Lady's Book* folded in 1898.
5. Bok, *The Americanization of Edward Bok*, 163. Bok was not the *Journal*'s first editor; from 1883 to 1889, it was edited by publisher Cyrus Curtis's wife, Louisa Knapp Curtis.
6. According to Bok himself, in *The Americanization of Edward Bok*, 169–71.
7. Scanlon, *Inarticulate Longings*, 2.
8. Biographical and professional information on Alice Barber Stephens comes from Brown, *Alice Barber Stephens;* Huber, *The Pennsylvania Academy and Its Women;* Mayer, *Women Artists in the Howard Pyle Tradition;* "Alice Barber Stephens, Illustrator," 49–53; and Walt Reed, *The Illustrator in America, 1900–1960s*.
9. Walt Reed, *The Illustrator in America, 1900–1960s*, 37.
10. Cited here are "the old" *Cosmopolitan* and *Life* magazines, the former a literary/general interest publication and the latter a humor magazine.
11. Harry Goldberg, "Art Means Pursuit of Beauty," *Philadelphia Press Fiction Magazine*, Sept. 26, 1915, 1, quoted in Brown, *Alice Barber Stephens*, 31–32.
12. Stephens was well paid by standards of this era, earning $125 for each of the six drawings; by comparison, Charles Dana Gibson received $150 for each of eleven interior illustrations he did for the *Journal* in 1896 (Financial records, July 14, 1896, Curtis Publishing Company Records, University of Pennsylvania, Philadelphia).
13. Welter, *Dimity Convictions*, 21; Blair, *The Torchbearers*, 12.
14. Bok, "On Being 'Old-Fashioned,'" 14.
15. Moody, "Mr. Moody's Bible Class," 21.
16. "Of a Personal Nature, by the Editors," Mar. 1897, 28, and Feb. 1897, 26; Gottheil, "The Jewess as She Was and Is," 21.
17. Scovil, "Suggestions for Mothers," Sept. 1897, 30; ads in the Mar., Apr., Sept., and Dec. 1897 issues; "Of a Personal Nature, by the Editors," May 1897, 36.
18. For more on the importance of pianos in nineteenth-century life, see Loesser, *Men, Women and Pianos*.
19. Ashmore, "What to Expect from a Young Man," 22.
20. Isaacs, "These Long Evenings in the Home," 18; "Droch's Literary Talks" (various issues). The *LHJ* Literary Bureau was promoted in the Jan. 1897 issue ("Of a Personal Nature, by the Editors," 27).

21. "The Gossip of the Editors," *LHJ,* Oct. 1897, 36, and Nov. 1897, 40.
22. Mulvey, "Visual Pleasure and Narrative Cinema," 6–18; Berger, *Ways of Seeing,* 47. In Mulvey's view, women were "simultaneously looked at and displayed, with their appearance coded for strong visual and erotic impact so that they can be said to connote *to-be-looked-at-ness*" (11). The role of a "female gaze" in contemporary media is explored in an anthology of critical essays, *The Female Gaze,* ed. Gamman and Marshment. "This shift from what an image did to women to what women could do with women's images allowed for a more complex attitude to femininity," writes Christine Geraghty, who has studied female audiences' use of television and film ("Feminism and Media Consumption," 318). Scholars also have used this notion—or at any rate, have considered the significance of a female audience in the meaning of popular culture imagery—to analyze popular literature; see, for instance, Baym, *Woman's Fiction,* and Radway, *Reading the Romance.* Given that magazines have catered to female audiences more than any other mass medium, and given the domination, historically and currently, of women's titles within the magazine industry, the role of a gendered "gaze" in the creation and reception of media imagery deserves more consideration in magazine scholarship.
23. Ashmore, "The Social Position of the Girl Who Works," 28. Writing as Isabel A. Mallon, she further suggested in a fashion feature on what to wear for "visiting day" ("The Visitor and the Hostess," 21) that "society" meant the company of other women.
24. Mallon, "The Gowns to Be Worn This Winter," 35.
25. Such as Rorer, "Handling the Family Wash," 22; "Mrs. Rorer's Household Council," 24; "Small Leakages of a Household," 24; and "Mrs. Rorer's Cooking Lessons," 25.
26. These articles appeared in the Feb., Mar., Apr., July, Sept., and Dec. issues of the *Journal.* According to Marsh (*Suburban Lives,* 94), the average cost of a home and lot in Philadelphia was $3,000 in 1895. Thousands of these homes—known as *"Ladies' Home Journal* houses"—were actually built (Bok, *The Americanization of Edward Bok,* 239, 242).
27. Ashmore, "Side-Talks with Girls," *LHJ,* from issues throughout 1897.
28. Orvell, *The Real Thing,* 49.
29. "The Gossip of the Editors," *LHJ,* Oct. 1897, 36, and Sept. 1897, 36.
30. Ads in the Feb., May, Nov., and Mar. 1897 issues of *LHJ.*
31. "Droch's Literary Talks," *LHJ,* Sept. 1897, 15; "Of a Personal Nature, by the Editors" [promoting "What Victoria Has Seen"], May 1897, 36; Fiske, "When the Prince of Wales Was in America," 3–4.
32. Jordan, "The Greatest Nation on Earth"; Palmer, "The Women's Patriotic Societies," 7–8, 10.
33. Beard, "In Camp and on House-Boat," 17; ads in the Jan., Mar., May, June, and Sept. 1897 issues of *LHJ.*
34. *LHJ,* Feb. 1897, 26, and Mar. 1897, 21.
35. Bok, "Breaking Down the Fences," 14.

36. Bok, *LHJ*, Apr. 1893, n.p., quoted in Damon-Moore, *Magazines for the Millions*, 92.

37. The origin of the word "magazine" is noted in many sources, including Ohmann, *Selling Culture*, 223–29, and Garvey, *The Adman in the Parlor*, 3–5. Ohmann notes that Bok himself made this comparison, quoting this from his autobiography: "A successful magazine is exactly like a successful store: it must keep its wares constantly fresh and varied to attract the eye and hold the patronage of its customers" (*The Americanization of Edward Bok*, 292–93; 229 in Ohmann).

38. Historian Daniel Boorstin has described department stores of this era as "Palaces of Consumption" (*The Americans*, 101). Folklorist Simon Bronner believes that mass-produced goods helped create a sense of community in an increasingly urban and unsettling society at the turn of the century. "Shared goods meant having more in common," he writes, and goods shared on a national scale increased Americans' sense "of belonging to the nation" ("Reading Consumer Culture," 13–53).

39. Robert Snyder and Rebecca Zurier call department stores of this era "Adamless Edens" ("Picturing the City," 150). Other scholars who have written about the gendering of department stores include Benson, *Counter Cultures*, and Leach, *Land of Desire: Merchants*.

40. Friedberg, *Window Shopping*. She writes that "the department store offered a protected site for the empowered gaze of the flâneuse" (37).

41. Ohmann, *Selling Culture*, 271–72.

42. Bok, *LHJ*, Apr. 1893, n.p., quoted in Damon-Moore, *Magazines for the Millions*, 92.

43. Peiss, *Cheap Amusements*, 38.

44. Benson, *Counter Cultures*, 23, 143; Leach, *Land of Desire*, 121.

45. Peiss, *Cheap Amusements*, 38–39; Benson, *Counter Cultures*, 209.

46. "The Gossip of the Editors," *LHJ*, Sept. 1897, 36, and Dec. 1897, 40.

47. Humphreys, "The Business Girl's Luncheon," 30; Ashmore, "The Social Position of the Girl Who Works," 28.

CHAPTER TWO

1. Article in the *New York World*, quoted in Sullivan, *Our Times*, 195. As Welter (*Dimity Convictions*) and others have noted, there were literary types of "the American Girl" in the nineteenth century, but the Gibson Girl was the first famous visual type.

2. Downey, *Portrait of an Era*, 100–101.

3. "Gibson rarely drew an unattractive woman well," notes Gelman (Introduction, *The Best of Charles Dana Gibson*, vii).

4. Downey, *Portrait of an Era*, 312; Best, "Charles Dana Gibson," 13; Meyer, *America's Great Illustrators*, 216–17, 222.

5. Meyer, *America's Great Illustrators*, 8; Mott, *A History of American Maga-*

zines, vol. 4: *1885–1905*, 456; Walt Reed, *The Illustrator in America, 1900–1960s*, 24.

6. David E. E. Sloan, "*Life*," in *American Humor Magazines and Comic Periodicals*, 146; Mott, *A History of American Magazines*, 4:453–79.

7. Pitz, "Charles Dana Gibson: Delineator of an Age," vii.

8. Earnest, *The American Eve in Fact and Fiction*, 230. Biographical information is from Downey, *Portrait of an Era;* Pitz, "Charles Dana Gibson: Delineator of an Age"; and Platt, "The Gibson Girl," 112–17.

9. Banner, *American Beauty*, 164.

10. Roosevelt, "The Strenuous Life."

11. "Charles Dana Gibson: The Man and His Art," 8.

12. *New York World* article cited in Sullivan, *Our Times*, 195.

13. Pitz, "Charles Dana Gibson: Creator of a Mode," 52. Elsewhere, Pitz describes Gibson's audience as "a rapidly expanding middle class, busily climbing up the social ladder" ("Charles Dana Gibson: Delineator of an Age," xi). One of Gibson's book collections was actually titled *The Social Ladder*.

14. Meyer, *America's Great Illustrators*, 212; Klein, "Charles Dana Gibson," 146.

15. Davis, "The Origin of a Type of the American Girl," 6, 8.

16. *Life* magazine and the P. F. Collier publishing company repackaged Gibson's magazine work in eighteen book collections over two decades, some editions selling as many as 20,000 copies (Meyer, *America's Great Illustrators*, 225). *Life*'s first such offer, in 1894, contained eighty-four drawings and sold for either five or fifteen dollars; for the higher price, the purchaser received one of only 100 "Edition[s] de Luxe . . . printed on special woodcut paper, each copy numbered and signed by the artist" (Advertisement, *Life* 24, no. 9 [Dec. 1894]: 29). Actual originals of Gibson drawings were for sale, too (by Gibson), but only to the truly elite: by 1903, they went for as much as $3,000 apiece (Klein, "Charles Dana Gibson," 8).

17. The model for the drawing was Evelyn Nesbit, then fourteen years old and later a well-known actress who would be at the center of one of the new century's most celebrated murder cases, the shooting of Stanford White by Harry K. Thaw (Best, "Charles Dana Gibson," 17).

18. Hope, "Mr. C. D. Gibson on Love and Life," 869.

19. Gilman, *Women and Economics*, 148.

20. Ticknor, "The Steel-Engraving Lady and the Gibson Girl," 105–8.

21. "As the all-American Girl, the Gibson Girl might play golf, but she certainly didn't play politics," notes Martha Patterson ("'Survival of the Best Fitted,'" 74).

22. Downey, *Portrait of an Era*, 300–301.

23. Hope, "Mr. C. D. Gibson," 870.

24. In 1905, when he was earning $65,000 a year, Gibson sailed for England with the intent of abandoning illustration and becoming a serious painter. The U.S. financial panic of 1907 forced him to return home, and he accepted illustration assignments for Hearst's *Cosmopolitan*, which in 1910

proclaimed that "Charles Dana Gibson still enjoys the unprecedented vogue that he established for himself twenty years ago" ("Worth-While People," 699). This was not true. Gibson would indeed remain well known, would continue to draw for national publications, and would even take over ownership and direction of *Life* during the 1920s. But neither he nor his creations would again enjoy the enormous popularity they experienced in the years just around the turn of the century.

25. According to Alice Sheppard (*Cartooning for Suffrage*, 137–39) and James R. McGovern ("The American Woman's Pre–World War I Freedom," 323), this phrase was first coined by another artist, the nationally syndicated newspaper cartoonist Nell Brinkley, a suffragist. The phrase was initially meant to have a progressive connotation.

26. All the illustrators to whom this article referred were men.

27. "Modern Picture Making," *Philadelphia Public Ledger.*

28. Downey, *Portrait of an Era*, 239; "Modern Picture Making."

29. "Modern Picture Making."

30. Christy, *The American Girl*, 156.

31. "Modern Picture Making."

32. In 1903, the *Ladies' Home Journal* became the first American magazine to reach the million mark in monthly circulation. The *Saturday Evening Post* reached a million in late 1908 and was at 1.25 million a year later. *Cosmopolitan*, which had averaged about 350,000 readers a month since the 1890s, saw circulation rise with its inclusion of muckraking articles and its purchase by Hearst in 1905: readership was at 450,000 by 1906 and at 750,000 by 1911. The *Woman's Home Companion* also averaged around 750,000 readers by 1912. (Tebbel and Zuckerman, *The Magazine in America;* Cohn, *Covers of the* Saturday Evening Post, 2; Schneirov, *The Dream of a New Social Order,* 206, 252; Zuckerman, *A History of Popular Women's Magazines in the United States,* 29.)

33. McCabe, "Poor Girls Who Marry Millions," 250. The author's choice of the word "sordid" may have had to do with urbanization but also no doubt referred to the impending financial panic of 1907. Few of the young women profiled in this article had been truly working-class; most had held white-collar jobs such as salesgirl, telephone operator, or secretary. Several had been stage actresses when they were "discovered" by their future husbands. One of the featured women was Pittsburgh-born actress Evelyn Nesbit, who had modeled for Gibson (notably for the drawing of the woman with the question-mark hair; see note 17).

34. Banta, *Imaging American Women*, 496.

35. Cott, *The Grounding of Modern Feminism*, 40.

36. Christy, *The American Girl*, 13, 38.

37. Bok, *LHJ*, Apr. 1897, 14.

38. Christy was successful in promoting himself as the reigning arbiter of feminine beauty: when the Miss America pageant began in the early 1920s, he was its first judge. Later in the 1920s, Christy would be joined by Norman

Rockwell and John Held Jr. (Walt Reed and Roger Reed, *The Illustrator in America, 1880–1980*, 77; Sommer, *Norman Rockwell*, 9.)

39. Miley, *Howard Chandler Christy*, n.p.
40. Reed, *The Illustrator in America, 1900–1960s*, 50. Though at first she was a composite—and some 800 women applied to be the artist's model—the Christy Girl who gained popularity from 1900 to 1920 was based mainly on the women who became Christy's first and second wives, Maybelle Thompson and Nancy Palmer (who initially tried out as a model for Gibson); it was Palmer's face that appeared on Christy's war posters (Miley, *Howard Chandler Christy*, n.p.; Meyer, *America's Great Illustrators*, 240–44).
41. Miley, "Howard Chandler Christy," n.p.
42. Christy, *The American Girl*, 46–47.
43. Gordon, "The Gibson Girl Goes to College," 215, 226.
44. Mrozek, "Sport in American Life," 27; Lears, "From Salvation to Self-Realization."
45. Clark, "The Need of the Business Woman for Body Culture," 6.
46. Dix, "The Girl of Today," 289.
47. Gates, "The Girl Who Travels Alone."
48. Tompkins, "Why Women Don't Marry," 471.
49. This term was coined by St. Louis newspaper editor William Marion Reedy, whose comments were quoted that year in *Current Opinion* ("Sex O'Clock in America").

CHAPTER THREE

1. Helen Benedict uses this dichotomy in examining news coverage in *Virgin or Vamp*.
2. Kery, *Great Magazine Covers of the World*, 239.
3. Dix, "The Girl of Today," 288.
4. George H. Douglas, *The Smart Magazines*, 45–46; David E. E. Sloan, "*Life*," 141–53.
5. Grant, "*Judge*," 115.
6. The term cited here is from Kathy Peiss's history of the same name, *Cheap Amusements*.
7. Muncy, *Creating a Female Dominion*.
8. Nancy Schrom Dye writes about the tensions that surfaced in these alliances: while upper-class participants urged "uplift" activities on working-class members, the latter were more interested in strategies that would lead directly to improvement in working conditions and wages ("Creating a Feminist Alliance," 347). In *Cheap Amusements*, Kathy Peiss similarly argues that native-born reformers wanted to inculcate American middle-class values and family structure into the lives of immigrants.
9. Sklar, "The Historical Foundations of Women's Power," 78.
10. Perry, "'The General Motherhood of the Commonwealth.'"

11. For a fuller discussion of the animal dances and their origins, see Peiss, *Cheap Amusements*, 101–2; Erenberg, "Everybody's Doin' It"; and Castle, *Castles in the Air*.

12. "Have You Tried the 'Long Boston' Dance?," 10.

13. Peiss, *Cheap Amusements*, 88, 95.

14. Millions of American women followed suit. In Boston, the hair-cutting fad took a criminal twist: a man reporters called "Jack the Snipper" snuck up on girls and cut their hair ("Stranger Cuts Girls' Curls," 2).

15. Chalmers, "Facts and Figures," 38. The writer explained that a woman still needed a corset—but a new model that gave her an entirely new shape. "The corset of former years gave a woman a mature, well-developed, matronly figure. The corset of to-day makes her look like a very young girl."

16. Erenberg, "Everybody's Doin' It," 155.

17. Bailey, *From Front Porch to Back Seat*, 6, 80–81, 88–89. Bailey also notes that around 1910 magazine writers began to shift the responsibility for controlling sexual behavior—and the blame for sexual misconduct—from the man to the woman.

18. Quoted in Solomon, *In the Company of Educated Women*, 102.

19. Quoted in Higashi, *Virgins, Vamps, and Flappers*, 61.

20. Both were 1914 films, the first starring Pickford, who was publicized as "America's Sweetheart," and the second starring Lillian Gish and her sister Dorothy. Bara's "vamp" character appeared in films with titles such as *A Fool There Was* (1915) and *The Vixen* (1916).

21. Bathrick, "The True Woman in the Family-Film," 15.

22. Ibid., 125–26.

23. Ibid., 15. Bathrick notes that "in sharp contrast [to the vamp], the True Woman is often seen in duplicate—near or surrounded by the sisters, the daughters, the mothers who constitute her community." This description applies to the older women in Flagg's vamp cover image as well as the communities of women in Alice Barber Stephens's work.

24. Jowett, *Film: The Democratic Art*.

25. Flagg, *Roses and Buckshot*, 175.

26. Ibid., 112–13, 152–53; Meyer, *James Montgomery Flagg*, 21. Later in his career, Flagg was known for his caricatures of movie stars and other celebrities, published in magazines such as *Collier's* and *Cosmopolitan* (Walt Reed, *Great American Illustrators, 1900–1960s*, 66).

27. Meyer, *James Montgomery Flagg*, 16, 19, 259; Walt Reed, *The Illustrator in America, 1900–1960s*, 55; Flagg, *Roses and Buckshot*, 76, 161.

28. "Saucy" is the word used by Susan Meyer in her biography of the artist (*James Montgomery Flagg*, 261).

29. Owen Johnson, Foreword, *The Salamander*, n.p. In his study of American womanhood in this era, historian James R. McGovern calls this popular culture type "a determined pleasure-seeker" ("The American Woman's Pre–World War I Freedom," 325).

30. Some of these are reproduced in Schau, *"All-American Girl."* Covers Phillips

drew for the *Post* in the early 1920s are reprinted in Cohn, *Covers of the* Saturday Evening Post. According to Schau (46), in 1911 Phillips contracted to do every *Good Housekeeping* cover for the next five years, but he renegotiated after two years. After 1913, he was one of several cover artists until Jessie Willcox Smith gained the job exclusively in 1917. Flagg, too, did frequent illustration work for *Good Housekeeping*'s fiction pages.

31. The Fadeaway Girl was as much an element of graphic design as an illustration, and design was Phillips's main interest: "That he made his reputation as a painter of pretty girls was more accident than anything else," claimed his wife, Teresa (who nevertheless was his model). She is quoted in Johnston, "Coles Phillips' 'Fade Away Girls,'" 29.

32. Schau, *"All-American Girl,"* 23, 46; Rockwell, *My Adventures as an Illustrator,* 196.

33. Phillips, Introduction, *A Young Man's Fancy,* n.p., quoted in Schau, *"All-American Girl,"* 24.

34. On the cover of the sheet music for a song titled "We All Fall," little men who represented a woman's marriage choices—from the old rhyme "rich man, poor man, beggar man, thief, doctor, lawyer, Indian chief"—sought the favor of a well-dressed woman whose attention seemed to be elsewhere. Similarly, tuxedoed gents on their knees appealed to a larger woman, perched above them on a pile of coins, on the cover of "The High Cost of Loving." The "girlie" on the cover of the music for "Oh, What Wonderful Things One Little Girlie Can Do" kept miniature, gift-bearing suitors on strings, like Gibson's kite-flyers. One song title—the sheet-music cover of which showed a woman dropping one little man while stepping on another—suggested that the man who failed to please the modern woman knew that "Somebody Else Is Getting It." (Goodwin and Meyer, "We All Fall"; Bryan and Meyer, "The High Cost of Loving"; Yellen, Schuster, and Glogau, "Oh, What Wonderful Things One Little Girlie Can Do"; Sterling and Von Tilzer, "Somebody Else Is Getting It.")

35. Kay Sloan, "Sexual Warfare in the Silent Cinema," 417. Women were shown diapering men in *The Suffragettes' Revenge* (Gaumont, 1914) (421 n. 16).

36. Haskell, *From Reverence to Rape,* 69.

37. Dubbert, *A Man's Place,* 198–99. Some historians disagree with this characterization of the era, arguing that, since men retained political power and the family structure remained essentially the same, there was never any real "crisis" of masculinity; see, for instance, Griffen, "Reconstructing Masculinity."

38. Mills, *White Collar,* xi–ii.

39. Mott, *A History of American Magazines,* vol. 4: *1885–1905,* 688.

40. Lorimer, "Is Success Personal?," 30.

41. Rockwell, *My Adventures as an Illustrator,* 143.

42. Steine and Taraba, *American Illustrators Poster Book: The J. C. Leyendecker Collection,* 12.

43. Schau, *J. C. Leyendecker,* 25, 28, 72, 127; Steine and Taraba, *American Illus-*

trators Poster Book: The J. C. Leyendecker Collection, 10–11; Walt Reed, *The Illustrator in America, 1900–1960s,* 60; Meyer, *America's Great Illustrators,* 141. Leyendecker also did interior work for these magazines, as well as *Scribner's* and the *Delineator,* plus forty-eight covers for *Collier's.* Scholars differ in their reports of how many *Post* covers Leyendecker did and whether he or Norman Rockwell holds the record. Schau and Meyer put Leyendecker's career cover output at 321 and Rockwell's at 322, while Steine and Taraba reverse those numbers, maintaining that because Rockwell revered Leyendecker, he stopped at 321 so as not to break his mentor's record.

44. Schau, *J. C. Leyendecker,* 34.
45. Ibid., 43.
46. Meyer, *America's Great Illustrators,* 139.
47. Roosevelt, "The Strenuous Life."
48. Hantover, "The Boy Scouts and the Validation of Masculinity," 293. Hantover is quoting Burgess, "Making Men of Them," 12.
49. Burgess, "Making Men of Them," 3.
50. Segal, "Norman Rockwell and the Fashioning of American Masculinity," 633.
51. Schau, *J. C. Leyendecker,* 73–74.
52. Rockwell, *My Adventures as an Illustrator,* 167.
53. Filene, *Him/Her/Self,* 101.
54. Kaye, *Good Clean Violence.*
55. Dubbert, *A Man's Place,* 179. That Leyendecker should have been the one to create such a symbol for millions of male magazine readers is particularly interesting in light of the artist's likely homosexuality and his use of his long-term partner, Frank Beach, as a frequent model (Steine and Taraba, *American Illustrators Poster Book: The J. C. Leyendecker Collection,* 10; Rockwell, *My Adventures as an Illustrator,* 167). This irony is underscored by the increasing public preoccupation with sexual behavior and identity during the second decade of the twentieth century. Through the popularization of Freudian psychology in America, homosexuality was, for the first time, publicly discussed and labeled pathological (D'Emilio and Freedman, *Intimate Matters,* 193–94).
56. Dubbert, *A Man's Place,* 164.

CHAPTER FOUR

1. Lessing, "The Emancipation of Sarah."
2. Sheppard, *Cartooning for Suffrage;* Tickner, *The Spectacle of Women,* 167, 169.
3. An excellent history of the cultural use of female allegorical forms, in Europe as well as America, is Marina Warner's *Monuments and Maidens.*
4. The trio of art editors for the *Woman Citizen*—Fredrikke Palmer, Blanche

Ames, and Mayme B. Harwood—were also artists themselves. Other female artists who specialized in suffrage imagery in this era included Lou Rogers, Cornelia Barns, May Wilson Preston, Ida Sedgwick Proper, Mary Ellen Sigsbee, Alice Beach Winter, Marietta Andrews, Edwina Dumm, and Nina Evans Allender (who belonged to the National Woman's Party and drew for its more radical publications); among other male artists who significantly contributed to suffrage magazines were Maurice Becker and Boardman Robinson. Several of these artists were also socialists who contributed work to the *Masses*. (Sheppard, *Cartooning for Suffrage*.)

5. "What We Are Fighting For," 30–31.

6. Reinforcing the messages in these drawings were graphic devices that tied them to mainstream media imagery of the time. One was the framing of both the wartime railway conductor and the sisters Justice and Mercy inside circles, a common device on the covers of the conservative and popular *Saturday Evening Post*. The circle-frame was especially common in the *Post* cover art of J. C. Leyendecker and Norman Rockwell. Another visual link was color: both the *Woman Citizen* and the *Post* used a black-and-orange theme for their covers during this era.

7. Blackwell, "Antis Outdo Bolsheviki," 27. Blackwell was playing to the increasing anticommunist feeling in the United States after the Russian Revolution. Ironically, when this fervor peaked in the early 1920s, it would be turned against former suffragists, who were listed on the government's "Spider Web chart" of individuals accused of being anti-American.

8. "Will They Never Learn," 7.

9. Doughty, "Taking Uncle Sam's Foster Children into the Family," 650–51; Blackwell, "Americanize the Mother," 7.

10. For a fuller discussion of such tensions, see Peiss, *Cheap Amusements*.

11. Advertisements in various issues of the *Woman Citizen*, 1919 and 1920. The railworkers article and fur coat ad appeared in Feb. 21, 1920, 895.

12. The peak circulation of the *Masses* was 40,000 according to Lougherty, *John Sloan*, 182; 20,000 according to Tebbel and Zuckerman, *The Magazine in America*, 125; and 12,000 according to Scott and Bullard, *John Sloan*, 30.

13. O'Neill, *Echoes of Revolt*, 19.

14. The frontispiece was a "second cover" in the front of the magazine, meant to be a freestanding visual statement. This was a common device in magazines of this era.

15. Zurier, *Art for the* Masses, 178. Fischer also did illustration work for mainstream magazines, including *Scribner's*, *Everybody's*, *Collier's*, and the *Saturday Evening Post*, as well as *Cosmopolitan* and *Life*.

16. "The Cheapest Commodity on the Market," 5.

17. *New York Globe*, May 24, 1913, quoted in Clifford, "Drawing on Women," 101.

18. Lougherty, *John Sloan*, 197; Brooks, *John Sloan*, 96; Goodrich, *John Sloan*, 44.

19. Lougherty, *John Sloan;* Herford, "Pen and Inklings," 28, quoted in Zurier,

Art for the Masses, 49. Writing in the *Masses,* editor Max Eastman called the mainstream cover women "a pattern, a conventionalized symbol" and specifically named Gibson, Fisher, and Christy as good artists who had sold out, who had "given up their profession of realizing in line the varieties of life and gone into the manufacturing business. They are now turning out an article that will sell widely in competition . . . and while they may find it profitable to vary the model a little from year to year, as progressive manufacturers do, the main lines were laid down in the first big sale, and no risks will be taken" ("Magazine Art," 34, 41).

20. Clifford, "Drawing on Women," 1.
21. Fishbein, "The Failure of Feminism in Greenwich Village," 276.
22. Elsie Clews Parsons, "Facing Race Suicide," *Masses,* June 1915, and Emma Goldman, "Emma Goldman's Defense," *Masses,* June 1916, both reprinted in O'Neill, *Echoes of Revolt,* 206–12; May Wood Simon, "Co-operation and Housewives," 11; "I Make Cheap Silk," *Masses,* Nov. 1913, 7.
23. Eastman, "Knowledge and Revolution," *Masses,* Jan. 1913, reprinted in O'Neill, *Echoes of Revolt,* 132.
24. O'Neill, *Echoes of Revolt,* 179.
25. Dell, "Feminism for Men," 19.
26. Some radical feminists interpreted Freud's theories, along with newly published works by "sexologists" such as Havelock Ellis, as both a legitimization of their own sexuality and a confirmation that women were "natural" mothers, meant to nurture men as well as children.
27. For a fuller discussion of immigrant family life in Greenwich Village, see Ware, *Greenwich Village.*
28. Goldman, "Emma Goldman's Defense," 210. This was actually a speech Goldman gave when she was sentenced to a short prison term after giving a public lecture on birth control.
29. Linda Gordon, "Birth Control and Social Revolution," 461–62.
30. Zurier, *Art for the* Masses, 100.
31. See, for instance, James Henle, "A Strange Meeting," and John Reed, "A Daughter of the Revolution," both reprinted in O'Neill, *Echoes of Revolt.* The third description is Rebecca Zurier's characterization of one part of Hutchins Hapgood's views on the subject (*Art for the* Masses, 13).
32. James Henle, "Nobody's Sister," *Masses,* Jan. 1915, reprinted in O'Neill, *Echoes of Revolt,* 191–92.
33. His compassion for prostitutes most likely was real, given that his (then-) wife, Dolly, was a former prostitute. She was a radical feminist and a socialist who organized suffrage, birth control, and labor demonstrations. She also served as business manager for the *Masses.* (Lougherty, *John Sloan,* 165, 172–76, 198, 221.)
34. The other seven members of "the Eight" were Robert Henri, George Luks, Everett Shinn, Maurice Prendergast, William Glackens, Ernest Lawson, and Arthur B. Davies. They were later called "Ashcan" realists because of their gritty scenes of working-class neighborhoods. For more on these

artists, see Perlman, *Painters of the Ashcan School,* and Zurier, Snyder, and Mecklenburg, *Metropolitan Lives.*

35. Sloan also did illustration work for mainstream magazines during this era. Most of these commissions came from *Harper's Weekly* and *Collier's,* though his drawings also appeared in *Century, Scribner's, Everybody's, Munsey's, Good Housekeeping,* and even the *Saturday Evening Post*—which he privately called "the magazine that looks and feels like a dead fish" (Scott and Bullard, *John Sloan,* 31; Lougherty, *John Sloan,* 162, 184; Brooks, *John Sloan,* 46–47; David Scott, *John Sloan,* 71).

36. Scott and Bullard, *John Sloan,* 80; Elzea and Hawkes, *John Sloan,* 110–11; Hills, "John Sloan's Images of Working-Class Women," 168.

37. The same issue of the *Masses,* Aug. 1913, contained a play "about prostitutes and the unfair court system" (Elzea and Hawkes, *John Sloan,* 112).

38. Goodrich, *John Sloan,* 44. Scholars who similarly see this illustration as uniformly positive—even apolitical—include Lougherty (*John Sloan,* 113) and Hills ("John Sloan's Images of Working-Class Women," 168, 189). Janice Marie Coco interprets it differently, seeing this "happy" girl as in fact threatened ("John Sloan and the Female Subject").

39. Snyder and Zurier, "Picturing the City," in *Metropolitan Lives,* ed. Zurier, Snyder, and Mecklenburg, 135.

40. Kinser, "Prostitutes in the Art of John Sloan," 233.

41. Snyder, "City in Transition," in *Metropolitan Lives,* ed. Zurier, Snyder, and Mecklenburg, 45–46.

42. Kinser, "Prostitutes in the Art of John Sloan," 234.

43. Lougherty, *John Sloan,* 183.

44. One example was Sloan's March 1913 cover drawing titled "The Idle Rich," which showed an overweight, unattractive woman at the opera and which poked fun at not just wealth but idleness. As an extra insult, he put a feather in her hair, subtly suggesting that wealthy women were equally prostitutes to men who paid their way.

45. They included the *Colored American* and the *Crusader,* published in New York; three Chicago-based magazines, the *Upreach,* the *Favorite,* and the *Half Century;* and the *Competitor,* published in Pittsburgh. In 1917, A. Phillip Randolph, head of the Pullman Porters Union, began the *Messenger,* a labor publication intended as an African American version of the *Masses,* though not overtly socialist. And, in 1923, the National Urban League began *Opportunity,* "a journal of Negro life." (Charles S. Johnson, "The Rise of the Negro Magazine.")

46. Ibid., 14.

47. Du Bois, "Votes for Women," *Crisis* 4 (Sept. 1912): 334, in *Writing in Periodicals Edited by W. E. B. Du Bois,* vol. 1: *1911–1925.*

48. "A Woman's Suffrage Symposium," 244.

49. "Votes for Women: A Symposium," 178–92.

50. See, for instance, Du Bois's editorials in the Sept. 1912 (234), Aug. 1914 (179–80), Apr. 1915 (285), and Nov. 1915 (29–30) issues of the *Crisis,* in *Writing in*

Periodicals Edited by W. E. B. Du Bois, 1:41, 79–80, 92, 111–12. The *Crisis* also ran a column called "Talks about Women," whose author, Mrs. John E. Milholland, wrote on girls' training in "domestic science" and women's choice to be full-time homemakers; she approved of both (*Crisis* 1, no. 6 [Apr. 1911]: 27; 1, no. 5 [Mar. 1911]: 29).

51. Covers, *Crisis* 4, no. 5 (Sept. 1912); 10, no. 4 (Aug. 1915).

52. *Crisis* 22, no. 3 (July 1921). Mossell is identified on the table of contents page.

53. This is Miles Orvell's comment on Americans' interpretation of these two media in this era (*The Real Thing*).

54. Patterson, " 'Survival of the Best Fitted,' " 82.

55. Advertisement, *Crisis* 22, no. 2 (June 1921): back cover.

56. Advertisement, *Crisis* 30, no. 2 (June 1925): 103.

57. Moore, "Making a Spectacle of Suffrage," 94.

58. Ibid.

59. The magazine was reincarnated in the 1920s as the *New Masses,* but, claims Leslie Fishbein, it was a poor imitation, weighed down by "pedestrian proletarian art and prose" (*Rebels in Bohemia,* 207).

CHAPTER FIVE

1. Jasen, *Tin Pan Alley;* Isenberg, *War on Film.*

2. Rawls, *Wake Up, America!,* 12.

3. Indeed, in his autobiography, Norman Rockwell remembered World War I as "a poster war" (*My Adventures as an Illustrator,* 121).

4. Rawls, *Wake Up, America!,* 137–38.

5. This chapter includes war poster work by Gibson, Fisher, Christy, Flagg, Leyendecker, McMein, and Rockwell. Although not discussed here, Alice Barber Stephens, whose son Owen fought in the war, contributed a single poster, "War Gardens," to encourage homefront support, Coles Phillips promoted energy conservation on posters for the U.S. Fuel Administration, and Jessie Willcox Smith, whose *Good Housekeeping* cover art is discussed in Chapter 7, lent her signature cherub-child to a Red Cross poster (Brown, *Alice Barber Stephens,* 34; Schau, *"All-American Girl,"* 46; Schnessel, *Jessie Willcox Smith*).

6. Rawls, *Wake Up, America!,* 167; Darracott, *The First World War in Posters,* vii.

7. Gibson also headed a New York organization called the Vigilantes Club, a patriotic society "formed by a group of artists pledged to contribute their efforts toward winning the war" (Siple, "The Gibson Girl Admits to 75," 32). The artists' participation in the war effort helped pull together a professional community that had become fragmented. The Society of Illustrators had been founded in 1901 in the hope that it would represent illustrators' interest in disputes with increasingly powerful art directors. But after only

a decade, the group had taken on a mostly social function. During the war, the Society again served to elevate illustrators' stature. In turn, the artists became invested in war propaganda: "Under the patriotic, tactful and witty guidance of Gibson," notes a history of the group, "the artists gladly put the Government work ahead of everything else." (*The Society of Illustrators, 1901–1928.*)

8. Rawls, *Wake Up, America!*, 12.
9. Darracott, *The First World War in Posters*, vii.
10. Meyer, *James Montgomery Flagg*, 53. Flagg also wrote official promotional films for the U.S. Marines and the Red Cross during World War I.
11. Flagg, *Roses and Buckshot*, 158.
12. Miley, *Howard Chandler Christy*, n.p.
13. Meyer, Introduction, *The James Montgomery Flagg Poster Book*, n.p.; Flagg, *Roses and Buckshot*, 157, 158.
14. Flagg, *Roses and Buckshot*, 158. The idea for this image, however, probably came from a 1914 British war recruitment poster by Alfred Leete titled "Your Country Needs You" and showing a pointing Lord Kitchener, Britain's secretary of state for war (Rawls, *Wake Up, America!*, 12).
15. Meyer, *James Montgomery Flagg*, 37.
16. Higham, *Writing American History*, 82.
17. Meyer, Introduction, *The James Montgomery Flagg Poster Book*, n.p. War themes in J. C. Leyendecker's magazine cover art similarly attempted to create "community" among viewers through idealism, notes art scholar Richard Martin: "This was Leyendecker's war: a story of heroes, women in distress, people like us, but not quite us" ("The Great War and the Great Image," 74).
18. W. J. T. Mitchell, *Iconology*, 41.
19. Downey, *Portrait of an Era*, 324. Frederick Platt also notes that "World War I brought back the Gibson Girl" and her Victorian purity and respectability ("The Gibson Girl," 116).
20. Banta, *Imaging American Women*, 484.
21. Norman Rockwell served in the navy but was stationed in Charleston, S.C., for the duration of the war. As a troop entertainer in France, McMein was caught in several air raids and in direct fire from enemy vehicles. Though she would do her most important magazine work for *McCall's* in the 1920s and 1930s, her cover art for the *Saturday Evening Post* was already well enough known to inspire a jingle among soldiers:

> "Have you heard of the show at the Y tonight?"
> Said Sergeant O'Grady to me.
> "Why no" sez I, "an' what's at the Y?"
> "Sure it's Neysa McMein" sez he.
> ". . . She has broken the hearts of a million of lovers
> Who fell in love with the girls on the covers

Of the magazines way back home," sez he.

". . . She's the party that places those wonderful faces

On the *Saturday Evening Post*."

(Gallagher, *Anything Goes*, 47–48.)

22. Kirkwood, "The Girl in the War," 120.
23. Banta, "They Shall Have Faces," 254.
24. "Woman-in-the-War Number." An article also jokingly praised women for wearing skirts "shorter than they were last year, showing a willingness to save cloth that produces some astonishing effects" (744).
25. Dr. Harvey Wiley, "Mobilize the Women," 51; "To the American Woman! An Appreciation," 17.
26. Dr. Harvey Wiley, "Mobilize the Women," 51.

CHAPTER SIX

1. Erens, "The Flapper," 134.
2. Ford, *The Time of Laughter*, 4–6.
3. Hoffman, *The Twenties*; Armitage, *John Held, Jr.*; Meyer, *America's Great Illustrators*, 1978; Merkin, Introduction, *The Jazz Age*; Weinhardt, "Introduction: The Rise of the Mormon Kid," 12–19.
4. David E. E. Sloan, "*Life*," 150.
5. Downey, *Portrait of an Era*, 350.
6. I am borrowing the term used by Roland Barthes in *Image, Music, Text*, 39.
7. Bliven, "Flapper Jane," 65, 67.
8. Filene, *Him/Her/Self*, 262.
9. Shuttlesworth, "John Held, Jr. and His World," 30.
10. Quoted in Hoffman, *The Twenties*, 110. Hoffman cites Fitzgerald, "Descriptions of Girls."
11. Higashi, *Virgins, Vamps, and Flappers*, 11.
12. Yellis, "Prosperity's Child," 44.
13. Cowley, "Memoranda of a Decade," 33.
14. Stuart Ewen includes this female body ideal among various types of evidence supporting his argument that modernism was based on immateriality and was signified by imagery "freed from the liabilities of substance." The "streamlined" flapper, he writes, looked as if "she might transcend the force of gravity, dissolving into the weightless ecstasy of some modernistic frenzy" (*All Consuming Images*, 183, 174).
15. Marchand, *Advertising the American Dream*, 146, 182, 155. Marchand attributes the information on the height of actual women of this era to fashion economist Paul Mystrom (184).
16. Ibid., 146.
17. Shelley Armitage makes this observation in *John Held, Jr.*
18. Marchand, *Advertising the American Dream*, 184.

19. Banner, *American Beauty*, 279.
20. Ann Douglas, *Terrible Honesty*, 252. Douglas calls this urge on the part of young women of the 1920s "feminicide."
21. For example, Armitage, *John Held, Jr.;* Meyer, *America's Great Illustrators;* Yellis, "Prosperity's Child."
22. Hooper, "Flapping Not Repented Of," 13.
23. Cited in Mowry, *The Twenties*, 186.
24. Erens, "The Flapper," 134.
25. Bailey, *From Front Porch to Back Seat*, 80–81.
26. Haskell, *From Reverence to Rape*, 45.
27. From a 1971 interview with the actress, quoted in Rosen, *Popcorn Venus*. Rosen cites Angela Taylor, "This Flapper's Altered Fashion's Course," *New York Times*, Oct. 26, 1971.
28. White, "The Flapper's Boyfriend."
29. Yellis, "Prosperity's Child," 49.
30. Hawkins and Nakayama, "Discourse on Women's Bodies," 62.
31. "Most every star who came to popularity in the twenties played a lingerie scene," notes Mary P. Ryan ("The Projection of a New Womanhood," 116).
32. Stevenson, "Flappers and Some Who Were Not Flappers," 123.
33. Rapp and Ross, "The Twenties' Backlash," 104.
34. Fitzgerald, "Echoes of the Jazz Age," 464.
35. Stevenson, *Babbitts and Bohemians*, 142.
36. Lynd and Lynd, *Middletown*, 159.
37. Brumberg, *Fasting Girls;* Mazur, "U.S. Trends in Feminine Beauty and Overadaptation."
38. "In the 1920s," writes Michael Schudson, "cigarettes came to be a personal and social marker for 'the new woman,' a sign of divorce from the past and inclusion in the group of the new, young, and liberated" (*Advertising, the Uneasy Persuasion*, 196). The Lucky Strike ad is quoted in Hawkins and Nakayama, "Discourse on Women's Bodies," 67.
39. Rosen, *Popcorn Venus*, 89.

CHAPTER SEVEN

1. Between 1890 and 1920, the U.S. marriage rate rose steadily, and until the Great Depression fewer than 10 percent of wives were in the work force (May, *Great Expectations*, 117, 167).
2. Women's increasing interest in sexual satisfaction has been documented by several social historians, who attribute the change to several factors that occurred simultaneously during this era: the availability of birth control, franker discussion (and better understanding) of sex thanks to the popularization of Freudian theory in the United States; the relatively new phenomenon of dating before marriage; and the new morality of the postwar "youth culture" (in other words, many young wives of the 1920s *were* flap-

pers before marriage). See Bailey, *From Front Porch to Back Seat;* D'Emilio and Freedman, *Intimate Matters;* Filene, *Him/Her/Self;* and May, *Great Expectations.*

3. Pumphrey, "The Flapper, the Housewife and the Making of Modernity," 101.

4. This "companionate" model of marriage did not necessarily characterize the unions of working-class spouses. In her study of immigrant families living in Greenwich Village in the 1920s, Caroline Ware wrote: "The girls who faced the camera on their wedding day with that characteristic expression of impersonal and fearless resignation bore eloquent testimony to the persistence of the outlook on marriage which their mothers had had" (*Greenwich Village*, 408).

5. Marsh and Ronner, *The Empty Cradle*, 112–13. In *Suburban Lives*, Marsh dates this cultural and family emphasis on children to the turn of the century, while other historians, such as Pumphrey ("The Flapper, the Housewife and the Making of Modernity"), consider it a phenomenon of the twenties.

6. Gallagher, *Anything Goes*, 89, 155; Walt Reed, *Great American Illustrators*, 104.

7. Gallagher, *Anything Goes*, 97.

8. Zuckerman, "*McCall's*," 221.

9. This estimate is based on Mary Ellen Zuckerman's ("*McCall's*") claim that the magazine's circulation rose from just over a million during the teens to 2.5 million at the end of the 1920s—figures she attributes to a brochure by a later editor of *McCall's*, Lenore Hershey ("The Pace and the Pattern," n.p.).

10. Mott, *A History of American Magazines*, vol. 4: *1885–1905*, 585.

11. Zuckerman, "*McCall's*," 218–25; Mott, *A History of American Magazines*, 4:580–88. The magazine initially had different titles—the *Queen* and then the *Queen of Fashion*—until it was named for its founder, Scottish immigrant James McCall, in 1897. During the 1920s, editor Harry Payne Burton commissioned fiction by well-known writers such as Zane Grey, Mary Roberts Rinehart, Harold Bell Wright, and Booth Tarkington.

12. Gallagher, *Anything Goes*, 70–83; Baragwanath, *A Good Time Was Had*, 78; Woollcott, *Enchanted Aisles*, 37. Baragwanath was McMein's husband.

13. Coward, *Present Indicative*, 176.

14. Quoted in Ferris and Moore, *Girls Who Did*, 114–15. This quote is an interesting explanation of an artist's vision stemming from a "study" of representational patterns that were already in place.

15. Interviewers mentioned McMein's devotion to her daughter, Joan (see, for instance, Van Santvoord, "What My Home Means to Me," 440), and her husband wrote in his memoirs that "she was wrapped up in our little daughter" (Baragwanath, *A Good Time Was Had*, 130).

16. Gaines, *Wit's End*, 81. The League was named for nineteenth-century activist Lucy Stone, who kept her maiden name after marriage.

17. She is the unidentified suffrage-parade marcher carrying the American flag in a photograph that appeared in the suffrage periodical the *Woman Citizen* (Dec. 8, 1917, 25) and has since been frequently reprinted—for instance, it is used as the cover of a recent biographical dictionary, *American Women's History*, ed. Weatherford. This book's claim that "[t]ruth lies in the details" (iii) is ironic, given that McMein is neither identified as the cover subject nor profiled in the book.

18. Woollcott, *Enchanted Aisles*, 35.

19. Gallagher, *Anything Goes*, 90. Because of this realism and the possibility that magazine readers could actually look like these cover girls, Gallagher considers McMein's type "the antithesis of the Gibson Girl" (90).

20. Ibid., 92. In 1937, McMein drew a similar *McCall's* cover series that included Amelia Earhart, Dorothy Thompson, Helen Hayes, and Edna St. Vincent Millay (Walt Reed, *Great American Illustrators*, 104).

21. "Looking Back, January 1925," 10; Gallagher, *Anything Goes*, 93.

22. In the 1930s, McMein, whose advertising work is discussed in Chapter 8, drew the prototype for Betty Crocker, though the image was recast by other artists in later decades ("Looking Back, January 1925," 10; Gallagher, *Anything Goes*, 99).

23. Lee, "With a College Education," 798.

24. One reason may have been the fact that Anna Kelton Wiley—wife of Dr. John Wiley, the director of the Good Housekeeping Institute—was a member of the militant Woman's Party. In February 1918, the magazine published her views in "Why We Picketed the White House," beginning with an italicized disclaimer that "*Good Housekeeping* does not believe in picketing the White House" (29, 124–25). Through 1914, the magazine ran a series called "The Advance of Militancy" by British suffragist Emmeline Pankhurst.

25. For instance, Frazer, "Say It with Ballots." The magazine published a monthly report from Washington by Frances Parkinson Keyes, a popular novelist who was the wife of a New Hampshire senator and wrote not only about the social life of the nation's capital but also about political issues of the day. In 1923, Keyes covered the International Women's Suffrage Alliance meeting in Rome for the magazine (Mott, *A History of American Magazines*, vol. 5: *1905–1930*, 134).

26. Mrs. Charles Dana Gibson, "When a Child Adopts You."

27. Marsh and Ronner, *The Empty Cradle*, 120.

28. Sheila Rothman makes this observation in *Woman's Proper Place*, 213–14. Even so, working-class mothers continued to receive advice (often unsolicited) from middle-class reformers through the federal Children's Bureau, a welfare network funded by the 1921 Sheppard-Towner Maternity and Infancy Protection Act, and through Mother's Clubs, in which native-born women could "teach the newcomers American ways" (Muncy, *Creating a Female Dominion*; Peiss, *Cheap Amusements*, 102).

29. Ladd-Taylor, *Mother-Work*, 44.

30. I am borrowing this term from Rothman, *Woman's Proper Place,* 177.

31. Advertisement, *Good Housekeeping,* Feb. 1916, 13.

32. Hogan, "Mothers and Children."

33. Zuckerman, *A History of Popular Women's Magazines in the United States,* 29; Mott, *A History of American Magazines,* 5:133, 136.

34. Smith was well paid for her part in the magazine's success, earning between $1,500 and $1,800 for each of her covers, plus additional income from subsequent commercial uses of her cover images. From *Good Housekeeping* alone, she made more than a quarter of a million dollars, in addition to what she earned illustrating books and painting portraits of the children of the Philadelphia elite (Schnessel, *Jessie Willcox Smith,* 135; Gene Mitchell, *The Subject Was Children,* 3; Jessie Willcox Smith papers, Pennsylvania Academy of the Fine Arts, Philadelphia; Philadelphia Art Alliance Records, University of Pennsylvania, Philadelphia).

35. Smith also illustrated several children's books, including a 1905 edition of Robert Louis Stevenson's *A Child's Garden of Verses;* Carolyn Wells's *The Seven Ages of Childhood* (1909; some of these illustrations ran in the *Ladies' Home Journal*); *Dickens' Children* (1910; some ran in *Scribner's*); a 1915 edition of Louisa May Alcott's *Little Women;* the 1916 edition of Charles Kingsley's *The Water-Babies;* and her own *The Little Mother Goose* (1915).

36. Stryker, *The Studios at Cogslea,* 12. For more on Smith's personal and professional background, see Carter, *The Red Rose Girls;* Schnessel, *Jessie Willcox Smith;* Gene Mitchell, *The Subject Was Children;* Nudelman, *Jessie Willcox Smith;* Jessie Willcox Smith, "Jessie Willcox Smith"; Likos, "The Ladies of the Red Rose"; Huber, *The Pennsylvania Academy and Its Women;* and Smith's *New York Times* obituary ("Miss Jessie Smith, Illustrator, Dead," 13).

37. The writer added, however, that Smith considered a single woman's sphere as wide as a man's. The remarks are taken from a typed magazine-article manuscript in the Jessie Willcox Smith papers. It is unclear whether or where the article was published, but it carries a notation that it was "possibly an enclosure belonging with letter from Louise Hillyer Armstrong [evidently the interviewer] to JWS, Jan. 31, 1927."

38. The ad further warned, somewhat threateningly, "It's not only in the thirties and the forties that Youth Preservation presents itself as a problem. It starts in the late *'teens* and the early twenties" (Advertisement, *Good Housekeeping,* Nov. 1927, n.p., in the Alice Marshall Women's History Collection, Pennsylvania State University, Harrisburg).

39. Lucy Van Haney, Brooklyn, NY, to *Good Housekeeping,* d. Nov. 28, 1926, in Jessie Willcox Smith papers; Schnessel, *Jessie Willcox Smith,* 124.

40. Constance Bell Pearson, Beverly, Mass., to Jessie Willcox Smith, c/o *Good Housekeeping,* d. Oct. 28, 1926, in Jessie Willcox Smith papers. More likely this illustration was a portrait of children of the artist's suburban Philadelphia neighbors, whom she used as models.

41. Zuckerman, *A History of Popular Women's Magazines in the United States,* 132–34. Zuckerman cites J. Walter Thompson, "Analysis of the Subscription Circulation of 44 Magazines" (1922), and Curtis Publishing Company, "A Study of City Markets, 1928–1929" (1930), 1.

42. Marsh, *Suburban Lives,* 69.

43. Ibid., 144, 146.

44. Buechner, *Norman Rockwell: A Sixty Year Retrospective,* 52.

45. Ibid., 42, 44; Moffat, *Norman Rockwell;* Walton, *A Rockwell Portrait,* 89; Flythe, *Norman Rockwell and the* Saturday Evening Post *(1916–1928),* 5; Sommer, *Norman Rockwell,* 9; Walt Reed, *Great American Illustrators,* 132.

46. Rockwell, *My Adventures as an Illustrator,* 34.

47. Cohn, *Covers of the* Saturday Evening Post, 2. These goals did not stop him from printing critical articles in the early 1920s about the "hordes" of foreigners in the United States and promoting works by eugenicists, including Madison Grant's *The Passing of the Great Race* and Lothrop Stoddard's *The Rising Tide of Color,* "both of which predicted the defeat of the white race at the hands of people of color" (Cohn, *Creating America,* 154–55).

48. Flythe, Foreword, *The* Saturday Evening Post *Norman Rockwell Book,* vii.

49. Advertisement, *Saturday Evening Post,* Jan. 20, 1923, 86–87.

50. Mott, *A History of American Magazines,* 4:692; Damon-Moore, *Magazines for the Millions,* 154.

51. Cohn, *Creating America,* 204.

52. Mott, *A History of American Magazines,* 4:696.

53. Cohn, *Creating America,* 165.

54. Rockwell, *My Adventures as an Illustrator,* 34.

55. Quoted in Cott, *The Grounding of Modern Feminism,* 170.

56. Flythe, *Norman Rockwell and the* Saturday Evening Post *(1916–1928),* 27.

57. I am again using the terms of Segal, "Norman Rockwell and the Fashioning of American Masculinity," 633. His analysis is discussed more fully in Chapter 3.

58. Quoted in Guptill, *Norman Rockwell, Illustrator,* 152.

59. Kimmel, *Manhood in America,* 164. Kimmel is referring to claims made in psychologist G. Stanley Hall's 1904 *Adolescence.*

60. Kimmel, "The Contemporary 'Crisis' of Masculinity in Historical Perspective," 149.

61. Cohn, *Creating America,* 11.

62. Advertisement, *Saturday Evening Post,* May 19, 1923, 94–95.

63. Pendergast, "'Horatio Alger Doesn't Work Here Any More,'" 64.

64. Also note the American eagle figurine attached to the side of the car. This cover, in addition, symbolized American progress through technology, a unifying theme in Rockwell's art, notes Moffat ("Norman Rockwell: Illustrator of America's Heritage," 30–31). Some of his other cover scenes focused on trains, the telephone, radio, and, eventually, television. One of his last magazine covers depicted the 1969 moon landing.

CHAPTER EIGHT

1. Among scholars who make this argument are Richard Ohmann (*Selling Culture*) and Judith Williamson ("Decoding Advertisements").
2. Brown, *Alice Barber Stephens*, 27–28.
3. Meyer, *James Montgomery Flagg*, 24.
4. Letter from Harry W. Brown, Procter & Gamble executive, to Alice Barber Stephens, d. April 26, 1902, Collection of Mr. and Mrs. Samuel S. Starr, quoted in Brown, *Alice Barber Stephens*, 29.
5. Buechner, *The Norman Rockwell Treasury*, 23; Rockwell, *My Adventures as an Illustrator*, 182.
6. Steine and Taraba, *American Illustrators Poster Book: The J. C. Leyendecker Collection*, 10.
7. Schau, *J. C. Leyendecker*, 28–30.
8. Steine and Taraba, *American Illustrators Poster Book: The J. C. Leyendecker Collection*, 5; Walt Reed, *The Illustrator in America, 1900–1960s*, 60.
9. Segal, "Norman Rockwell and the Fashioning of American Masculinity," 646.
10. Jan Cohn also notes this transformation of the Arrow Man into a World War I doughboy, arguing that his combination of clean-shaven and rugged looks helped define wartime masculinity as "cheerful, modest, but entirely manly" (*Creating America*, 125).
11. Steine and Taraba, *American Illustrators Poster Book: The J. C. Leyendecker Collection*, 10. Other products for which Leyendecker did advertising illustrations included Kellogg's Corn Flakes, Ivory Soap, and Overland automobiles (Schau, *J. C. Leyendecker*, 81–125).
12. This ad is reproduced in Steine and Taraba, *American Illustrators Poster Book: The J. C. Leyendecker Collection*, n.p.
13. A two-page 1920 *Saturday Evening Post* ad drawn by James Montgomery Flagg made a similar suggestion about the American businessman. This promotion of Royal Tailor suits showed several well-dressed businessmen in an office setting. One man had his jacket off and sleeves rolled up—like Flagg's war-poster man so enraged by "Huns" killing women and children that he was determined to enlist. Here, that gesture signified the man's determination to work hard. Yet the ad copy suggested that his *appearance* would ultimately determine his professional fate: success came to "discerning men" who wore "the best made-to-order clothes." (Advertisement, *Saturday Evening Post*, Mar. 6, 1920, 146–47.)
14. Schau, *"All-American Girl,"* 45–46, 57.
15. Phillips's bird motif may have been meant to portray women themselves as birdlike and flighty, with their hair and dress as plumage. Yet it could also have been part of the broader use of animal references in popular discourse about sexuality during this era, epitomized by the fox trot, the bunny hug, the turkey trot, and other animal dances of the era. The small-type ad copy

under one version of this ad (not the version shown in Figure 8.4) noted that Holeproof Hosiery came in colors named "Airedale" and "Jack Rabbit."

16. In the 1890s and early 1900s, it was common for a major publication such as the *Journal* to retain an art staff who prepared ads according to advertisers' stipulations.

17. Schnessel, *Jessie Willcox Smith*, 196.

18. There was no indication of where this drawing first appeared, though most likely it was in *Collier's*, for which Smith was working in 1902, the copyright date of the ad.

19. Advertisement, *Atlantic Monthly Advertiser*, n.d., 80. The phrase "It floats" was the company's ad campaign tagline in this era, always ending the ad copy. This and the other Ivory Soap ad shown here are held in the Alice Marshall Women's History Collection, Pennsylvania State University, Harrisburg.

20. McClintock, "Soft-Soaping Empire," 131–54.

21. Roosevelt, "The Strenuous Life."

22. Goodrum and Dalrymple, *Advertising in America*, 36.

23. This text is also strikingly similar to an article explaining the new Boy Scouts of America in a 1912 issue of *Leslie's Weekly:* "The REAL Boy Scout is not a 'sissy.' He is not a hothouse plant, like Little Lord Fauntleroy. . . . Instead of being a puny, dull, or bookish lad, who dreams and does nothing, he is full of life, energy, enthusiasm, bubbling over with fun, full of ideas as to what he wants to do and knows how he wants to do it. . . . He is not hitched to his mother's apronstrings. While he adores his mother, and would do anything to save her from suffering or discomfort, he is self-reliant, sturdy and full of vim" (J. E. West, "The Real Boy Scout," *Leslie's Weekly,* n.d., 1912, 448, quoted in Hantover, "The Boy Scouts and the Validation of Masculinity," 295–96).

24. Dubbert, "Progressivism and the Masculinity Crisis," 312.

25. Advertisement, *Saturday Evening Post,* Mar. 13, 1920, 145.

26. Horowitz, *The Morality of Spending.* He explains that consumption did not stop in the postwar recession years, but was more likely to be characterized by discrimination, a prioritizing of family spending on "'elevating' consumer goods and experiences" (118).

27. McMein's advertising clients not named in the main text included Palm Oil Shampoo, Lucky Strike cigarettes, Wallace Silver, Scranton Lace Curtains, and Cadillac automobiles (Gallagher, *Anything Goes,* 99). In 1936, McMein also drew the original version of Betty Crocker—though her unsmiling, matronly, depression-era rendition of the icon was made younger, more glamorous, and more pleasant-looking by other artists in subsequent decades (Goodrum and Dalrymple, *Advertising in America,* 40).

28. Gallagher, *Anything Goes,* 100.

29. Advertisement, *Woman's Home Companion,* Oct. 1917, 67, Alice Marshall Women's History Collection.

30. The presence of this female figure was erased by the ad copy, however, which was selling *men's* clothing and which explained that men returning from war would need to buy "civilian clothes of the right kind . . . inspiring the confidence of others in you" (Advertisement, *Literary Digest*, Apr. 19, 1919, 76–77, Alice Marshall Women's History Collection).

31. Advertisement, *American Magazine*, n.d., 1919, 183, Alice Marshall Women's History Collection.

EPILOGUE AND DISCUSSION

1. The New Year's Baby, like the Arrow Collar Man, has been preserved; in 2000, the U.S. Post Office issued postage stamps featuring Leyendecker's baby to celebrate the millennium.

2. Quoted in Goodrum and Dalrymple, *Advertising in America*, 255.

3. Abbott, "What the Newest New Woman Is," 154.

4. Genn, "The Bachelor Girl: Is She a Menace?," 564. The expert quoted here was not a psychologist or a working mother, but a male statistician for the Metropolitan Life Insurance Company. Despite the nature and audience of this magazine, the title of the article and the expert's note that the typical man had a "natural reluctance to marry a woman better educated than himself" were a warning for women in college and the professions.

5. By the 1920s, birth control was available to many American women, so childbearing had become another aspect of women's "will." This choice, still unavailable to most working-class women, further distinguished "the New Woman" of the 1920s as middle-class.

6. It was in the new ideals of beauty and fashion that commerce most clearly intersected with visual representations of the American woman/girl. In 1921, beauty became "a national ritual," celebrated by the new Miss America pageant. That the contestants were expected to resemble the "types" of beauty created in mass media was clear in the selection of the era's famous illustrators as the pageant's first judges. For the first year's contest, the sole judge was Howard Chandler Christy; in the second year, he was joined by James Montgomery Flagg, Coles Phillips, and Norman Rockwell. John Held Jr. was added to the group later in the decade—and made Miss Louisiana of 1927 his third wife. (Banner, *American Beauty*, 16; Rockwell, *My Adventures as an Illustrator*, 175, 179; Armitage, *John Held, Jr.*, 49; Weinhardt, "Introduction: The Rise of the Mormon Kid," 12–19.)

7. Bromley, "Feminist—New Style," 552, 556.

8. Lee, "Care to Join Me in an Upwardly Mobile Tango?," 168.

9. Film scholar Marsha McCreadie used this phrase to describe Hayworth (*The American Movie Goddess*).

10. Cheever, "Twiggy," 74. Ironically—perhaps in light of 1990s "third wave" postfeminism at the time she wrote this—Cheever saw this figure in a posi-

tive light, as a revolutionary challenge to conventional femininity of the midcentury.

11. Friedan, *The Feminine Mystique*.

12. As a general interest magazine, *Life* would become one of the casualties of color television, losing much of its weekly circulation of eight million in 1972. It was again resurrected in 1978, published as a monthly until folding once more in 2000.

13. Women's and teen fashion-and-beauty magazines continued to depict the idealized reader on their covers, using photographs of models to do so, until the mid-1990s, when women's fashion magazines switched to female celebrities, and the late 1990s, when magazines for teenage girls switched first to female celebrities and then *male* celebrities. This was a drastic shift in cover philosophy, in which the cover image ceased to reveal who the girl might become and instead was a fantasy image of the boy she might date. For a fuller explanation of magazine history during the midcentury, see Tebbel and Zuckerman, *The Magazine in America*. The more recent information here (and the information on men's magazines later in this chapter) is based on my own experience as an editor for eleven years at American women's magazines and my contact with editors and study of the industry since then.

14. Susan J. Douglas, *Where the Girls Are;* Dow, *Prime-Time Feminism*.

15. Susan J. Douglas, *Where the Girls Are*, 121.

16. Kuczynski, "That Girl, All Grown Up."

17. Susan J. Douglas, *Where the Girls Are*, 126, 137.

18. Dow, *Prime-Time Feminism*, 60–79, 82.

19. Ibid., 51–52.

20. One exception to this shift from working-class to middle-class heroines was the popular 1980s sitcom *Roseanne*, about a working-class (and working) mother. But it is important to note that this comedy was based on the title character's loud and excessive (she was overweight) personality and on her cynicism about domesticity and motherhood. Like the working-class women portrayed on the covers of the *Masses* (see Chapter 4), she was the anti-ideal who knew it and didn't care—and that was what made her funny.

21. Faludi, *Backlash*, 160–67. In 1998, psychologist Carol Tavris complained that reading the many current books about motherhood "makes me feel like Rip Van Winkle, awakening to the exact same arguments about working mothers that modern feminists were raising in the 1970s—and that *their* predecessors were in the 1920s" ("Goodbye to Momism," 16).

22. Dow, *Prime-Time Feminism*, 52.

23. Flora Davis, *Moving the Mountain*, 433–44.

24. Waters and Huck, "Networking Women," 48–54.

25. Waters and Huck, "Shedding a Glacial Identity," 55.

26. *Time*, Dec. 4, 1989, cover; Wallis, "Onward, Women!," 81.

27. Wolf, *Fire with Fire*, 66, 135–38.

28. Ricapito, "'Girl' Makes a Comeback."

29. Some scholars contend that feminism survived even in media imagery of the midcentury. Using the same type of source material as Betty Friedan—magazine editorial (though looking at nonfiction rather than fiction)—in the same time period, Joanne Meyerowitz saw a very different image of womanhood than Friedan had, a celebration of women's achievement in Horatio Alger–type tales through which the magazines conveyed "overt admiration for women whose individual striving moved them beyond the home" ("Beyond the Feminine Mystique," 1458).

30. Dow, *Prime-Time Feminism*, 173.

31. Historian Garry Wills writes that John Wayne "was the conduit [audiences] used to communicate with their own desired selves or their own imagined past. When he was called *the* American, it was a statement of what his fans wanted America to be" (*John Wayne's America*, 14).

32. *Maxim* originated in the United Kingdom.

33. I am borrowing "hypermasculinity" from historian Clyde Griffen. Writing about the 1910s "crisis of masculinity," Griffen argues that signs of this phenomenon could be seen during other eras, including the preceding nineteenth century and the later twentieth century, and that, since the balance of societal power between men and women did not significantly change, "calling it a 'crisis' seems misleading" ("Reconstructing Masculinity," 200).

34. Covert, "Journalism History and Women's Experience," 6.

Bibliography

PRIMARY SOURCES

Magazines (Sources for Artwork)

American Magazine, The
Collier's
Crisis, The
Good Housekeeping
Judge
Ladies' Home Journal, The
Life

Literary Digest, The
McCall's
Masses, The
Motor
Saturday Evening Post, The
Woman Citizen, The

Archives and Collections

Chadds Ford, Pa.
  Brandywine River Museum.
    Holdings on Neysa McMein, Norman Rockwell, Jessie Willcox Smith,
      and Alice Barber Stephens.
Harrisburg, Pa.
  Alice Marshall Women's History Collection, Pennsylvania State
    University at Harrisburg.
    Holdings on James Montgomery Flagg, Charles Dana Gibson,
      John Held Jr., Neysa McMein, Coles Phillips, and Jessie Willcox
      Smith; advertising files; *The Woman Citizen;* sheet music files.
New York, N.Y.
  The Arrow Company, a division of Cluett, Peabody & Co., Inc.
    Holdings on J. C. Leyendecker.
Philadelphia, Pa.
  Pennsylvania Academy of the Fine Arts.
    Holdings on John Sloan, Jessie Willcox Smith, and Alice Barber
      Stephens.
  Special Collections, Van Pelt Library, University of Pennsylvania.
    Curtis Publishing Company Records (Coll. 51). Holdings on
      Charles Dana Gibson and Alice Barber Stephens.
    Philadelphia Art Alliance Records (Coll. 53, Folder 624). Holdings
      on John Sloan and Jessie Willcox Smith.
Stockbridge, Mass.
  Norman Rockwell Museum at Stockbridge.
    Holdings on Norman Rockwell.
Urbana-Champaign, Ill.
  D'Arcy Collection, Communications Library, University of Illinois at
    Urbana-Champaign.

Holdings on Coles Phillips.
Washington, D.C.
  Archives of American Art, Smithsonian Institution.
    Holdings on most of the artists discussed in this book.
  General Collection and Prints and Photographs Division, Library of
      Congress.
    Holdings on all of the artists discussed in this book.
Winterthur, Del.
  Winterthur Museum and Library.
    Holdings on Howard Chandler Christy, J. C. Leyendecker, Neysa
      McMein, Norman Rockwell, Jessie Willcox Smith, and Alice Barber
      Stephens.

Exhibition Catalogs

Brown, Ann Barton. *Alice Barber Stephens: A Pioneer Woman Illustrator,*
    Mar. 17–May 20, 1984. Chadds Ford, Pa.: Brandywine River Museum,
    1984.
Elzea, Rowland, and Elizabeth Hawkes. *John Sloan: Spectator of Life,*
    Apr. 26–Dec. 31, 1981. Wilmington: Delaware Art Museum, 1988.
Goodrich, Lloyd. *John Sloan, 1871–1951,* Jan. 10–June 8, 1952. New York:
    Whitney Musem of American Art, 1952.
Gregg, Richard N., ed. *Salute to Norman Rockwell.* Columbus Gallery of Fine
    Arts, Oct. 7–31, 1976; Allentown Art Museum, Nov. 20, 1976–Jan. 1, 1977.
    Allentown, Pa.: Allentown Art Museum 1976.
Huber, Christine Jones. *The Pennsylvania Academy and Its Women, 1850–*
    1920, May 3–June 16, 1973. Philadelphia: Pennsylvania Academy of the
    Fine Arts, 1974.
Mayer, Anne E. *Women Artists in the Howard Pyle Tradition,* Sept. 6–Nov. 23,
    1975. Chadds Ford, Pa.: Brandywine River Museum, 1975.
Merkin, Richard. *The Jazz Age, as Seen through the Eyes of Ralph Barton,*
    Miguel Covarrubias, and John Held, Jr., Sept. 25–Nov. 10, 1968.
    Providence: Museum of Art, Rhode Island School of Design, 1968.
Miley, Mimi C. *Howard Chandler Christy: Artist/Illustrator of Style,*
    Sept. 25–Nov. 6, 1977. Allentown, Pa.: Allentown Art Museum, 1977.
Scott, David W., and E. John Bullard. *John Sloan, 1871–1951: His Life and*
    Paintings, His Graphics, Sept. 18–Oct. 31, 1971. Washington, D.C.:
    National Gallery of Art, 1971.
Stryker, Catherine Connell. *The Studios at Cogslea,* Feb. 20–28, 1976.
    Wilmington: Delaware Art Museum, 1976.

Published Collections of Illustrations

Buechner, Thomas, ed. *Norman Rockwell: A Sixty Year Retrospective.* New
    York: Harry N. Abrams, 1972.
————. *The Norman Rockwell Treasury.* New York: Galahad Books, 1979.

Christy, Howard Chandler. *The American Girl as Seen and Portrayed by Howard Chandler Christy.* New York: Da Capo, 1976. Originally published New York: Moffat, Yard, 1906.

Cohn, Jan. *Covers of the* Saturday Evening Post: *Seventy Years of Outstanding Illustration from America's Favorite Magazine.* New York: Viking, 1995.

Darracott, Joseph, ed. *The First World War in Posters.* New York: Dover, 1974.

Finch, Christopher. *Norman Rockwell: 322 Magazine Covers.* New York: Abbeville, 1979.

Flythe, Starkey, Jr., ed. *Norman Rockwell and the* Saturday Evening Post: *The Early Years, May 1916–July 1928.* New York: MJF Books, 1994.

———. *The* Saturday Evening Post *Norman Rockwell Book.* New York: Bonanza Books, 1986.

Gelman, Woody, ed. *The Best of Charles Dana Gibson.* New York: Crown, 1969.

Gibson, Charles Dana. *The Social Ladder.* New York: Russell, 1902.

Gillon, Edmund Vincent, ed. *The Gibson Girl and Her America: The Best Drawings of Charles Dana Gibson.* New York: Dover, 1969.

Guptill, Arthur. *Norman Rockwell, Illustrator.* New York: Watson-Guptill, 1946.

Held, John, Jr. *The Most of John Held, Jr.* Brattleboro, Vt.: Stephen Greene, 1972.

Kery, Patricia Frantz. *Great Magazine Covers of the World.* New York: Abbeville, 1982.

Life Publishing Company. *Catalog of Charles Dana Gibson Drawings.* New York: Life Publishing Co., 1898.

Meyer, Susan E., ed. *The James Montgomery Flagg Poster Book.* New York: Watson-Guptill, 1975.

Mitchell, Gene. *The Subject Was Children: The Art of Jessie Willcox Smith.* New York: E. P. Dutton, 1979.

Moffat, Laurie Norton. *Norman Rockwell: A Definitive Catalogue.* Hanover, N.H.: University Press of New England, 1986.

Phillips, Coles. *A Young Man's Fancy.* Indianapolis: Bobbs-Merrill, 1912.

Rawls, Walton. *Wake Up, America! World War I and the American Poster.* New York: Abbeville, 1988.

Schau, Michael. *"All-American Girl": The Art of Coles Phillips.* New York: Watson-Guptill, 1975.

———. *J. C. Leyendecker.* New York: Watson-Guptill, 1974.

Sommer, Robin Langley, ed. *Norman Rockwell: A Classic Treasury.* London: Bison Books, 1993.

Steine, Kent, and Frederic B. Taraba. *American Illustrators Poster Book: The J. C. Leyendecker Collection.* Portland, Ore.: Collectors Press, 1996.

Contemporary Commentary and Memoirs

"Alice Barber Stephens, Illustrator." *Woman's Progress* 2, no. 2 (Nov. 1893): 49–53.

Ashmore, Ruth [Isabel Mallon]. "The Girl Who Aspires to Art." *Ladies' Home Journal,* Sept. 1897, 17–18.

———. "Side-Talks with Girls." *Ladies' Home Journal.* [Ongoing editorial feature during the 1890s.]

———. "The Social Position of the Girl Who Works." *Ladies' Home Journal,* Dec. 1897, 28.

———. "What to Expect from a Young Man." *Ladies' Home Journal,* June 1897, 22.

Baragwanath, John. *A Good Time Was Had.* New York: Appleton-Century-Crofts, 1962.

Beard, Daniel C. "In Camp and on House-Boat." *Ladies' Home Journal,* May 1897, 17.

Blackwell, Alice Stone. "Americanize the Mother." *Woman Citizen,* June 7, 1919, 7.

———. "Antis Outdo Bolsheviki." *Woman Citizen,* Dec. 18, 1917, 27.

———. "A. S. B.'s Page." *Woman Citizen,* Dec. 21, 1918, 607.

———. "Women and Wages." *Woman Citizen,* June 7, 1919, 8–9.

Bliven, Bruce. "Flapper Jane." *New Republic,* Oct. 9, 1925, 65–67.

Bok, Edward. *The Americanization of Edward Bok: The Autobiography of a Dutch Boy Fifty Years After.* New York: Scribner's, 1920.

———. "Breaking Down the Fences." *Ladies' Home Journal,* Aug. 1897, 14.

———. "On Being 'Old-Fashioned.' " *Ladies' Home Journal,* Sept. 1897, 14.

———. "Where America Fell Short with Me." *Saturday Evening Post,* Mar. 13, 1920, 29, 46, 49–50.

———. [Untitled editorial page.] *Ladies' Home Journal,* Oct. 1897, 14.

Bromley, Dorothy Dunbar. "Feminist—New Style." *Harper's Monthly Magazine* 155 (Oct. 1927): 552–60.

Bryan, Alfred, and George W. Meyer. "The High Cost of Loving" [sheet music]. New York: Leo Feist, n.d. [ca. 1910–1920]. Alice Marshall Women's History Collection, Pennsylvania State University, Harrisburg.

Burgess, Thornton W. "Making Men of Them." *Good Housekeeping* 59 (July 1914): 3–12.

Castle, Irene, as told to Bob and Wanda Duncan. *Castles in the Air.* Foreword by Ginger Rogers. New York: Doubleday, 1958.

Chalmers, Eleanor. "Facts and Figures: What You Ought to Know about the New Corsets from the Standpoint of Fashion and Health." *Delineator* 84 (Apr. 1914): 38–39.

"Charles Dana Gibson: The Man and His Art." *Collier's Weekly* 29 (Nov. 29, 1902): 8–9.

"Cheapest Commodity on the Market, The." *Masses,* Dec. 1911, 5.

Clark, Marion Wiltbank. "The Need of the Business Woman for Body Culture." *Philadelphia Press,* Sept. 26, 1915.

Coward, Noël. *Present Indicative.* Garden City, N.Y.: Doubleday, Doran, 1937.

Davis, Richard Harding. "The Origin of a Type of the American Girl." *Quarterly Illustrator* 3, no. 9 (Jan. 1895): 3–8.

Dell, Floyd. "Feminism for Men." *Masses,* July 1914, 19.

Dix, Dorothy. "The Girl of Today." *Good Housekeeping* 62 (Mar. 1916): 288–91.

Doughty, Isabel. "Taking Uncle Sam's Foster Children into the Family." *Woman Citizen,* Jan. 4, 1919, 650–51.

Downey, Fairfax. *Portrait of an Era as Drawn by C. D. Gibson: A Biography.* New York: Scribner's, 1936.

"Droch's Literary Talks." *Ladies' Home Journal.* [Ongoing editorial feature during the 1890s.]

Du Bois, W. E. B. *Writing in Periodicals Edited by W. E. B. Du Bois,* vol. 1: *1911–1925.* Edited by Herbert Aptheker. Millwood, N.Y.: Kraus-Thompson, 1983.

Eastman, Max. "Magazine Art." In Max Eastman, *Journalism versus Art.* New York: Knopf, 1916. Originally published in the *Masses,* no date given.

"Exclusively for *Colliers.*" *Collier's,* Oct. 14, 1905, 21.

Ferris, Helen Josephine. *Girls Who Did: Stories of Real Girls and Their Careers.* New York: E. P. Dutton, 1933.

Fiske, Stephen. "When the Prince of Wales Was in America." *Ladies' Home Journal,* Jan. 1897, 3–4.

Fitzgerald, F. Scott. "Echoes of the Jazz Age." *Scribner's* 90, no. 5 (Nov. 1931): 459–65.

Flagg, James Montgomery. *Roses and Buckshot.* New York: Harper & Row, 1946.

Frazer, Elizabeth. "Say It with Ballots." *Good Housekeeping* 74 (June 1922): 27–28, 186, 189–90.

Gates, Eleanor. "The Girl Who Travels Alone." [Three-part series.] *Cosmopolitan* 42 (Nov. 1906–May 1907): 1–13, 163–72, 308–15.

Genn, Lillian G. "The Bachelor Girl: Is She a Menace?" *Independent Woman* 7 (Dec. 1928): 538, 563–64.

Gibson, Mrs. Charles Dana. "When a Child Adopts You." *Good Housekeeping* 85 (July 1927): 79, 133–34, 136, 139.

Gilman, Charlotte Perkins. *Women and Economics.* Edited by Carl N. Degler. New York: Harper & Row, 1966. Originally published Boston: Maynard, 1898.

Goldberg, Harry. "Art Means Pursuit of Beauty Says Alice Barber Stephens." *Philadelphia Press Fiction Magazine,* Sept. 26, 1915, 1. Quoted in Ann Barton Brown, *Alice Barber Stephens: A Pioneer Woman Illustrator* (exhibition catalog), Mar. 17–May 20, 1984. Chadds Ford, Pa.: Brandywine River Museum, 1984.

"Gossip of the Editors, The." *Ladies' Home Journal.* [Ongoing editorial feature during the 1890s.]

Gottheil, Gustav. "The Jewess as She Was and Is." *Ladies' Home Journal,* Dec. 1897, 21.

Hale, Helen. "Hints to Young but Ambitious Artists from Some of the Most Famous Women Illustrators." *Chicago Examiner,* Jan. 22, 1906. Elizabeth

Shippen Green Elliott Collection, Archives of American Art, Smithsonian Institution, Washington, D.C.

Hall, G. Stanley. *Adolescence: Its Psychology and Its Relations to Physiology, Anthropology, Sociology, Sex, Crime, Religion, and Education.* 2 vols. New York: Appleton.

"Have You Tried the 'Long Boston' Dance?" *New York Times Sunday Magazine,* Jan. 29, 1911, 10.

Hewitt, Emma Churchman. "The 'New Woman' in Her Relation to the 'New Man.'" *Westminster Review* 147 (Mar. 1897): 335–37.

Hogan, Louise. "Mothers and Children." *Good Housekeeping* 62 (Mar. 1916): 321–25.

Hooper, Ruth. "Flapping Not Repented Of." *New York Times,* July 16, 1922.

Hope, Anthony. "Mr. C. D. Gibson on Love and Life." *McClure's* 9 (Aug. 1897): 869–75.

"Housewifely Husbands." *Woman's Home Companion,* June 1919, n.p. Alice Marshall Women's History Collection, Pennsylvania State University, Harrisburg.

Humphreys, Phebe Westcott. "The Business Girl's Luncheon." *Ladies' Home Journal,* Apr. 1897, 30.

"I Make Cheap Silk." *Masses,* Nov. 1913, 7.

Isaacs, Prof. A. S. "These Long Evenings in the Home." *Ladies' Home Journal,* Jan. 1897, 18.

Johnson, Owen. *The Salamander.* Indianapolis: Bobbs-Merrill, 1914.

Johnston, Frances Benjamin. "What a Woman Can Do with a Camera." *Ladies' Home Journal,* Sept. 1897, 6–7.

Jordan, William George. "The Greatest Nation on Earth." *Ladies' Home Journal,* July 1897, 7–8.

Keyes, Francis Parkinson. "Letters from a Senator's Wife." *Good Housekeeping.* [Ongoing editorial feature during the 1920s.]

Kirkwood, Edith. "The Girl in the War." *Western Magazine* 12, no. 3 (Sept. 1918): 118–20.

Lee, Jennette. "With a College Education." *Good Housekeeping* 58 (June 1914): 796–805.

Lessing, Bruno. "The Emancipation of Sarah." *Cosmopolitan* 46 (Dec. 1908–May 1909): 554–60.

Lorimer, George Horace. "Is Success Personal?" *Saturday Evening Post,* Apr. 10, 1920, 30.

Lynd, Robert S., and Helen M. Lynd. *Middletown: A Study in American Culture.* New York: Harcourt, Brace, 1929.

McCabe, Lida Rose. "Poor Girls Who Marry Millions." *Cosmopolitan* 41 (May–Oct. 1906): 249–59.

Mallon, Isabel. "The Gowns to Be Worn This Winter." *Ladies' Home Journal,* Sept. 1897, 35.

———. "The Visitor and the Hostess." *Ladies' Home Journal,* Jan. 1897, 21.

Milholland, Mrs. John E. "Talks about Women." *Crisis.* [Ongoing editorial feature during the period 1910–1920.]

"Miss Jessie Smith, Illustrator, Dead." *New York Times,* May 4, 1935.

Mitchell, John Ames. "Contemporary American Caricature." *Scribner's* 6, no. 6 (Dec. 1889): 728–45.

"Modern Picture Making and Its Generous Rewards: How a Group of Illustrators Is Reaping Fortunes by Drawing Pictures of the 'Modern Girl.'" *Philadelphia Public Ledger,* Feb. 6, 1910. Elizabeth Shippen Green Elliott Collection, Archives of American Art, Smithsonian Institution, Washington, D.C.

Moody, Dwight L. "Mr. Moody's Bible Class." *Ladies' Home Journal,* Sept. 1897, 21.

"Of a Personal Nature, by the Editors." *Ladies' Home Journal.* [Ongoing editorial feature during 1890s.]

Palmer, Marion van Riper. "The Women's Patriotic Societies." *Ladies' Home Journal,* July 1897, 10.

Pankhurst, Emmeline. "The Advance of Militancy." *Good Housekeeping* 58–59. (Series running in several issues through 1914.)

Rockwell, Norman. *My Adventures as an Illustrator.* New York: Harry N. Abrams, 1988.

Roosevelt, Theodore. "The Strenuous Life." In *The Strenuous Life. Essays and Addresses.* New York: Century, 1901.

Rorer, Sarah Tyson. "Handling the Family Wash." *Ladies' Home Journal,* Nov. 1897, 22.

———. "Mrs. Rorer's Cooking Lessons." *Ladies' Home Journal.* [Ongoing editorial feature during the 1890s.]

———. "Mrs. Rorer's Household Council." *Ladies' Home Journal.* [Ongoing editorial feature during the 1890s.]

———. "Small Leakages of a Household." *Ladies' Home Journal,* Sept. 1897, 24.

Scovil, Elisabeth Robinson. "Suggestions for Mothers." *Ladies' Home Journal,* Sept. 1897, 30.

"Sex O'Clock in America." *Current Opinion,* Aug. 1913, 113–14.

Simon, May Wood. "Co-operation and Housewives." *Masses,* Dec. 1911, 11.

Smith, Jessie Willcox. "Jessie Willcox Smith." *Good Housekeeping* 65 (Oct. 1917): 190.

Society of Illustrators, 1901–1928, The. New York: Society of Illustrators, 1928.

Sterling, Andrew B., and Harry Von Tilzer. "Somebody Else Is Getting It" [sheet music]. New York: Harry Von Tilzer Music Publishing Co., 1912. Alice Marshall Women's History Collection, Pennsylvania State University, Harrisburg.

"Stranger Cuts Girls' Curls." *New York Times,* Dec. 22, 1911.

Sullivan, Mark. *Our Times.* New York and London: Scribner's, 1929.

Ticknor, Caroline. "The Steel-Engraving Lady and the Gibson Girl." *Atlantic Monthly* 88 (July 1901): 105–8.

Tompkins, Juliet Wilbor. "Why Women Don't Marry." *Cosmopolitan* 42 (Nov. 1906–Apr. 1907): 468–71.

"To the American Woman! An Appreciation." *Good Housekeeping* 66, no. 5 (May 1918): 17.

Van Santvoord, Wilma. "What My Home Means to Me." [Interview with Neysa McMein.] *American Home* 1, no. 5 (Feb. 1929): 391, 440, 498.

"Votes for Women: A Symposium by Leading Thinkers of Colored America." *Crisis* 10, no. 4 (Aug. 1915): 178–92.

Ware, Caroline F. *Greenwich Village, 1920–1930: A Comment on American Civilization in the Post-War Years.* Berkeley: University of California Press, 1994. Originally published Boston: Houghton Mifflin, 1935.

"What We Are Fighting For." *Woman Citizen,* Dec. 8, 1917, 30–31.

Wiley, Anna Kelton. "Why We Picketed the White House." *Good Housekeeping* 66 (Feb. 1918): 29, 124–25.

Wiley, Dr. Harvey. "Mobilize the Women." *Good Housekeeping* 66 (Apr. 1918): 51–52, 132.

"Will They Never Learn." *Woman Citizen,* June 7, 1919, 7.

Woman Citizen, Dec. 8, 1917, 25.

"Woman-in-the-War Number." *Life* 70, no. 1828 (Nov. 8, 1917).

"Woman's Suffrage Symposium, A." *Crisis* 4, no. 5 (Sept. 1912): 240–47.

Woollcott, Alexander. *Enchanted Aisles.* New York: Putnam's, 1924.

"Worth-While People." *Cosmopolitan* 49 (June–Nov. 1910): 699.

Yellin, Jack, Ira Schuster, and Jack Glogau. "Oh, What Wonderful Things One Little Girlie Can Do" [sheet music]. New York: Leo Feist, 1917. Alice Marshall Women's History Collection, Pennsylvania State University, Harrisburg.

Young, Rose. "What Is Feminism?" *Good Housekeeping* 58 (May 1914): 679–84.

SECONDARY SOURCES

Books

Armitage, Shelley. *John Held, Jr.: Illustrator of the Jazz Age.* Syracuse: Syracuse University Press, 1987.

Bailey, Beth L. *From Front Porch to Back Seat: Courtship in Twentieth-Century America.* Baltimore: Johns Hopkins University Press, 1988.

Banner, Lois. *American Beauty.* New York: Knopf, 1983.

Banta, Martha. *Imaging American Women: Idea and Ideals in Cultural History.* New York: Columbia University Press, 1987.

Barthes, Roland. *Image, Music, Text.* Translated by Stephen Heath. New York: Hill and Wang, 1977.

Baym, Nina. *Woman's Fiction: A Guide to Novels by and about Women in America, 1820–1870.* Ithaca, N.Y.: Cornell University Press.

Benedict, Helen. *Virgin or Vamp: How the Press Covers Sex Crimes.* New York: Oxford University Press, 1993.

Benson, Susan Porter. *Counter Cultures: Saleswomen, Managers, and Customers in American Department Stores, 1880–1940.* Urbana: University of Illinois Press, 1986.

Berger, John. *Ways of Seeing.* New York: Penguin, 1972.

Best, James J. *American Popular Illustration: A Reference Guide.* Westport, Conn.: Greenwood, 1984.

Blair, Karen J. *The Torchbearers: Women and Their Amateur Arts Associations in America, 1890–1930.* Bloomington: Indiana University Press, 1994.

Boorstin, Daniel J. *The Americans: The Democratic Experience.* New York: Random House, 1973.

Brooks, Van Wyck. *John Sloan: A Painter's Life.* New York: E. P. Dutton, 1955.

Brumberg, Joan Jacobs. *Fasting Girls: The Emergence of Anorexia Nervosa as a Modern Disease.* Cambridge, Mass.: Harvard University Press, 1988.

Carter, Alice A. *The Red Rose Girls: An Uncommon Story of Art and Love.* New York: Harry N. Abrams, 2000.

Cohn, Jan. *Creating America: George Horace Lorimer and the* Saturday Evening Post. Pittsburgh: University of Pittsburgh Press, 1989.

Cott, Nancy F. *The Grounding of Modern Feminism.* New Haven: Yale University Press, 1987.

Damon-Moore, Helen. *Magazines for the Millions: Gender and Commerce in the* Ladies' Home Journal *and the* Saturday Evening Post, *1880–1910.* Albany: State University of New York Press, 1994.

Davis, Flora. *Moving the Mountain: The Women's Movement in America since 1960.* New York: Simon & Schuster, 1991.

D'Emilio, John, and Estelle B. Freedman. *Intimate Matters: A History of Sexuality in America.* New York: Harper & Row, 1988.

Douglas, Ann. *Terrible Honesty: Mongrel Manhattan in the 1920s.* New York: Farrar, Straus and Giroux, 1995.

Douglas, George H. *The Smart Magazines: 50 Years of Literary Revelry and High Jinks at* Vanity Fair, *the* New Yorker, Life, Esquire, *and the* Smart Set. Hamden, Conn.: Archon Books, 1991.

Douglas, Susan. *Where the Girls Are: Growing Up Female with the Mass Media.* New York: Times Books, 1994.

Dow, Bonnie J. *Prime-Time Feminism: Television, Media Culture, and the Women's Movement since 1970.* Philadelphia: University of Pennsylvania Press, 1996.

Dubbert, Joe L. *A Man's Place: Masculinity in Transition.* Englewood Cliffs, N.J.: Prentice-Hall, 1979.

Earnest, Ernest. *The American Eve in Fact and Fiction, 1775–1914.* Urbana and Chicago: University of Illinois Press, 1974.

Ewen, Stuart. *All Consuming Images: The Politics of Style in Contemporary Culture.* New York: Basic Books, 1988.

Faludi, Susan. *Backlash: The Undeclared War against American Women.* New York: Crown, 1991.

Filene, Peter G. *Him/Her/Self: Gender Identities in Modern America.* 3d ed. Baltimore: Johns Hopkins University Press, 1998.

Fishbein, Leslie. *Rebels in Bohemia: The Radicals of the* Masses, *1911–1917.* Chapel Hill: University of North Carolina Press, 1982.

Ford, Corey. *The Time of Laughter.* Boston: Little, Brown, 1967.

Friedan, Betty. *The Feminine Mystique.* New York: Norton, 1963.

Friedberg, Anne. *Window Shopping: Cinema and the Postmodern.* Berkeley: University of California Press, 1993.

Gaines, James R. *Wit's End: Days and Nights of the Algonquin Round Table.* New York: Harcourt Brace Jovanovich, 1977.

Gallagher, Brian. *Anything Goes: The Jazz Age Adventures of Neysa McMein and Her Extravagant Circle of Friends.* New York: Times Books, 1987.

Gamman, Lorraine, and Margaret Marshment, eds. *The Female Gaze: Women as Viewers of Popular Culture.* Seattle: Real Comet Press, 1989.

Garvey, Ellen Gruber. *The Adman in the Parlor: Magazines and the Gendering of Consumer Culture, 1880s to 1910s.* New York: Oxford University Press, 1996.

Gombrich, E. H. *Art and Illusion: A Study in the Psychology of Pictorial Representation.* Princeton: Princeton University Press, 1960.

Goodrum, Charles, and Helen Dalrymple. *Advertising in America: The First 200 Years.* New York: Harry N. Abrams, 1990.

Haskell, Molly. *From Reverence to Rape: The Treatment of Women in the Movies.* New York: Penguin, 1973.

Heller, Adele, and Lois Rudnick, eds. *1915, the Cultural Moment: The New Politics, the New Woman, the New Psychology, the New Art, and the New Theatre in America.* New Brunswick, N.J.: Rutgers University Press, 1991.

Higashi, Sumiko. *Virgins, Vamps, and Flappers: The American Silent Movie Heroine.* Brattleboro, Vt.: Eden Press Women's Publications, 1978.

Higham, John. *Writing American History: Essays on Modern Scholarship.* Bloomington: Indiana University Press, 1970.

Hoffman, Frederick J. *The Twenties: American Writing in the Postwar Decade.* Rev. ed. New York: Free Press, 1965.

Horowitz, Daniel. *The Morality of Spending: Attitudes toward the Consumer Society in America, 1875–1940.* Baltimore: Johns Hopkins University Press, 1985.

Isenberg, Michael T. *War on Film: The American Cinema and World War I.* Rutherford, Madison, and Teaneck, N.J.: Fairleigh Dickinson University Press, 1981.

Janello, Amy, and Brennon Jones. *The American Magazine.* New York: Harry N. Abrams, 1991.

Jasen, David A. *Tin Pan Alley: The Composers, the Songs, the Performers, and Their Times.* New York: Donald I. Fine, 1988.

Jowett, Garth. *Film: The Democratic Art.* Boston: Little, Brown, 1976.

Kaye, Ivan N. *Good Clean Violence: A History of College Football.*
    Philadelphia: Lippincott, 1973.
Kimmel, Michael. *Manhood in America: A Cultural History.* New York: Free
    Press, 1996.
Ladd-Taylor, Molly. *Mother-Work: Women, Child Welfare, and the State, 1890–
    1930.* Urbana: University of Illinois Press, 1994.
Leach, William. *Land of Desire: Merchants, Power, and the Rise of a New
    American Culture.* New York: Vintage Books, 1993.
Lears, T. J. Jackson. *Fables of Abundance: A Cultural History of Advertising in
    America.* New York: Basic Books, 1994.
Lemons, J. Stanley. *The Woman Citizen: Social Feminism in the 1920s.*
    Charlottesville: University Press of Virginia, 1990.
Loesser, Arthur. *Men, Women and Pianos.* New York: Simon & Schuster,
    1954.
Loughery, John. *John Sloan: Painter and Rebel.* New York: Henry Holt, 1995.
McCreadie, Marsha. *The American Movie Goddess.* New York: John Wiley,
    1973.
Marchand, Roland. *Advertising the American Dream: Making Way for
    Modernity, 1920–1940.* Berkeley: University of California Press, 1985.
Marsh, Margaret. *Suburban Lives.* New Brunswick, N.J.: Rutgers University
    Press, 1990.
Marsh, Margaret, and Wanda Ronner. *The Empty Cradle: Infertility in
    America from Colonial Times to the Present.* Baltimore: Johns Hopkins
    University Press, 1996.
May, Elaine Tyler. *Great Expectations: Marriage and Divorce in Post-Victorian
    America.* Chicago: University of Chicago Press, 1980.
Meyer, Susan E. *America's Great Illustrators.* New York: Harry N. Abrams,
    1978.
————. *James Montgomery Flagg.* New York: Pitman, 1974.
————. *Norman Rockwell's People.* New York: Harry N. Abrams, 1981.
Mills, C. Wright. *White Collar: The American Middle Classes.* New York:
    Oxford University Press, 1953.
Mitchell, W. J. T. *Iconology: Images, Text, Ideology.* Chicago and London:
    University of Chicago Press, 1986.
Mott, Frank Luther. *A History of American Magazines.* 5 vols. Cambridge,
    Mass.: Harvard University Press, 1957.
Mowry, George E., ed. *The Twenties: Fords, Flappers and Fanatics.*
    Englewood Cliffs, N.J.: Prentice-Hall, 1963.
Muncy, Robyn. *Creating a Female Dominion in American Reform, 1890–1935.*
    New York: Oxford University Press, 1991.
Nudelman, Edward D. *Jessie Willcox Smith: A Bibliography.* Gretna, La.:
    Pelican Publishing, 1989.
Ohmann, Richard. *Selling Culture: Magazines, Markets, and Class at the Turn
    of the Century.* London and New York: Verso, 1996.

O'Neill, William. *Echoes of Revolt: The* Masses, *1911–1917.* Chicago: Quadrangle Books, 1966.

Orvell, Miles. *After the Machine: Visual Arts and the Erasing of Cultural Boundaries.* Jackson: University Press of Mississippi, 1995.

———. *The Real Thing: Imitation and Authenticity in American Culture, 1880–1940.* Chapel Hill: University of North Carolina Press, 1989.

Panofsky, Erwin. *Meaning in the Visual Arts.* Garden City, N.Y.: Doubleday Anchor Books, 1955.

Peiss, Kathy. *Cheap Amusements: Working Women and Leisure in New York City, 1880 to 1920.* Philadelphia: Temple University Press, 1985.

Perlman, Bennard B. *Painters of the Ashcan School: The Immortal Eight.* New York: Dover, 1979.

Radway, Janice. *Reading the Romance.* Chapel Hill: University of North Carolina Press, 1984.

Reed, Walt. *Great American Illustrators.* New York: Abbeville, 1979.

———. *The Illustrator in America, 1900–1960s.* New York: Reinhold, 1966.

Reed, Walt, and Roger Reed. *The Illustrator in America, 1880–1980.* New York: Madison Square Press, 1984.

Riesman, David. *The Lonely Crowd: A Study of the Changing American Character.* New Haven: Yale University Press, 1950.

Rosen, Marjorie. *Popcorn Venus: Women, Movies and the American Dream.* New York: Coward, McCann & Geoghegan, 1973.

Rothman, Sheila M. *Woman's Proper Place: A History of Changing Ideals and Practices, 1870 to the Present.* New York: Basic Books, 1978.

Ryan, Mary P. *Womanhood in America: From Colonial Times to the Present.* New York: New Viewpoints, 1975.

Scanlon, Jennifer. *Inarticulate Longings: The* Ladies' Home Journal, *Gender, and the Promises of Consumer Culture.* London and New York: Routledge, 1995.

Schneirov, Matthew. *The Dream of a New Social Order: Popular Magazines in America, 1893–1914.* New York: Columbia University Press, 1994.

Schnessel, S. Michael. *Jessie Willcox Smith.* New York: Thomas Y. Crowell, 1977.

Schudson, Michael. *Advertising, the Uneasy Persuasion: Its Dubious Impact on American Society.* New York: Basic Books, 1984.

Scott, David W. *John Sloan.* New York: Watson-Guptill, 1975.

Sheppard, Alice. *Cartooning for Suffrage.* Albuquerque: University of New Mexico Press, 1994.

Smith-Rosenberg, Carroll. *Disorderly Conduct: Visions of Gender in Victorian America.* New York: Oxford University Press, 1985.

Solomon, Barbara Miller. *In the Company of Educated Women.* New Haven: Yale University Press, 1985.

Stevenson, Elizabeth. *Babbitts and Bohemians: The American 1920s.* New York: Macmillan, 1967.

Strasser, Susan. *Satisfaction Guaranteed: The Making of the American Mass Market*. Washington, D.C.: Smithsonian Institution Press, 1989.

Tebbel, John, and Mary Ellen Zuckerman. *The Magazine in America, 1741–1990*. New York: Oxford University Press, 1991.

Tickner, Lisa. *The Spectacle of Women: Imagery of the Suffrage Campaign, 1907–1914*. London: Chatto & Windus, 1987.

Walton, Donald. *A Rockwell Portrait: An Intimate Biography*. New York: Bantam, 1978.

Ware, Susan. *Still Missing: Amelia Earhart and the Search for Modern Feminism*. New York: Norton, 1993.

Warner, Marina. *Monuments and Maidens: The Allegory of the Female Form*. London: Weidenfeld and Nicolson, 1985.

Weatherford, Doris, ed. *American Women's History*. New York: Prentice Hall General Reference, 1994.

Welter, Barbara. *Dimity Convictions: The American Woman in the Nineteenth Century*. Athens: Ohio University Press, 1976.

Williams, Raymond. *The Long Revolution*. London: Chatto & Windus, 1961.

Wilson, Margaret Gibbons. *The American Woman in Transition: The Urban Influence, 1870–1920*. Westport, Conn.: Greenwood, 1979.

Wolf, Naomi. *Fire with Fire: The New Female Power and How It Will Change the 21st Century*. New York: Random House, 1993.

Zuckerman, Mary Ellen. *A History of Popular Women's Magazines in the United States, 1792–1995*. Westport, Conn.: Greenwood, 1998.

Zurier, Rebecca. *Art for the Masses: A Radical Magazine and Its Graphics, 1911–1917*. Philadelphia: Temple University Press, 1988.

Zurier, Rebecca, Robert W. Snyder, and Virginia M. Mecklenburg, eds. *Metropolitan Lives: The Ashcan Artists and Their New York*. New York: Norton, 1995.

Articles, Essays, and Magazine Special Issues

Banta, Martha. "They Shall Have Faces, Minds, and (One Day) Flesh: Women in Late Nineteenth-Century and Early Twentieth-Century American Literature." In *What Manner of Woman: Essays on English and American Life and Literature*, edited by Marlene Springer, 235–70. New York: New York University Press, 1977.

Bellfante, Ginia. "Feminism: It's All about Me!" *Time*, June 29, 1998, 54–60.

Best, Gary A. "Charles Dana Gibson." *Bulletin of Bibliography* 41, no. 1 (Mar. 1984): 12–18.

Bonard, Carolyn Ann. "The Women's Movement in the 1920s: American Magazines Document the Health and Progress of Feminism." In *The American Magazine: Research Perspectives and Prospects*, edited by David Abrahamson, 231–40. Ames: Iowa State University Press, 1995.

Bronner, Simon J. "Reading Consumer Culture." In *Consuming Visions: Accumulation and Display of Goods in America, 1880–1920*, edited by Simon J. Bronner, 13–53. New York: Norton, 1989.

Brown, Michael. "The Popular Art of American Magazine Illustration, 1885–1917." *Journalism History* 24, no. 3 (Autumn 1998): 95–103.

Cheever, Susan. "Twiggy: A Stick Figure." *New York Times Magazine* (*Special Issue. Heroine Worship: Inventing an Identity in the Age of Female Icons*), Nov. 24, 1996, 74.

Cook, Blanche Wiesen. "Female Support Networks and Political Activism: Lillian Wald, Crystal Eastman, Emma Goldman." *Chrysalis* 3 (1977): 43–61.

Cott, Nancy F. Introduction. In *Root of Bitterness: Documents of the Social History of American Women*, edited by Nancy F. Cott, 3–28. New York: E. P. Dutton, 1972.

Covert, Catherine L. "Journalism History and Women's Experience: A Problem in Conceptual Change." *Journalism History* 8, no. 1 (Spring 1981): 2–6.

Cowan, Ruth Schwartz. "Two Washes in the Morning and a Bridge Party at Night: The American Housewife between the Wars." In *Decades of Discontent: The Women's Movement, 1920–1940*, edited by Lois Scharf and Joan M. Jensen, 177–96. Westport, Conn.: Greenwood, 1983.

Cowley, Malcolm. "Memoranda of a Decade." *American Heritage*, Aug. 1965, 33–40.

Dubbert, Joe L. "Progressivism and the Masculinity Crisis." In *The American Man*, edited by Elizabeth H. Pleck and Joseph H. Pleck, 303–20. Englewood Cliffs, N.J.: Prentice-Hall, 1980.

Dye, Nancy Schrom. "Creating a Feminist Alliance: Sisterhood and Class Conflict in the New York Women's Trade Union League, 1903–1914." In *Our American Sisters: Women in American Life and Thought*, 4th ed., edited by Jean E. Friedman, William G. Shade, and Mary Jane Capozzoli, 341–58. Lexington, Mass.: D. C. Heath, 1987.

Erenberg, Lewis A. "Everybody's Doin' It: The Pre–World War I Dance Craze, the Castles, and the Modern American Girl." *Feminist Studies* 3, nos. 1/2 (Fall 1975): 155–70.

Erens, Patricia. "The Flapper: Hollywood's First Liberated Woman." In *Dancing Fools and Weary Blues: The Great Escape of the Twenties*, edited by Lawrence R. Broer and John D. Walther, 130–39. Bowling Green, Ohio: Bowling Green State University Popular Press, 1990.

Fishbein, Leslie. "The Failure of Feminism in Greenwich Village before World War I." *Women's Studies* 9 (1982): 275–89.

Fleming, E. McClung. "The American Image as Indian Princess, 1765–1783." *Winterthur Portfolio* 2 (1965): 65–81.

———. "From Indian Princess to Greek Goddess: The American Image, 1783–1815." *Winterthur Portfolio* 3 (1966): 37–66.

Geraghty, Christine. "Feminism and Media Consumption." In *Cultural Studies and Communications*, edited by James Curran, David Morley, and Valerie Walkerdine, 306–22. London: Arnold, 1996.

Gibbs, Nancy. "The War against Feminism." *Time*, Mar. 9, 1992, 50–55.

Gordon, Linda. "Birth Control and Social Revolution." In *A Heritage of Her Own: Toward a New Social History of American Women,* edited by Nancy F. Cott and Elizabeth H. Pleck, 445–75. New York: Simon & Schuster, 1979.

Gordon, Lynn D. "The Gibson Girl Goes to College: Popular Culture and Women's Higher Education in the Progressive Era, 1890–1920." *American Quarterly* 39, no. 2 (Summer 1987): 211–30.

Grant, Thomas. "*Judge.*" In *American Humor Magazines and Comic Periodicals,* edited by David E. E. Sloan, 111–20. Westport, Conn.: Greenwood, 1987.

Griffen, Clyde. "Reconstructing Masculinity from the Evangelical Revival to the Waning of Progressivism: A Speculative Synthesis." In *Meanings for Manhood: Constructions of Masculinity in Victorian America,* edited by Mark C. Carnes and Clyde Griffen, 183–204. Chicago: University of Chicago Press, 1990.

Hantover, Jeffrey P. "The Boy Scouts and the Validation of Masculinity." In *The American Man,* edited by Elizabeth H. Pleck and Joseph H. Pleck, 285–301. Englewood Cliffs, N.J.: Prentice-Hall, 1980.

Hawkins, Margaret A., and Thomas K. Nakayama. "Discourse on Women's Bodies: Advertising in the 1920s." In *Constructing and Reconstructing Gender: The Links among Communication, Language, and Gender,* edited by Linda A. M. Perry, Lynn H. Turner, and Helen M. Sterk, 61–71. Albany: State University of New York Press, 1992.

Hills, Patricia. "John Sloan's Images of Working-Class Women." *Prospects: An Annual of American Cultural Studies* 5 (1980): 156–96.

Hynes, Terry. "Magazine Portrayal of Women, 1911–1930." *Journalism Monographs,* no. 72 (May 1981).

Johnson, Charles S. "The Rise of the Negro Magazine." *Journal of Negro History* 13, no. 1 (Jan. 1928): 7–21.

Johnston, Patricia C. "Coles Phillips' 'Fade Away Girls.'" *American History Illustrated* 16, no. 6 (1981): 29–33.

Kimmel, Michael S. "The Contemporary 'Crisis' of Masculinity in Historical Perspective." In *The Making of Masculinities: The New Men's Studies,* edited by Harry Brod, 121–53. Boston: Allen & Unwin, 1987.

Kinser, Suzanne L. "Prostitutes in the Art of John Sloan." *Prospects* 9 (1984): 231–54.

Kitch, Carolyn. "Changing Theoretical Perspectives on Women's Media Images: The Emergence of Patterns in a New Area of Historical Scholarship." *Journalism & Mass Communication Quarterly* 74, no. 3 (Autumn 1997): 477–89.

Kuczynski, Alex. "That Girl, All Grown Up." *New York Times,* Feb. 24, 1998.

Labi, Nadya. "Girl Power." *Time,* June 29, 1998, 60–62.

Lears, T. J. Jackson. "From Salvation to Self-Realization: Advertising and the Therapeutic Roots of the Consumer Culture, 1880–1930." In *The*

Culture of Consumption: Critical Essays in American History, 1880–1980,
edited by Richard Wightman Fox and T. J. Jackson Lears, 1–38. New
York: Pantheon, 1983.

Lee, Janet. "Care to Join Me in an Upwardly Mobile Tango? Postmodernism
and the 'New Woman.'" In *The Female Gaze: Women as Viewers of Popular
Culture,* edited by Lorraine Gamman and Margaret Marshment, 166–72.
Seattle: Real Comet Press, 1989.

Likos, Patricia. "The Ladies of the Red Rose." *Feminist Art Journal* 5 (Fall
1976): 11–15, 43.

"Looking Back, January 1925: Our Covers Capture a Woman's Life."
McCall's, Jan. 1995, 10.

McClintock, Anne. "Soft-Soaping Empire: Commodity Racism and Imperial
Advertising." In *Travelers' Tales: Narratives of Home and Displacement,*
edited by George Robertson et al., 131–54. London: Routledge, 1994.

McGovern, James R. "The American Woman's Pre–World War I Freedom in
Manners and Morals." *Journal of American History* 55, no. 2 (Sept. 1968):
315–33.

Martin, Richard. "The Great War and the Great Image: J. C. Leyendecker's
World War I Covers for the *Saturday Evening Post.*" *Journal of American
Culture* 20, no. 1 (Spring 1997): 55–74.

Marzolf, Marion. "American Studies—Ideas for Media Historians."
Journalism History 5, no. 1 (Spring 1978): 1, 13–16.

Mazur, Allan. "U.S. Trends in Feminine Beauty and Overadaptation."
Journal of Sex Research 22, no. 3 (Aug. 1986): 281–303.

Meyerowitz, Joanne. "Beyond the Feminine Mystique: A Reassessment of
Postwar Mass Culture, 1946–1958." *Journal of American History* 79, no. 4
(Mar. 1993): 1455–82.

Meyers, John A. "A Letter from the Publisher." *Time,* Feb. 22, 1982, 3.

Moffat, Laurie Norton. "Norman Rockwell: Illustrator of America's
Heritage." *American History Illustrated* 21, no. 8 (1986): 24–33.

Moore, Sarah J. "Making a Spectacle of Suffrage: The National Woman
Suffrage Pageant, 1913." *Journal of American Culture* 20, no. 1 (Spring
1997): 89–103.

Mrozek, Donald J. "Sport in American Life: From National Health to
Personal Fulfillment, 1890–1940." In *Fitness in American Culture: Images
of Health, Sport, and the Body, 1830–1940,* edited by Kathryn Grover,
18–46. Amherst: University of Massachusetts Press, 1989.

Mulvey, Laura. "Visual Pleasure and Narrative Cinema." *Screen* 16 (1975):
6–18.

Patterson, Martha. "'Survival of the Best Fitted': Selling the American New
Woman as Gibson Girl, 1895–1910." *ATQ* 9, no. 1 (Mar. 1995): 73–87.

Pendergast, Tom. "'Horatio Alger Doesn't Work Here Any More':
Masculinity and American Magazines, 1919–1940." *American Studies* 38,
no. 1 (Spring 1997): 55–80.

Perkins, Teresa E. "Rethinking Stereotypes." In *Ideology and Cultural*

Production, edited by Michèle Barrett, Philip Corrigan, Annette Kuhn, and Janet Wolff, 135–59. New York: St. Martin's, 1979.

Perry, Elisabeth I. "'The General Motherhood of the Commonwealth': Dance Hall Reform in the Progressive Era." *American Quarterly* 37, no. 5 (Winter 1985): 719–35.

Pitz, Henry C. "Charles Dana Gibson: Creator of a Mode." *American Artists* 20 (Dec. 1956): 50–55.

———. "Charles Dana Gibson: Delineator of an Age." In *The Gibson Girl and Her America*, edited by Edmund Vincent Gillon, vii–xi. New York: Dover, 1969.

Platt, Frederick. "The Gibson Girl." *Art & Antiques* 4, no. 6 (1981): 112–17.

Pumphrey, Martin. "The Flapper, the Housewife and the Making of Modernity." *Cultural Studies* 1 (May 1987): 179–94.

Rapp, Rayna, and Ellen Ross. "The Twenties' Backlash: Compulsory Heterosexuality, the Consumer Family, and the Waning of Feminism." In *Class, Race, and Sex: The Dynamics of Control*, edited by Amy Swerdlow and Hanna Lessinger, 93–107. Boston: G. K. Hall, 1983.

Reed, J. D. "The New Baby Bloom." *Time*, Feb. 22, 1982, 52–58.

Ricapito, Maria. "'Girl' Makes a Comeback, Even on Madison Avenue." *Chicago Tribune*, Jan. 18, 1998.

Ryan, Mary P. "The Projection of a New Womanhood: The Movie Moderns in the 1920's." In *Decades of Discontent: The Women's Movement, 1920–1940*, edited by Lois Scharf and Joan M. Jensen, 113–30. Westport, Conn.: Greenwood, 1983.

Segal, Eric J. "Norman Rockwell and the Fashioning of American Masculinity." *Art Bulletin* 78, no. 4 (1996): 633–46.

Shuttlesworth, Jack. "John Held, Jr. and His World." *American Heritage*, Aug. 1965, 29–32.

Siple, Walter H. "The Gibson Girl Admits to 75: The Artist Celebrates His Birthday at the Cincinnati Museum." *ARTnews* 41, no. 18 (Oct. 1–14, 1942): 14–15, 32, 34.

Sklar, Kathryn Kish. "The Historical Foundations of Women's Power in the Creation of the American Welfare State, 1830–1930." In *Mothers of a New World: Maternalist Politics and the Origins of Welfare States*, edited by Seth Koven and Sonya Michel, 43–93. New York and London: Routledge, 1993.

Sloan, David E. E. "*Life.*" In *American Humor Magazines and Comic Periodicals*, edited by David E. E. Sloan, 141–53. Westport, Conn.: Greenwood, 1987.

Sloan, Kay. "Sexual Warfare in the Silent Cinema: Comedies and Melodramas of Woman Suffragism." *American Quarterly* 33, no. 4 (Fall 1981): 412–36.

Stevenson, Elizabeth. "Flappers and Some Who Were Not Flappers." In *Dancing Fools and Weary Blues: The Great Escape of the Twenties*, edited by Lawrence R. Broer and John D. Walther, 120–29. Bowling Green, Ohio: Bowling Green State University Popular Press, 1990.

Tavris, Carol. "Goodbye to Momism." *New York Times Book Review*, May 3, 1998, 16.

Time. Special Issue: "The American Woman." Mar. 20, 1972.

Time. Special Issue: "The Road Ahead." 1989 [no month and day].

Time. Special Issue: "Women of the Year." Jan. 5, 1976.

Tuchman, Gaye. "Introduction: The Symbolic Annihilation of Women by the Mass Media." In *Hearth and Home: Images of Women in the Mass Media*, edited by Gaye Tuchman, Arlene Kaplan Daniels, and James Benét, 3–38. New York: Oxford University Press, 1978.

Vanek, Joann. "Time Spent in Housework." In *A Heritage of Her Own: Toward a New Social History of American Women*, edited by Nancy F. Cott and Elizabeth H. Pleck, 499–506. New York: Simon & Schuster, 1979.

Wallis, Claudia. "Onward, Women!" *Time*, Dec. 4, 1989, 80–89.

Waters, Harry F., and Janet Huck. "Networking Women." *Newsweek*, Mar. 13, 1989, 48–54.

———. "Shedding a Glacial Identity." *Newsweek*, Mar. 13, 1989, 55.

Weinhardt, Carl J. "Introduction: The Rise of the Mormon Kid." In *The Most of John Held, Jr.*, 12–19. Brattleboro, Vt.: Stephen Greene, 1972.

Williamson, Judith. "Decoding Advertisements." In *Looking On: Images of Femininity in the Visual Arts and Media*, edited by Rosemary Betterton, 49–52. London: Pandora Press, 1987.

Yellis, Kenneth A. "Prosperity's Child: Some Thoughts on the Flapper." *American Quarterly* 21 (Spring 1969): 44–64.

Zuckerman, Mary Ellen. "*McCall's*." In *Women's Periodicals in the United States*, edited by Kathleen L. Endres and Therese L. Lueck, 218–25. Westport, Conn.: Greenwood, 1995.

Dissertations and Theses

Bathrick, Serafina Kent. "The True Woman and the Family-Film: The Industrial Production of Memory." Ph.D. diss., University of Wisconsin–Madison, 1981.

Clifford, Marie. "Drawing on Women: Representations of Women and Suffrage Imagery in *The Masses*, 1913–1917." M.A. thesis, University of Alberta, 1991.

Coco, Janice Marie. "John Sloan and the Female Subject." Ph.D. diss., Cornell University, 1993.

Klein, Vera McHenry. "Charles Dana Gibson: A Study of an Artist as Social Historian." M.A. thesis, California State University, Northridge, 1978.

Ward, Douglas B. "Tracking the Culture of Consumption: Curtis Publishing Company, Charles Coolidge Parlin, and the Origins of Market Research, 1911–1930." Ph.D. diss., University of Maryland, 1996.

White, Kevin Francis. "The Flapper's Boyfriend: The Revolution in Morals and the Emergence of Modern American Male Sexuality, 1910–1930." Ph.D. diss., Ohio State University, 1990.

Index

Italic page numbers refer to illustrations.

Abbey, Edwin Austin, 39
Advertising: and femininity, 1, 181; and mass media, 4, 7; and Smith, 6, 16, 144, 160, 169; and Leyendecker, 6, 16, 160, 161–63, 166; and Phillips, 6, 16, 160, 163, 166–67; and Gibson Girl, 6, 41; and New Woman, 13, 179, 184–85; and Rockwell, 16, 160, 161, 162, 173; and McMein, 16, 160, 177, 179, 217 (n. 27); and editorial content, 16, 161, 172, 179, 181; and magazine covers, 16, 177, 181; and *Ladies' Home Journal*, 20, 22, 28, 99, 169, 177; and music, 24, 150; and class status, 28, 162–63; and outdoor settings, 31; and upward mobility, 58, 181; and alternative magazines, 82; and African Americans, 99; and World War I, 102; and flapper, 122, 132–33; and children, 144, 160; and aging, 145, 214 (n. 38); and *Saturday Evening Post*, 150, 151, 162, 176, 183; and businessmen, 158–59, 162, 163, 216 (n. 13); and Flagg, 161, 216 (n. 13); and clothing, 162, 166, 176–77, 179, 218 (n. 30); and sexuality, 166; and motherhood, 169, 176; and race, 172, 176; and housework, 172–73; and television, 186; and feminism, 189
African Americans, 59, 72, 75, 92–93, 95, 99, 148, 207 (n. 45); female, 9, 15, 93
American Boy, 150
American Farm and Fireside, 150
American Magazine, 61, 150

Americanness, 4, 40, 148, 182, 191
Anthony, Susan B., 1
Ashmore, Ruth, 18, 24, 26, 35–36
Athletics: and crisis of masculinity, 11; and Fisher Girl, 14, 48, 51; and women's imagery, 14, 48, 54, 138; and masculinity, 14, 70, 72; and Gibson Girl, 39, 44; and *Good Housekeeping*, 53; and working-class women, 88
Atlantic Monthly, 44
Ayer, N. W., 133

Bankhead, Tallulah, 137
Banner, Lois, 40, 130
Banta, Martha, 7, 48, 107, 113
Bara, Theda, 60, 202 (n. 20)
Barrymore, Ethel, 138
Barrymore, John, 61, 163
Batchelor, C. D., 77, 78, *79, 81*
Bathrick, Serafina, 61
Berger, John, 26
Berlin, Irving, 5, 101, 137
Birth control, 9, 11, 86, 87, 143, 184, 206 (n. 28), 218 (n. 5)
Blackwell, Lucy Stone, 76, 205 (n. 7)
Blair, Karen, 20
Bok, Edward, 18, 20, 24, 31–32, 34, 35, 44, 48, 172
Bow, Clara, 131
Boy Scouts of America, 11, 70, 72, 104, 154, 217 (n. 23)
Boy's Life, 150
Brice, Fanny, 137
Brokaw, Tom, 190
Businessmen: and and masculinity, 10, 11, 14, 69, 159; and *Saturday Evening Post*, 150; and Rockwell,

154, 158; and advertising, 158–59, 162, 163, 216 (n. 13)

Call, 87
Castle, Irene, 59, 138
Castle, Vernon, 59
Century, 19, 39, 69, 144
Chaplin, Charlie, 67, 137
Chase, William Merritt, 39
Cheever, Susan, 185–86
Children: and family, 15, 136, 137, 143–44, 148, 150, 212 (n. 5); and Good Housekeeping, 15, 143, 144, 150, 160–61, 184; and Smith, 15–16, 144, 145, 148, 150, 160–61, 169, 179, 182; and suffrage movement, 80, 82; and Masses, 86; and consumption, 136, 172; and McMein, 140; and Rockwell, 150, 151–52, 173–74, 176; and New Woman, 183
Children's Aid Society, 10
Christy, Howard Chandler: and advertising, 6; and women's imagery, 14, 29; style of, 44, 45–46, 51; earnings of, 45; philosophies on young women, 45–46, 48, 53, 200–201 (n. 38); "Our Girl Graduate," 48, 51; "The Soldier's Dream," 48, 51; Motor, 52; and education, 93, 123; and war posters, 103, 107, 113; "Fight or Buy Bonds," 107, 110, 112; "Your Angel of Mercy," 107, 111, 112; "Gee!!! I Wish I Were a Man," 113, 114; "I Want You for the Navy," 115
Christy Girl, 6, 14, 48, 51, 63, 78, 93, 99, 113, 117
City life, 11, 35, 55, 59
Class status: and media imagery, 4; and suffrage movement, 9, 80; and New Woman, 13, 185; and women's imagery, 26, 28; and advertising, 28, 162–63; and outdoor settings, 31; and department

stores, 34, 35; and womanhood, 36, 58; and Gibson Girl, 39–40; and Fisher Girl, 46; and gender, 58; and dance craze, 59; and Masses, 83, 88, 92; and Sloan, 87, 88; and war posters, 104; and flapper, 131; and Lorimer, 150; changes in, 182, 183–84; and feminism, 188; history of, 192. See also Upward mobility
Clothing: and editorial content, 7; and flapper, 12, 122, 132, 133, 183; and Ladies' Home Journal, 18; and outdoor settings, 31; and Gibson Girl, 39, 41; and men's imagery, 40, 159; and Fisher Girl, 46; and Christy Girl, 48, 51; and physical fitness, 53; and dance craze, 59; and vamps, 61; and fashion reform, 86; and African Americans, 95; and war posters, 107, 112, 113, 117; and McCall's, 137; and advertising, 162, 166, 176–77, 179, 218 (n. 30); and class status, 163
Cluett, Peabody & Company, 162
Cohan, George M., 137
Cohn, Jan, 154
Collier's, 5, 6, 13, 39, 40, 41, 63, 69, 144, 150
Committee on Public Information, 102
Congressional Union, 76
Consumption: and magazines, 4, 18; and women, 8, 12; and masculinity, 11, 159; and New Woman, 13, 182, 183, 185; and upward mobility, 28; and department stores, 32, 34, 198 (n. 38); and flapper, 133, 135; and children, 136, 172; and motherhood, 172; and thrift, 177, 217 (n. 26)
Cosmopolitan: and advertising, 4; and Fisher Girl, 14, 46; and Stephens, 19; and Gibson Girl, 39; readership of, 46, 82, 200 (n.

32); and Christy Girl, 48; editorial content of, 54; and Flagg, 62; and literature, 75; and flapper, 121
Cott, Nancy, 10
Country Gentleman, 150
Covert, Catherine, 16, 191
Cowan, Ruth Schwartz, 11
Coward, Noël, 137
Creel, George, 102
Crisis, 15, 92, 93, *94*, 95, *96*, *97*, *98*, 99, 100
Culture, American: and women's imagery, 6–7, 194 (n. 28); and immigrants, 7, 10, 75; feminiza-tion of, 14; and Gibson Girl, 41; and stereotypes, 92; and African Americans, 95; and flapper, 128; and mass media, 191–92. *See also* Middle-class: culture of
Curtis, Cyrus, 150
Curtis Publishing Company, 148

Dance craze, 59–60, 63
Dangerous women: as vamps, 14, 56, 60–61, 70, 95, 99, 107, 121, 126; and Fadeaway Girls, 14, 64–67; as playful women, 56, 58, 60, 121; and dance craze, 59–60, 63
Davis, Flora, 188
Davis, Richard Harding, 40, 41
Davis, Stuart, 83; "Gee, Mag, Think of Us Bein' on a Magazine Cover!," 85, *85*
Day, Doris, 185
Debs, Eugene V., 82
Delineator, 59
Dell, Floyd, 82, 86
Department stores, 32, 34, 198 (n. 38)
Dix, Dorothy, 14
Douglas, Ann, 130
Douglas, Susan, 186, 187
Douglass, Frederick, 93
Dow, Bonnie, 186, 187, 188, 189
Downey, Fairfax, 37, 107, 122

Downward mobility, 8, 58
Dressler, Marie, 103
Dubbert, Joe, 10, 68–69, 72, 176
Du Bois, W. E. B., 92, 93

Eakins, Thomas, 18
Earnest, Ernest, 39
Eastman, Max, 82, 86, 206 (n. 19)
Education: and women's status, 8; and crisis of masculinity, 10; and female schoolteachers, 11, 195 (n. 46); and Christy Girl, 14, 48, 51, 93; and Fisher Girl, 14, 48, 54–55, 93, 138; and women's imagery, 24, 26, 29, 44, 53, 54, 123; and same-sex friendships, 51, 53; and dance craze, 60; and men's imagery, 72; and *Crisis*, 93, 95; and McMein, 138, 140; and *Good Housekeeping*, 140, 143
Equal Rights, 76
Equal Rights Amendment, 1, 188
Erens, Patricia, 121
Esquire, 185
Eugenics, 40, 72, 215 (n. 47)

Fadeaway Girls, 6, 14, 64–67, 112, 163, 166, 203 (n. 31)
Faludi, Susan, 2, 12, 187, 190
Family: middle-class, 4, 8, 16, 22, 136, 137, 143, 148, 182, 190; ideal of, 11, 136, 184, 190; and women's status, 12; and children, 15, 136, 137, 143–44, 148, 150, 212 (n. 5); and womanhood, 15, 182; and masculinity, 16, 120; vamps as outside of, 61; and gender roles, 117, 119; and Rockwell, 117, 137, 151, 159, 167, 169; working-class, 143, 213 (n. 28); and *Saturday Evening Post*, 150, 159, 176; and Phillips, 166; and Smith, 169
Female gaze, 26, 54, 145, 197 (n. 22)
Feminine mystique, 11
Femininity: and advertising, 1, 181;

and media imagery, 4; ideal types
of, 6; changing ideas about, 11;
and flapper, 12; and music, 22, 24;
and outdoor settings, 31; and suffrage movement, 76; and magazine covers, 86; and World War I,
102, 107; and family, 120; and
McMein, 140; and Leyendecker,
163; and television, 188

Feminism: and popular culture
imagery, 1, 2, 3, 191; and *Time*,
1–3, 11, 12, 188, 189; viability
of, 1–4, 11–12, 189; and mass
media, 2, 3–4, 12, 191; early use
of term, 9; and socialism, 9, 86,
90; and sexuality, 12, 86, 87, 206
(n. 26); representational parallels, 16, 184; and Gibson Girl, 43,
44; and vamps, 60; and Jews, 75;
and *Masses*, 86, 90; as political
force, 100; and war posters, 102;
and editorial content, 183; and
motherhood, 183, 187, 219 (n. 21);
and media imagery, 184, 189, 220
(n. 29); and television, 187, 188,
189. *See also* Women: movement
for rights of
Filene, Peter, 10, 72
Fischer, Anton Otto: "The Cheapest
Commodity on the Market," 82
Fishbein, Leslie, 86
Fisher, Harrison: and women's
imagery, 14, 29, 46; and *Saturday
Evening Post*, 14, 46, *47*, 53–54;
and *Ladies' Home Journal*, 14, 46,
48, *49, 50*, 54–55, 138; and education, 14, 54–55, 93, 123, 138; style
of, 44, 46, 48, 51; earnings of, 45;
"I Summon You to Comradeship
in the Red Cross," 107, *108*
Fisher Girl, 14, 46, 48, 54–55, 63, 83,
93, 95, 138
Fitzgerald, F. Scott, 121, 123, 133,
137
Flagg, James Montgomery: style of,

5, 62–63; and vamps, 14, 60, 61,
95, 107; "Sweet Girl Graduate,"
56, *57*; and women's imagery,
56, 103, 122; earnings of, 61; and
movies, 61, 62, 202 (n. 26); and
Life, 61, 63, *64*; "Passed by the
Board of Censorship," 62, *62*;
Flagg Girl, 62, 63, 122, 151; and
Good Housekeeping, 62, 203 (n.
30); "Has This Ever Happened
to You?," 63, *64*; "I Want You
for U.S. Army," 103–4, 209 (n.
14); "Together We Win," 104,
104; "Vive La France!," *109*; and
advertising, 161, 216 (n. 13)
Flapper: and New Woman, 12, 122,
130–31, 132, 135, 183; and clothing, 12, 122, 132, 133, 183; and
sexuality, 15, 121, 122, 124, 130,
131, 132; and Held, 15, 121–33,
135, 151, 185; and Christy Girl,
51; and African Americans, 99;
and marriage, 120, 131, 132, 135,
211–12 (n. 2); and men's imagery,
122, 123, 125–28, 130–32; and
Gibson Girl, 122, 128, 130, 186;
proportions of, 128–30, 210 (n. 14);
and motherhood, 135, 159, 188;
Twiggy compared to, 185–86; and
television characters, 188
Foringer, Alonzo Earl: "The Greatest Mother in the World," 117,
118
Freud, Sigmund, 8–9, 14, 55, 67, 86,
204 (n. 55), 206 (n. 26)
Friedan, Betty, 1, 186
Friedberg, Anne, 32

Gallagher, Brian, 138, 177
Gender and gender roles: and men's
imagery, 4; and New Woman,
11, 29, 32; sex-role reversal
imagery, 14; and "The American
Woman" series, 17–18, 29, 36; and
Stephens, 36; and Gibson Girl, 41,

43; shifts in, 54, 182; in society, 54–55; and class status, 58; and crisis of masculinity, 68, 191; and *Masses*, 83, 88; and Sloan, 87; and World War I, 102, 117; and war posters, 113; and family, 117, 119; and flapper, 131; and advertising, 172; and television, 186

General Federation of Women's Clubs, 10

Gibson, Charles Dana: and *Life*, 5, 29, 37, 41, *45*, 107, 121, *129*; style of, 5, 37, 39, 70, 95, 122; earnings of, 5, 45, 196 (n. 12); and women's imagery, 13, 29, 113, 122; and World War I, 15; "Mr. Gibson's American Girl," 37, *38*; and men's imagery, 40, 44, 67; "The Eternal Question," 41, *42*; "Summer Sports," 43; "The Weaker Sex," 43, *43*; and bathing beauties, 44; dissociation from Gibson Girl, 44, 199–200 (n. 24); "The Turning of the Tide," *45*; and war posters, 102, 103, 107, 113, 208–9 (n. 7); and flapper, 121–22; "Thirty Years of Progress, 1896–1926," *129*

Gibson, Mrs. Charles Dana, 143

Gibson Girl: and *Life*, 6, 13, 29, 37, 41, 43, 107, 128, 199 (n. 16); and advertising, 6, 41; and upward mobility, 13, 41, 199 (n. 13); imitations of, 14; and *Ladies' Home Journal*, 37, 39, 44; as type, 37, 39; and class status, 39–40; meaning of, 43–44; and city life, 55; and ideal dancing body, 59; and Flagg Girl, 63; and suffrage movement, 78; and race, 99; and flapper, 122, 128, 130, 186; as cultural icon, 191

Gibson Man, 40, 44

Gilman, Charlotte Perkins, 44

Gish, Lillian, 61, 101, 202 (n. 20)

Godey's Lady's Book, 18

Goldman, Emma, 86, 87

Gombrich, Ernst, 8

Good Housekeeping: and Smith, 5, 6, 137, 144, 145, *146*, *147*, 148, *149*, 150, 160–61, 169, 203 (n. 30); and feminism, 9; and children, 15, 143, 144, 150, 160–61, 184; and Gibson Girl, 39; and athletics, 53; and Flagg, 62, 203 (n. 30); and Phillips, 63, 66, 163, 203 (n. 30); editorial content of, 70, 137, 143; readership of, 102, 144; and World War I, 117; and education, 140, 143; and politics, 143, 213 (n. 25); and suffrage movement, 143, 213 (n. 24)

Gordon, Linda, 87

Gordon, Lynn D., 53

Great Depression, 185

Hairstyles: and Gibson Girl, 13, 37, 39, 41; and *Ladies' Home Journal*, 18; and Fisher Girl, 46; and Christy Girl, 51; and flapper, 51, 122, 123, 133; and dance craze, 59; and suffrage movement, 78; and African Americans, 95; and McMein, 138

Hantover, Jeffrey, 70

Harper's Weekly, 7, 19, 39, 48, 61–62, 86, 184,

Hart, William S., 61

Haskell, Molly, 67, 131

Hawkins, Margaret, 132

Hayes, Helen, 137

Hayworth, Rita, 185

Held, John, Jr.: and *Life*, 15, 121–28, *124*, *125*, *126*, *127*, *129*, 132, *134*, 135, 185; and flapper, 15, 121–33, 135, 151, 185; and World War I, 102; "The Girl Who Gave Him the Cold Shoulder," 123; "The Laughing Stock," 123; "Where the Blue Begins," 123; "The Sweet Girl Graduate," 123, *124*; "Hold

'Em," 123, *125*; "A Heavy Date," 123–24; "Sitting Pretty," 124–25, *126*; "She Missed the Boat," 125; "Teaching Old Dogs New Tricks," 127, *127*; style of, 129–30; "Thirty Years of Progress, 1896–1926," *129*

Henle, James, 87

Higashi, Sumiko, 128

Higham, John, 14

Hitler, Adolf, 103

Homosexuality, 204 (n. 55)

Hooper, Ruth, 130

Hope, Anthony, 43–44

Horowitz, Daniel, 177

Housework: and editorial content, 7; as professional, 11; and New Woman, 13, 184; and upward mobility, 28; and McMein, 140; and advertising, 172–73

Iconology, 8, 16, 76, 99, 191–92

Illustrations: engraving process, 4, 193 (n. 13); and magazine covers, 5, 7; and dance craze, 59; and World War I, 102; and advertising, 160; photography compared to, 169

Illustrators: styles of, 5, 137, 182; and advertising, 6, 16, 160–61, 181; and war posters, 15, 102, 208–9 (n. 7); and types, 44–45, 181; and education, 53; and full-length portraits, 60; and suffrage movement, 76, 78, 204–5 (n. 4); and family, 136–37. *See also* names of specific illustrators

Immigrants and immigration: and American culture, 7, 10, 75; and New Woman, 8, 32; and race suicide, 14, 40; and women's imagery, 15, 83; and working women, 34; and city life, 55; and Progressive Era reformers, 58, 201 (n. 8); and athletics, 72; and suffrage movement, 82; and public life, 88; and magazines, 148; and marriage, 212 (n. 4)

Independent Woman, 183

Jews, 22, 75, 148

Johnson, Charles, 92

Johnson, Owen, 63

Judge, 14, 56, *57*, 58, 61, *62*, 63, 121, 123, 150

Keaton, Buster, 67

Kery, Patricia Frantz, 56

Kimmel, Michael, 6, 154

Kinser, Suzanne, 90

Kipling, Rudyard, 60

Ku Klux Klan, 100

Ladies' Home Journal: readership of, 4, 17, 18, 46, 56, 102, 200 (n. 32); and Stephens, 5, 13, 17, 19–36, *21*, *23*, *25*, *27*, *30*, *32*, 37; "The American Woman" series, 13, 17, 19–36, 37; and Fisher, 14, 46, 48, *49*, *50*, 54–55, 138; editorial content of, 18, 20, 22, 24, 28, 29, 31–32, 35, 48, 137, 160, 183; and religion, 20, 22; and advertising, 20, 22, 28, 99, 169, 177; and motherhood, 22, 24; and outdoor settings, 29, 31–32; and department stores, 34–35; and Gibson, 37, *38*; and Gibson Girl, 37, 39, 44; and Phillips, 63; and Smith, 144, 169; and race, 148

Ladies' World, 137

Langhorne, Irene, 39

Lears, T. J. Jackson, 13, 53

Lee, Janet, 184–85

Leslie's Weekly, 19, 39, 48, 62, 104, 150

Lewis, Sinclair, 61

Leyendecker, J. C.: and manhood, 6, 14, 16, 70; and advertising, 6, 16, 160, 161–63, 166; and *Saturday Evening Post*, 6, 69, 70, *71*, 72,

73, 161, 204 (n. 43); and magazine covers, 69–70, 204 (n. 43); and men's imagery, 70, 72, 151, 182, 204 (n. 55); style of, 70, 205 (n. 6); and war posters, 104, 209 (n. 17); "Hailing You for U.S. Navy," *106*; Arrow Collars and Shirts advertisement, 161–63, *162*, *164*; and women's imagery, 163; "New Year's Baby," 182, 218 (n. 1)

Liberty, 62, 63, 121

Life: and Gibson, 5, 29, 37, 41, *45*, 107, 121, *129*; and Gibson Girl, 6, 13, 29, 37, 41, 43, 107, 128, 199 (n. 16); and Phillips, 6, 63, 64–65, *65*, *66*, 66–67, *68*, 138, 163; and dangerous women, 14, 56; and Held, 15, 121–28, *124*, *125*, *126*, *127*, *129*, 132, *134*, 135, 185; and flapper, 15, 121–28, 132, 135, 185; and Stephens, 19; readership of, 56, 58, 122; and Flagg, 61, 63, *64*; and Rockwell, 113, *116*, 117, *119*, 150; and World War I, 113, 117; and women's imagery, 113, 122; and television, 186, 219 (n. 12)

Lincoln, Abraham, 93

Literary Digest, 69, 150, 154, *157*, 167, 169

Literature: and mass media, 7; and True Woman, 20; and *Ladies' Home Journal*, 24; and Anglophilia, 28; and *Collier's*, 39; and dance craze, 59; and Flagg, 63; and men's imagery, 69; and *Saturday Evening Post*, 69, 151; and *Cosmopolitan*, 75; and flapper, 121, 128, 133; and McMein, 137

Lorimer, George Horace, 69, 150–51, 177

Love, Courtney, 2

Lucy Stone League, 138

Lynd, Helen, 133

Lynd, Robert, 133

McAllister, Ward, 39

MacArthur, Charlie, 137

McCall's: and New Woman, 15; and Gibson Girl, 39; and Phillips, 63; readership of, 102, 137, 212 (n. 9); and McMein, 113, 137, *139*, *141*, *142*, 177, 181; editorial content of, 137; and advertising, 177, 179

McClintock, Anne, 172

McClure's, 4, 39, 48, 144

McMein, Neysa: and New Woman, 15, 137, 179, 181; and advertising, 16, 160, 177, 179, 217 (n. 27); "One of the Thousand Y.M.C.A. Girls in France," *112*, 112–13; and *McCall's*, 113, 137, *139*, *141*, *142*, 177, 181; and World War I service, 113, 209–10 (n. 21); career of, 137–38; "Twelve Most Beautiful Women in America" series, 138; "Twelve Milestones in a Woman's Life" series, 138, 140; Smith compared to, 144, 145; and Gossard corsets advertisement, 177, *178*; and San-Tox Preparations advertisement, 179, *180*, 181

Magazines: growth of, 4, 7, 193–94 (n. 16); and illustrators, 5–6; marketing of, 7, 194 (n. 31); and Progressive reform movement, 10, 11; and dangerous women, 14; editorial and advertising imagery in, 16, 161, 172, 179, 181; and literature, 24; origin of word, 32, 198 (n. 37); and womanhood, 58; alternative, 75–76, 82; and patriotism, 102; and flapper, 121, 133; and family, 136–37; and motherhood, 144; and race, 148
—covers of: and readership, 4; and illustrations, 5, 7; and upward mobility, 5, 26; and Rockwell, 5, 204 (n. 43); and stereotypes, 13; and women's imagery, 15, 54, 60, 83, 85–86, 192, 206 (n. 19); and ad-

vertising, 16, 177, 181; frontispiece as second cover, 17, 82, 205 (n. 14); style of, 19; and audience, 54; and Flagg, 62, 63; and Phillips, 63–64, 67, 202–3 (n. 30); and Leyendecker, 69–70, 204 (n. 43); and gender roles, 117; and flapper, 121, 130; and celebrity photography, 186, 219 (n. 13)

Male gaze, 26

Mallon, Isabel, 18

Manhood: and Leyendecker, 6, 14, 16, 70; and popular culture imagery, 10; and types, 13; and race suicide, 14, 172; and media imagery, 15, 74; and boyhood, 16, 70; and athletics, 70, 72; and World War I, 101; and middle-class family, 182; and mass media, 191

Marchand, Roland, 128

Marriage: and companionship, 11, 136, 212 (n. 4); and feminism, 86–87, 183; and flapper, 120, 131, 132, 135, 211–12 (n. 2); marriage rate, 136, 211 (n. 1)

Marsh, Margaret, 11, 148

Marx, Harpo, 137

Marzolf, Marion, 13

Masculinity: and media imagery, 4, 189–90; as reactive to femininity's definition, 6; and New Woman, 8; and businessmen, 11, 14, 159; and athletics, 14, 70, 72; and family, 16, 120; and Rockwell, 16, 151–52, 154; and World War I, 102, 112, 119–20; and Flagg, 104; and advertising, 162, 181; and Leyendecker, 163

—crisis of: and psychology, 10–11, 154; and women's imagery, 14; and men's imagery, 67–70, 72; and World War I, 101; and advertising, 176; recurrence of, 190–91, 220 (n. 33); validity of, 203 (n. 37)

Masses: and women's imagery, 15, 82–83, 85–86, 92, 100, 101; readership of, 82; and Sloan, 82, 85, 87, 88, *89*, 90, *91*; and socialism, 82, 86, 90, 99; and Winter, 83, *84*; and gender, 83, 88; and Davis, 85, *85*; and children, 86; and birth control, 87; and working-class women, 88

Mass media: and feminism, 2, 3–4, 12, 191; and women's imagery, 3, 12–13, 37, 192; and literature, 7; and meaning, 16, 191; and men's imagery, 68, 189–91; and middle-class family, 182

—imagery in: and cultural ideals, 3, 5; and femininity, 4; and masculinity, 4, 189–90; and New Woman, 12, 182; and manhood, 15, 74; and family, 15, 136; and vamps, 56; and men as endangered sex, 60; and African Americans, 95; and World War I, 101–2, 112; and flapper, 122; and advertising, 160, 181; representational contradictions of, 182; in twenty-first century, 183; and feminism, 184, 189, 220 (n. 29); and suffrage movement, 184, 205 (n. 6); and good/bad women, 185. *See also* Men: imagery of; Women: imagery of

Maxim, 190

Men: socialization of, 11; and physical attributes, 40; and Gibson Girl, 41, 43; emasculation of, 43, 60, 184; and dangerous women, 56, 58, 59, 60, 61, 63, 70; middle-class, 59, 69, 72, 132, 136, 162; and feminism, 86; working-class, 104; and "men's movement," 190

—imagery of: and gender tensions, 4; and Rockwell, 6, 72, 151; and corporatization, 8; and popular culture, 10, 14, 67, 189; and fathers, 11, 22, 137, 158–59, 190; miniature men in, 14, 43, 63, 67–69, 70, 127; and war posters, 15, 101, 104, 190; and Flagg, 63, 104; and Phillips, 66–67; and mass media, 68, 189–91; and Leyendecker, 70, 72, 151, 182, 204 (n. 55); and suffrage movement, 76, 78; and Sloan, 88; and flapper, 122, 123, 125–28, 130–32; and stereotypes, 191

See also Manhood; Masculinity

Men's Health, 190

Meyer, Susan, 7, 70, 104

Middle class: culture of, 7–8, 177, 184. *See also* Family: middle-class; Men: middle-class; Women: middle-class

Miley, Mimi, 51

Mills, C. Wright, 69

Mitchell, W. J. T., 104, 107

Mobile gaze, 32

Modernity: and women's imagery, 5; and *Ladies' Home Journal*, 18; and Gibson Man, 40; and Fisher Girl, 51; and flapper, 128–30, 210 (n. 14); and McMein, 140; and Smith, 145; and Leyendecker, 163; and cultural icons, 191

Monroe, Marilyn, 185

Moody, Dwight, 20, 22

Moore, Colleen, 131–32

Moore, Sarah J., 99

Morality: and Bok, 18, 44; and True Woman, 20; and physical fitness, 53; and dating, 60; and good/bad women, 72; and suffrage movement, 82, 93; and magazine covers, 86; and feminism, 87; and Sloan, 88; and flapper, 121, 128

Mossell, Sadie Tanner, 93

Motherhood: as professional, 11; and family, 15, 137; and suffrage movement, 80; and *Masses*, 87; and World War I, 113, 117; and

marriage, 120; and flapper, 135, 159, 188; and McMein, 140; and *Good Housekeeping*, 143–44; and Smith, 145, 148, 169; and Rockwell, 151; and masculinity, 154, 176–77, 217 (n. 23); and Phillips, 166; and advertising, 169, 176; and feminism, 183, 187, 219 (n. 21); and television, 186, 187

Mother's Clubs, 143–44

Motor, 52

Movies: and women's imagery, 2, 61; and New Woman, 12; and flapper, 15, 121, 128, 131–32, 133; and dangerous women, 56, 60–61; and sexuality, 60; and Flagg, 61, 62, 202 (n. 26); and World War I, 101; and patriotism, 102

Mrozek, Donald, 53

Mulvey, Laura, 26, 197 (n. 22)

Muncy, Robyn, 58

Munsey's, 4

Music: and women's imagery, 2, 5, 6, 101; and dangerous women, 14, 67; and True Woman, 20, 24; and femininity, 22, 24; and advertising, 24, 150; and Gibson Girl, 41; and men's imagery, 67, 203 (n. 34); and patriotism, 102; and McMein, 137

Nakayama, Thomas, 132

National American Woman Suffrage Association, 9, 76

National Association for the Advancement of Colored People, 92

National Congress of Mothers, 10, 143–44

National Consumer's League, 10

National Woman's Party, 76

Nesbit, Evelyn, 199 (n. 17), 200 (n. 33)

New Republic, 122

Newsweek, 188

New Woman: and feminism, 1; and

television, 2, 188; and types, 8; and popular culture imagery, 8, 12, 14, 29, 117; and crisis of masculinity, 10, 67–68; and gender roles, 11, 29, 32; and flapper, 12, 122, 130–31, 132, 135, 183; and media imagery, 12, 182; and advertising, 13, 179, 184–85; and consumption, 13, 182, 183, 185; and class status, 13, 185; and working-class women, 13, 218 (n. 5); and Stephens, 19, 26, 36; and True Woman, 26, 36; and outdoor settings, 31, 177; and Gibson Girl, 41, 44; and Fisher Girl, 48; and sexuality, 55, 172, 184–85; and suffrage movement, 76, 182; and World War I, 101, 107; and marriage, 120; freedom of, 183

New Yorker, 121

New York Globe, 83, 85

New York Times, 130, 131

Nineteenth Amendment, 80, 122, 138

Normand, Mabel, 61

Ohmann, Richard, 8, 34

Orvell, Miles, 7, 28

Outdoor settings: and masculinity, 11; and editorial content, 29, 31–32; and women's imagery, 29, 53; and New Woman, 31, 177; and Fisher Girl, 46, 48; and Christy Girl, 48; and children, 145, 148; and Rockwell, 152, 154; and Leyendecker, 163

Parents, 151

Parent-Teacher Association, 10, 144

Parsons, Elsie Clews, 86

Patriotism, 29, 78, 80, 82, 102

Patterson, Martha, 95, 99

Paul, Alice, 76

Peiss, Kathy, 34

Pendergast, Tom, 159

Perkins, Teresa, 5

Petty Girl, 185

Philadelphia Press, 53

Philadelphia Press Fiction Magazine, 19

Phillips, Coles: and Fadeaway Girls, 6, 14, 64–67, 163, 166, 203 (n. 31); and advertising, 6, 16, 160, 163, 166–67; and *Life*, 6, 63, 64–65, *65*, *66*, 66–67, *68*, 138, 163; and dangerous women, 56, 60; "Net Results," 63, *65*, 166; and magazine covers, 63–64, 67, 202–3 (n. 30); style of, 64–66; earnings of, 65; "The Time of Her Life," *66*, 66–67; and men's imagery, 66–67; "The Butterfly Chase," 67, *68*; and Leyendecker, 69; and women's imagery, 122, 138, 163, 166–67, 169, 216–17 (n. 15); McMein compared to, 140; Community Plate Silverware advertisement, 163, *165*, 166; Holeproof Hosiery advertisement, 166–67, *167*, *168*

Photography, 5, 95, 169, 186, 219 (n. 13)

Physical fitness, 48, 53, 70, 104. *See also* Athletics

Pickford, Mary, 61, 101, 138, 202 (n. 20)

Pitz, Henry, 41

Politics: and middle-class women, 8; and types of womanhood, 14–15; and political radicalism, 100, 184; and flapper, 122, 132; and McMein, 138; and *Good Housekeeping*, 143, 213 (n. 25); and *Saturday Evening Post*, 151; and New Woman, 185; and television, 187

Popular culture imagery: and feminism, 1, 2, 3, 191; and New Woman, 8, 12, 14, 29, 117; and men's imagery, 10, 14, 67, 189;

and stereotypes, 13; and vamps, 14, 56; and music, 22, 24; and women as girls, 36; and unattractive women, 83; and World War I, 101; and fallen women, 107; and motherhood, 113, 117; and marriage, 120; and editorial and advertising imagery, 181; and women's rights movement, 183

Popular Monthly, 150

Progressive reform movement, 8, 9, 10, 35, 58, 59, 80, 82, 83, 144

Progressive Woman, 87

Prostitutes, 15, 59, 61, 87–88, 90–92, 207 (n. 44)

Psychology, 10–11, 67, 86, 151, 154, 204 (n. 55)

Public life: and Progressive reform movement, 9; and women's imagery, 13, 17–18, 19, 20, 32, 34, 35, 36; and vamps, 61; and working-class women, 88; and Sloan, 90; and television, 186

Puck, 121

Pure Food Association, 10

Race: and suffrage movement, 9, 92–93; and "race suicide," 14, 40, 86, 172; and dance craze, 59; and survival of whites, 60, 72; and American culture, 75; and *Crisis*, 92; and Ku Klux Klan, 100; and magazines, 148; and advertising, 172, 176; and New Woman, 185; and feminism, 188

Rapp, Rayna, 132

Rawls, Walter, 102–3

Reagan, Ronald, 188

Reed, John, 82

"Reflection hypothesis," 3

Religion, and women's imagery, 20

Rockwell, Norman: on cover illustrations, 5; and men's imagery, 6, 72, 151; and masculinity, 16, 151–52, 154; and advertising, 16, 160, 161, 162, 173; style of, 19, 205 (n. 6); and Leyendecker, 69, 72, 204 (n. 43); "The Lord Loveth a Cheerful Giver," 113, *116*; and *Life*, 113, *116*, 117, *119*, 150; and World War I, 113, 209 (n. 21); "Carrying On," 117, *119*; and *Saturday Evening Post*, 117, 137, 150, *152*, *153*, *155*, *156*, *158*, 159, 161, 173, 204 (n. 43); and family, 117, 137, 151, 159, 167, 169; and children, 150, 151–52, 173–74, 176; and *Literary Digest*, 150, 154, *157*, 167, 169; "Planning the Home," *157*; earnings of, 161; Orange Crush advertisement, 173, *174*; Black Cat Reinforced Hosiery advertisement, 173–74, *175*, 176, 177; and progress through technology, 215 (n. 64)

Rogers, Ginger, 103

Roosevelt, Theodore, 10, 40, 70, 172

Ross, Ellen, 132

Ryan, Mary P., 3, 6, 12

Saint-Gaudens, Augustus, 39

St. Nicholas, 150

Sanger, Margaret, 87

Sargeant, John Singer, 39

Saturday Evening Post: readership of, 4, 46, 56, 69, 82, 102, 150, 200 (n. 32); and Leyendecker, 6, 69, 70, *71*, 72, *73*, 161, 204 (n. 43); and Fisher, 14, 46, *47*, 53–54; and boyhood, 16; and Phillips, 63, 202–3 (n. 30); editorial content of, 69, 151, 177; and women's imagery, 95; and Rockwell, 117, 137, 150, *152*, *153*, *155*, *156*, *158*, 159, 161, 173, 204 (n. 43); and McMein, 137, 138; and race, 148; and advertising, 150, 151, 162, 176, 183; and children, 150; and family, 150, 159, 176; and television, 186; and suffrage movement, 205 (n. 6)

Scanlon, Jennifer, 18

Schau, Michael, 70, 161

Scribner's, 6, 7, 14, 19, 39, 48, 51, 61, 144

Sears, Roebuck, 133

Segal, Eric, 72, 162

Settlement-house work, 10, 58

Sexuality: of women, 9, 136, 202 (n. 17), 211–12 (n. 2); and feminism, 12, 86, 87, 206 (n. 26); and flapper, 15, 121, 122, 124, 130, 131, 132; and New Woman, 55, 172, 184–85; and playful woman, 58; and dance craze, 59, 60; and vamps, 61; and good/bad women, 72; and stereotypes, 87; and Sloan, 88; and war posters, 107, 112; and marriage, 136; and advertising, 166; and television, 187

Shearer, Norma, 61

Sheppard, Alice, 76

Shuttlesworth, Jack, 123

Sigsbee, Mary Ellen, 82

Sklar, Kathryn Kish, 9–10, 58

Sloan, John: and *Masses*, 82, 85, 87, 88, *89*, 90, *91*; "The Women's Night Court," 87–88; "'Circumstances' Alter Cases," 88; "At the Top of the Swing," 88, *89*; "Innocent Girlish Prattle— Plus Environment," 88, 90; and stereotypes, 88, 91–92; "The Return from Toil," 90, *91*; style of, 95

Smart Set, 121

Smith, Jaclyn, 1

Smith, Jessie Willcox: and *Good Housekeeping*, 5, 6, 137, 144, 145, *146*, *147*, 148, *149*, 150, 160–61, 169, 203 (n. 30); earnings of, 5, 214 (n. 34); style of, 6; and advertising, 6, 16, 144, 160, 169; and children, 15–16, 144, 145, 148, 150, 160–61, 169, 179, 182; Ivory Soap advertisement, 169, *170*, *171*, 172

Smoking, 133, 211 (n. 38)

Snyder, Robert, 88, 90

"Social housekeeping" movement, 58

Socialism: and feminism, 9, 86, 90; and alternative magazines, 75; and *Masses*, 82, 86, 90, 99; and women's imagery, 82–83; and children, 83; and Sloan, 87; as un-American, 100; and media imagery, 184

Socialist Party, 82

Spanish-American War, 51, 172

Steine, Kent, 163

Steinem, Gloria, 1, 187

Stephens, Alice Barber: and *Ladies' Home Journal*, 5, 13, 17, 19–36, *21*, *23*, *25*, *27*, *30*, *32*, 37; style of, 5, 18–19, 54; "The American Woman" series, 13, 17, 19–36, 37; earnings of, 19, 196 (n. 12); "The Woman in Religion," 20, *21*, 26; and religion, 20, 22; "The Beauty of Motherhood," 22, *23*, 29; "The Woman in the Home," 24, *25*; and True Woman, 24, 26, 36, 202 (n. 23); "The Woman in Society," 26, *27*, 29, 32, 34; "The American Girl in Summer," 29, *30*, 31; "The Woman in Business," 32, *33*, 34–35; and advertising, 160, 161

Stereotypes: and women's imagery, 3, 5, 37, 44–45, 92, 99, 100, 191, 192; and magazine covers, 13; and suffrage movement, 76, 99; and sexuality, 87; and Sloan, 88, 91– 92; and American culture, 92; racial, 95; and war posters, 102, 107; and flapper, 130; resurfacing of, 185; and men's imagery, 191

Stone, Lucy, 76

Suburbs, 11, 136, 145, 148, 183, 184

Success, 69

Suffrage movement: and women's imagery, 3, 15, 67; and women's

status, 8; and working-class
women, 9, 58, 82; perceptions
of failure of, 11–12; and alternative magazines, 75–76; and New
Woman, 76, 182; and children,
80, 82; and anticommunism, 80,
205 (n. 7); and feminism, 86; and
African Americans, 92–93; and
flapper, 132; and McMein, 138,
213 (n. 17); and *Good Housekeeping*, 143, 213 (n. 24); and media
imagery, 184, 205 (n. 6)

Suffragist, 76

Sweet, Blanche, 133

Taft, Helen, 59
Taraba, Frederic, 163
Tarkington, Booth, 61
Tebbel, John, 5
Television, 2, 16, 186–87
Terrell, Mary Church, 92–93
Thomas, Marlo, 187
Thompson, J. Walter, 148
Tickner, Lisa, 76
Time, 1–3, 11, 12, 188, 189
True Woman, 20, 24, 26, 36, 61, 136,
202 (n. 23)
Tubman, Harriet, 93
Tuchman, Gaye, 3
Twiggy, 185–86

Upward mobility: and magazine
covers, 5, 26; and aesthetic of imitation, 7–8, 28, 58; and Gibson
Girl, 13, 41, 199 (n. 13); and
Stephens, 19; and womanhood,
24; and women's imagery, 26, 28;
and New Woman, 32; and working women, 34; and Fisher Girl,
46, 200 (n. 33); and advertising,
58, 181; and Leyendecker, 69; and
athletics, 72; and flapper, 131; and
family, 150; and thrift, 177

Urbanization, 8, 11

Valentino, Rudolph, 162, 163
Vamps, 14, 56, 60–61, 70, 95, 99,
107, 121, 126
Vanity Fair, 121
Varga Girl, 185
Victoria (queen of England), 28
Victorian era: and womanhood, 10,
54; and women's imagery, 13, 51;
and Stephens, 18, 19; and Anglo-
philia, 28; and Gibson Man, 40;
and sexuality, 87; and public life,
88; and suffrage movement, 99
Villard, Fanny Garrison, 92
Villard, Oswald Garrison, 92
Vogue, 177
Vorse, Mary Heaton, 82

Walker, Madame C. J., 99
Wanamaker's, 32, 34
Warner, Marina, 6
War posters: and women's imagery,
6, 15, 101, 104, 107, 112–13, 117,
119–20; and illustrators, 6, 102,
208–9 (n. 7); and men's imagery,
15, 101, 104, 190; and propaganda
campaign, 102–3
Wayne, John, 190, 220 (n. 31)
Welter, Barbara, 20
Wharton, Edith, 39
White, Kevin, 132
Williams, Raymond, 3, 16
Winter, Alice Beach, 83
Winter, Charles Allen, "The Mili-
tant," 83, *84*
Wodehouse, P. G., 61
Wolf, Naomi, 188–89
Woman Citizen, 15, 76, *77*, 78, *79*, 80,
81, 82, 83, 205 (n. 6)
Womanhood: visual vocabulary
of, 3; Cult of True Womanhood,
10, 20, 24, 36; and Victorian
era, 10, 54; and types, 13, 14–15;
and family, 15, 182; and flapper,
15, 133; and children, 16; and
Ladies' Home Journal, 32; and

class status, 36, 58; and suffrage movement, 76; and *Masses*, 92, 100; and African Americans, 99; and war posters, 104, 107, 120; and American culture, 128; and McMein, 140, 177; and feminism, 184; and mass media, 191

Woman's Christian Temperance Union, 10

Woman's Home Companion, 46, 62, 63, 137, 144, 200 (n. 32)

Woman's Journal, 76

Women: working, 1, 32, 34–36, 53, 54, 86, 90, 188; and consumption, 8, 12; and women's club movements, 8, 35; sexuality of, 9, 136, 202 (n. 17), 211–12 (n. 2); upper-class, 10, 13, 32, 34, 41, 58, 123, 201 (n. 8); economic status of, 12, 19–20; as girls, 36; health of, 48, 53; same-sex friendships among, 51, 53; good/bad dichotomy, 56, 58, 72, 185; as playful woman, 56, 58, 121; older, 61, 113; unattractive, 83; feminist writing of, 86–87; and World War I, 113, 117

—imagery of: and types, 2, 3, 6, 8, 13, 14–15, 17, 29, 36, 37, 44–45, 60, 181, 186; and television, 2, 16, 186–87; and stereotypes, 3, 5, 37, 44–45, 92, 99, 100, 191, 192; and war posters, 6, 15, 101, 104, 107, 112–13, 117, 119–20; and American culture, 6–7, 194 (n. 28); approaches to, 12–13, 195 (n. 54); and public life, 13, 17–18, 19, 20, 32, 34, 35, 36; and Victorian era, 13, 51; and athletics, 14, 48, 54, 138; and magazine covers, 15, 54, 60, 83, 85–86, 192, 206 (n. 19); and *Crisis*, 15, 93, *94*, 95, *96*, *97*, *98*, 99; and *Masses*, 15, 82–83, 85–86, 92, 100, 101; and World War I, 15, 101, 107, 128; and "The American Woman" series, 17–18; and edu-

cation, 24, 26, 29, 44, 53, 54, 123; and upward mobility, 26, 28; and working-class women, 26, 34, 219 (n. 20); and Phillips, 122, 138, 163, 166–67, 169, 216–17 (n. 15); and family, 137; and beauty/fashion ideals, 218 (n. 6)

—middle-class: and politics, 8; and suffrage movement, 9, 82; and Progressive reform movement, 10; and New Woman, 13, 218 (n. 5); and "The American Woman" series, 18; Jews as, 22; and working women, 32, 34; and Sloan, 88; and flapper, 131, 133; and marriage, 136; and television, 187, 219 (n. 20)

—movement for rights of, 18; first and second wave of, 3, 12, 16, 186, 189; and sexuality, 60; and *Good Housekeeping*, 143; and popular culture imagery, 183; history of, 192 (*see also* Feminism; Suffrage movement)

—working-class: and suffrage movement, 9, 58, 82; and New Woman, 13, 218 (n. 5); Jews as, 22; and women's imagery, 26, 34, 219 (n. 20); and city life, 55; and dance halls, 59; and feminism, 86–87; and Sloan, 88, 90

Women's Trade Union League, 10, 58

Woollcott, Alexander, 138

World War I, 15, 51, 101, 102, 107, 128, 190. *See also* War posters

World War II, 184, 185, 190

Yellis, Kenneth, 128, 132

Youth's Companion, 150

Ziegfeld Follies, 44

Zuckerman, Mary Ellen, 5, 148

Zurier, Rebecca, 87, 88